Theoretical Logic in Sociology

Instead of a serious discussion among conflicting theories that, in their very conflict, demonstrate the intimacy with which they belong together, the commonness of their underlying convictions, and an unswerving belief in a true philosophy, we have a pseudo-reporting and a pseudo-criticizing, a mere semblance of philosophizing seriously with and for one another. . . . But how could actual study and actual collaboration be possible, where there are so many philosophers and almost equally many philosophies? To be sure, we still have philosophical congresses. The philosophers meet but, unfortunately, not the philosophies. The philosophies lack the unity of a mental space in which they might exist for and act on one another.

Edmund Husserl,
Cartesian Meditations

Theoretical Logic in Sociology

Volume One

POSITIVISM,
PRESUPPOSITIONS,
AND CURRENT
CONTROVERSIES

Jeffrey C. Alexander

University of California Press
Berkeley · Los Angeles

University of California Press
Berkeley and Los Angeles, California
© 1982 by
The Regents of the University of California
Printed in the United States of America

1   2   3   4   5   6   7   8   9

Library of Congress Cataloging in Publication Data

Alexander, Jeffrey C.
  Theoretical logic in sociology.

  Includes bibliographical references and index.
  Contents: v. 1. Positivism, presuppositions, and
current controversies.
  1. Sociology—Collected works. I. Title.
HM24.A465   301   75-17305
ISBN 0-520-03062-1 (set)   AACR2
ISBN 0-520-04480-0 (vol.1)

To my wife,
Ruth Hedi Bloch

CONTENTS—OVERVIEW

Volume Three
THE CLASSICAL ATTEMPT AT
THEORETICAL SYNTHESIS: MAX WEBER

Volume Four
THE MODERN RECONSTRUCTION OF
CLASSICAL THOUGHT: TALCOTT PARSONS

PREFACE AND ACKNOWLEDGMENTS

In the course of composing these four volumes I have incurred so many personal and intellectual debts that I am tempted simply to ask for a blanket pardon from parties unnamed. I have benefited greatly from so many small conversations and chance encounters that I cannot hope to do justice to all those whose acknowledgment I would like to make. It seems imperative, however, that some persons be singled out.

This project began as a dissertation at the University of California, Berkeley, but its history goes back further still. I was first confronted with the challenge of classical thought and sociological theory as a Harvard undergraduate in a sophomore tutorial called "Social Studies 10." I had some difficulty with the class, and in one sense the current work is an effort finally to come to terms with it. As the late 1960s unfolded, and I continued to mull over these theoretical questions, I was fortunate enough to encounter a teaching assistant in the first and last sociology course I took as an undergraduate. His name was Mark Gould and he alerted me to the significance of a modern theorist, Talcott Parsons. Soon after I entered graduate school at Berkeley, I made the lucky decision to attend Richard Lichtman's lectures on Marx, an experience which permanently affected my view of that theorist's work. Shortly after that, I had an equally decisive intellectual experience in the seminar that Leo Lowenthal conducted on Durkheim.

As my dissertation took shape it did so with the support and under the guidance of two men, Robert Bellah and Neil Smelser. I would never have continued to write it without their encouragement and I would not have been able to do so without their trenchant criticism and advice. They continued to be involved in the project after the completion of their

xi

formal obligations, and their contributions—most of all their intellectual examples—continued to sustain me.

In subsequent years, as the manuscript continued to develop, I benefited greatly from the critical readings of different scholars. At an early stage, Seymour Martin Lipset, S. N. Eisenstadt, and Alvin Gouldner each read the manuscript in its entirety. Also at an early point, Martin Jay read the section on Marx; Lewis Coser and Daniel Bell read the analysis at a later date. Donald N. Levine, Steven Seidman, Colin Loader, Talcott Parsons, and Gershon Shafir examined the Weber analysis at various points along the way. Warren Hagstrom, Gerald Holton, Ian Jarvie, and Jonathan Kerman critically commented upon the discussion of science. S. N. Eisenstadt examined the manuscript on Parsons; David Lane and Philippe Nonet read parts of it. Bernard Barber provided, throughout these years, vital intellectual support and enthusiasm for the task.

Seth Knoepler and Michael Hui provided much needed clerical assistance at critical points (Hui also prepared the indexes). Steven Seidman, Colin Loader, and Ken Rasmussen provided invaluable assistance in checking and translating German texts.

Grant Barnes, my editor at University of California Press, has shown the enormous patience that, it is to be hoped, marks the better part of wisdom. As a long manuscript became longer still, he also provided moral support without which the project would not have been completed in its present form. In more material terms, this work was generously supported by graduate fellowships from the Regents of the University of California and by Research Grants from the Faculty Senate of the University of California at Los Angeles. The final stages were completed while I enjoyed a fellowship from the John Simon Guggenheim Memorial Foundation. In more practical terms, I wish also to thank the women and men of the UCLA Stenographic Pool who gave of their time, dexterity, and intelligence not just in the typing of the final manuscript but in work on earlier drafts as well. Jesse M. Phillips, my copy editor for all four volumes, performed an arduous task with erudition and wit.

In critical stages of my work on this project I have been lucky enough to enjoy the intelligent and learned conversation of two colleagues, Jeffrey Prager and Steven Seidman. Their contributions are impossible to estimate.

My wife, Ruth Bloch, has not only provided the decisive intellectual context within which this work was created and decisive editorial criticism as well, but over this same period she shared with me the lived experience of which any intellectual work is, in the end, only a partial crystalization. Her doubt has been my inspiration, her approval my reward.

Los Angeles
June 1980

Theoretical Logic in Sociology

INTRODUCTION

If sociology could speak it would say, "I am tired." But how can a fledgling discipline, scarcely a hundred years old, already feel the onset of senility? Surely this old age is premature, an ennui brought on by the consciousness of great challenges posed by the founding fathers that have proven difficult to fulfill. But this pervasive fatigue is not stimulated only by the epigoni's fear of defeat, of the humiliation that is the lot of those who cannot live up to their parent's achievements. It has also been created by more proximate events: by the trivializing effect of the ever more powerful urge for "scientization," by the flood of well-intended but too often grossly misleading critiques, by the false promise of imminent transformation, and by the death of a great man.

The foundations of sociology were laid before the First World War. During the interwar period, the discipline lay relatively dormant. It began to build upon the classical foundations only after the Second World War: sociology was reconstructed much as were the Western democracies, and the processes were not unrelated. Talcott Parsons dominated this postwar period intellectually, though not politically and institutionally as some of his critics would contend. Parsons tried to incorporate the classical tradition but he sought to obliterate it at the same time. Despite the monumentality of his contribution, however, this was not to be. It turned out that while Parsons could claim to be the true peer of the founders of sociology, he was not meant to be their one true son. A flood of liberating criticism marked Parsons' decline. These critiques sought to renew various strands of the classical tradition, but they were more critical and programmatic than substantive and theoretical. More importantly, when taken together the critiques rested on claims that were themselves questionable and internally contradictory. The proof of this assessment is that in most respects the decade which followed, the 1970s, was a moribund one. Like the postrevolutionary King Louis XVIII, contemporary sociology seems to have forgotten nothing and learned nothing new. The tradition of Parsons is crippled; the traditions of Weber and Durkheim have only begun to be reinvented.

We live in a pessimistic time. The technocratic fetishism of empirical sociology is matched only by the defensiveness and tepid caution of the liberal creed upon whose vigor and courage the postwar revival was based. Quantification is in the empirical saddle, and Marxism is the only theoretical tradition that appears as a lively challenger. One wonders whether Marxism is up to the challenge. Sociology has always flourished alongside a vigorous and critical liberalism. But this ideological consideration is somewhat beside the point. There are analytic reasons for reservations about Marxism, reservations I will discuss at some length.

The present work has four parts. Volume 1, *Positivism, Presuppositions, and Current Controversies,* begins by challenging the bases of the recent scientization of sociology. Then, utilizing an alternative model of social science, it challenges some of the ambitious claims of recent theoretical debate. I argue for the importance of more generalized concerns and try to lay these general issues out in a precise and, I hope, not overly elaborated way. In concluding this volume, I set myself the challenge not only of reinterpreting the most important classical and modern sociological theories but of teasing out from the debates that continue to inform these traditions the elements of a more satisfactory, more inclusive approach to these general theoretical points.

Volume 2, *The Antinomies of Classical Thought: Marx and Durkheim,* explores the work of Marx and Durkheim, outlining the processes of theoretical reasoning that led them to create the fundamentally opposing strands of sociological materialism and idealism. Its focus is primarily on the most generalized elements in their thought, though I relate these presuppositions to empirical and ideological issues as well. While Marx manifested an early understanding of voluntaristic theory, in his mature analysis of capitalism he settled—for a mixture of ideological, empirical, and epistemological reasons—upon a more instrumental strand of structural analysis. Durkheim's early work was more ambiguous, but it demonstrated, in contrast, a strong materialist strain. As he matured, however, Durkheim clung as strongly to a voluntaristic kind of structuralism as the older Marx did to a deterministic one. But profound ambiguities exist even in these mature classical theories. Indeed, the finest students of Durkheim and Marx seized upon ambiguities in their teachers' works to revise these classical traditions in unacknowledged ways, rereading the founders' theories in more multidimensional and synthetic ways.

Volume 3, *The Classical Attempt at Synthesis: Max Weber,* analyzes

Weber's work in an attempt to disclose the elements in his theorizing which were designed to transcend the debilitating dichotomization that such classical antinomies produced. Weber was influenced in his early formation by both the instrumentalist and the idealist strands of German social theory, and although his early writing tended merely to reproduce these presuppositional bifurcations, his later work produced a powerful strand of synthetic and multidimensional theory. The analytical insights that allowed Weber to make this translation are critically important for the future of contemporary theory in the social sciences, and I try to analyze the logic of this theorizing in detail. I also spend a good deal of time analyzing the problems that remain in this later work, for I argue that in his synthesizing effort Weber was only partly successful. I conclude that the classical tradition has left to contemporary thought an ambiguous legacy, one that has never been fully and properly explored.

Volume 4, *The Modern Reconstruction of Classical Thought: Talcott Parsons*, tries to explain why Parsons, of all his generation, was the only true peer of the classical tradition, and also why he did not achieve his ambition of being its only legitimate son. I argue, on the one hand, that Parsons went even further than Weber in the attempt to reconcile the antinomies of classical thought, on the other that the internal contradictions of his work exacerbated the very polarizing tendencies he sought to reconcile. Sociology will never be subject to complete consensus, but it must strive for a general and synthetic theory nonetheless. This is the paradox that inspires the present work, and I hope that it is a fruitful one.

I have written one book. *Theoretical Logic in Sociology* has one major theme and one consistent theoretical ambition. Still, the single book consists of four distinctive parts. I have separated them because they can, indeed, be read independently of one another. Each presents a distinctive theoretical argument in its own right. The first volume is directed at the most contemporary problems and controversies, not only in "theory" but in the philosophy and sociology of science. The last three volumes make independent interpretations, confronting the individual theorists, and the secondary literature, on their own terms. A reader might prefer to start with one volume rather than another, and I have provided the necessary prefatory material to make this possible. For all that, of course, I would urge that all four parts be read through. My argument is cumulative, and I construct a new "theoretical logic" for sociology step-by-step. Each volume stands on its own, but its greater import and full ramification rest with its place in the larger whole.

Sociology is tired. It must be revived, or revivified. "There are those among us," Lenin wrote in *What Is To Be Done?*, "who strive . . . to belittle the significance of theory." Lenin responded that without a revolutionary theory there would be no revolution. On the critical role of theory I am in complete agreement: without a strong and vigorous sociological theory there will be no strong and vigorous sociology. To revive sociology, we must revivify its theory. The present work, I hope, is a small (if lengthy) contribution to this task.

POSITIVISM, PRESUPPOSITIONS, AND CURRENT CONTROVERSIES

Contents
VOLUME ONE
POSITIVISM,
PRESUPPOSITIONS,
AND CURRENT
CONTROVERSIES

Chapter One

THEORETICAL LOGIC
IN SCIENTIFIC
THOUGHT

The attempt to elaborate a general theoretical logic for sociology is confronted by two barriers. There is, of course, the truly imposing lack of agreement on what the general theoretical issues are and how they affect sociological formulations. I will discuss this issue in chapters 2 and 3. But before this problem can even be addressed, there is another obstacle which must first be overcome. This is the issue of theoretical thinking itself, not "how" general issues affect sociology but "whether" they do. Since sociology has for the most part measured itself against the standard of the natural sciences, the point at the center of this initial problem becomes the debate over the nature of science. If the independent role of general thinking in sociology is to be preserved, it is necessary to reinterpret the conventional understanding of the scientific process.

In the first section of this chapter, I present the outline of such a reformulation. Next, I articulate the principles of the prevailing "positivist persuasion," found in the work of a wide range of contemporary sociologists. In subsequent sections, I argue, first, that the traditional alternative to such positivism, the argument that sociology should not be conceived as a science, represents an inappropriate response, and I propose instead a series of counterpostulates to the positivist conception of science, counterpostulates derived from the work of those philosophers and histo-

NOTE: In addition to the citation of sources, the backnotes include numerous substantive discussions—refinements of points that occur in the main text and digressions about relevant issues and secondary literature. To enable the interested reader to turn immediately to this substantive annotation, I have distinguished these substantive notes by marking them with a dagger [†] following the note number. A ribbon bookmark is provided to facilitate such referral.

rians who, rather than leave science to its objectivist interpreters, have
begun to develop an alternative understanding of natural science itself.
In conclusion, I present the case for developing a conception of general
theoretical logic in sociology.

1. INTRODUCTION: SCIENTIFIC THOUGHT AS A TWO-DIRECTIONAL CONTINUUM

Science can be viewed as an intellectual process that occurs within
the context of two distinctive environments, the empirical observational
world and the non-empirical metaphysical one. Although scientific statements may be oriented more toward one of these environments than the
other, they can never be determined exclusively by either alone. The differences between what are perceived as sharply contrasting kinds of scientific arguments should be understood rather as representing different
positions on the same epistemological continuum (see fig. 1).[1†] Those scientific statements closer to the right-hand side of the continuum are said
to be "empirical" because their form is more influenced by the criterion
of precisely describing observation, hence the "specificity" of empirical
statements. Statements closer to the left-hand side are called "theoretical" because their form is concerned less with the immediate character
of the observations that inform them. One can, in fact, arrange all the
different components of scientific thought in terms of such degrees of
generality and specificity (fig. 2).[2†] This listing is intended to be sug-
gestive rather than exhaustive, an attempt to order the elements most
often mentioned in the social scientific literature as constituting independent points of focus. Each of these elements I have listed could themselves be further elaborated—for example, the methodological level into
"meta-methodological assumptions" and "technical orientations." Also,
the identity of different levels differs, to some degree, according to the
nature of the scientific activity. In the human sciences, the category of
"general presuppositions" should be divided into "presuppositions" and
"ideological assumptions," whereas this division does not apply to the
sciences of nature.

Figure 2 allows us to make several important points. First, it clarifies
further the relative character of the theory/data split. That "data" is a

Figure 1

THE CONTINUUM OF SCIENTIFIC THOUGHT

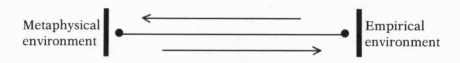

Figure 2

THE SCIENTIFIC CONTINUUM AND ITS COMPONENTS

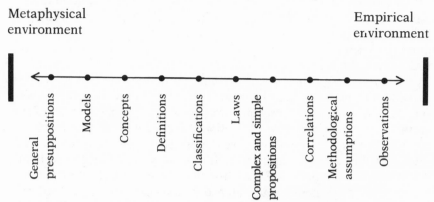

thoroughly relative formulation can be illustrated by the fact that as so-cial scientists we continually treat as data the more general "scientific" formulations of those around us—others' propositions, models, classifi-cations, and general assumptions about the empirical world. But it is also clear that "theory" is just as much a designational convenience. Different sociological theorists, like Talcott Parsons, John Rex, or Hans Zetterberg, take different levels of scientific formulation to be indicative of "real sci-entific theory" as distinguished from more general "speculation" on the one hand and mere "data" on the other. Thus, while Parsons defines proper theoretical thinking in sociology as focusing on "frames of refer-ence" (i.e., general presuppositions) and on "generalized conceptual sys-tems," Rex considers the "model" to be the level of generality at which any truly effective sociological theory must be directed.[3] And in sharp contrast to both of these theorists, Zetterberg claims the only legitimate focus for social scientific theorizing to be "multi-variate" axioms, as com-pared with mere simple propositions, on the one hand, and more general "social thought," on the other.[4†] Although data and theory are, thus, com-monly equated with qualitative positions on the more specific and gen-eral sides of the scientific continuum, it is more correct to understand them as quantitative distinctions: every formulation "leftward" of any given point of focus is called theory and every statement "rightward" of that point is claimed as data.

As this first clarification begins to indicate, the continuum concep-tualization also allows us to emphasize the interdependence of formula-tions at each of these levels. Although common sense and a certain body of scientific opinion inform us that these elements are qualitatively dis-crete, that is, completely independent of one another, in positioning the elements on this continuum I try to demonstrate precisely the opposite. "Generality" and "specificity" indicate orientations, or directions, of different kinds of scientific statements, but each element nevertheless contains references to both general and specific, empirical and nonempirical, properties. If these elements actually were completely qualitatively differentiated, they would represent "concrete" distinctions. They are, instead, "analytic" distinctions, separations established for the convenience of scientific discourse, made to facilitate communication and not to establish ontological qualities.

Every piece of actual scientific analysis contains implicit references to, and is at least influenced by, each of the other analytic levels of scientific thought. What appears, concretely, to be a difference in types of scientific statements—models, definitions, propositions—simply reflects the different emphasis within a given statement on generality or specificity. Even the most metaphysical theory of society, which explicitly focuses upon and elaborates only the most general properties, is influenced by implicit though undeveloped notions of models, propositions, and empirical correlations. Similarly, even for the most self-consciously neutral and precise scientific exercise, "empirical observations" represent only an explicit focus.[5†] Generalized presuppositions, definitions, classifications, and models—all levels influenced by more metaphysically oriented concerns—still affect such specific statements, even though their influence remains completely implicit.

This last point raises a final issue. While the continuum notion allows one to stress the interdependence of each analytical level, it illustrates also that these relationships are asymmetrical. This is implied by the very notions of generality and specificity: while elements at lower levels bring new information about observable reality to bear, they still represent specifications of more general assumptions. The general always subsumes the specific. Yet this asymmetry does not mean generality is more important. For science, especially, this is not the case. By themselves, "metaphysical" statements are not scientific, neither are models or definitions; each has scientific relevance only when coupled with commitments which are determined more directly by the empirical environment. Scientific status assures—to lift a phrase from Toulmin's early work—that "statements at one level have a meaning only *within the scope* of those in the level below."[6] It must be emphasized, then, that although the asymmetry of the scientific continuum has important implications, this intellectual hierarchy is not, for science, a hierarchy of relative importance, nor does it imply temporal priority for the allocation of scientific activity.

Although social and natural scientists continually do make imperial claims for the greater heuristic fruitfulness and determinate power of each of these different levels of analysis, it is more correct to regard every level as having its own partial autonomy. While the boundaries of each element are established by the "empirical" and "nonempirical" formulations on either side, each level performs a distinctive type of intellectual function and is subject for this reason to distinctive criteria of scientific merit. Only by understanding science in this manner can we preserve both the general and specific dimensions of scientific thought.

2. THE POSITIVIST PERSUASION IN SOCIAL SCIENCE: THE REDUCTION OF THEORY TO FACT

The position I have just articulated represents a minority viewpoint, and a steadily shrinking one, among American sociologists today. At least since the end of the Second World War, there has been a growing tendency toward conceptualizing and practicing social science as a one-directional process, as an inquiry that moves, in terms of the framework I have presented, only along the dimension from specificity to generality.[7†] I will call this tendency the positivist "persuasion" because in the context of contemporary sociology it represents much more of an amorphous self-consciousness than an articulate intellectual commitment; indeed, the formal methodological principles of classical positivism are today eschewed by most sophisticated sociological thinkers. Yet positivism in a more generic sense is, nonetheless, a persuasion that permeates contemporary social science.[8] In this section I will outline and elaborate its general postulates, and indicate what I regard as its debilitating ramifications.

The two postulates central to the positivist persuasion are, first, that a radical break exists between empirical observations and nonempirical statements, and, second, that because of this break, more general intellectual issues—which are called "philosophical" or "metaphysical"—have no fundamental significance for the practice of an empirically oriented discipline. The third postulate, which completes what might be called the triadic foundations of the positivist orientation, is that since such an elimination of the nonempirical reference is taken to be the distinguishing feature of the natural sciences, any true sociology must assume a "scientific" self-consciousness.[9†]

These first three fundamental propositions—unlike the fourth postulate, which I will discuss below—have in one form or another assumed such a self-evident role in much of contemporary sociology that they are rarely articulated. Perhaps the best illustration of how they do in fact present a logically interrelated perspective is provided by William R. Catton, Jr., whose book *From Animistic to Naturalistic Sociology* combines arguments about the history and philosophy of science with actual empirical practice in a manner that typifies the self-understanding of most American empirical sociology today. Contrary to the two-directional position outlined above, Catton defines "the issue of supra-empirical postulates" as the decisive distinction between scientific and nonscientific intellectual disciplines.[10] He locates the origins of the modern sociological discipline in the transition from the subjective study of society typified by such disciplines as philosophy and theology—pejoratively defined as "animistic" approaches—to what he considers the purely "naturalistic" approach, in which the investigator's commitments have no influence on his or her data and in which generalizations are based solely on objective evidence. On the basis of this perspective on contemporary sociology, Catton dismisses traditional epistemological and ontological issues on the grounds that "the operationally real is the observable," referring, for example, to the debate about materialism in the following manner: "Genuinely naturalistic sociology would simply say that there is no operationally verifiable meaning to the dichotomy 'material reality' versus 'immaterial reality.' "[11]

Although the starkness of these formulations represents Catton's commitment to the radically positivist perspective of operationalism, in a more general and less sectarian form his conception of the nature of the sociological science is widely shared. For example, although Hans Zetterberg views himself as in battle with operationalism and with narrowly empiricist views of sociological theory, his book *On Theory and Verification in Sociology* became a minor classic on the strength of its argument for a " 'scientific' conception of sociological theory" which can finally establish the separation of the concerns of "social thought" from those of social science.[12]

And to move one step further along the scientific continuum, even such a purposefully theoretical sociologist as William J. Goode lends his support to the foundations of the positivist perspective on science. In the introductory chapter to his collection of theoretical essays, Goode emphasizes what he considers the irrelevance of generalized metaphysical concerns to contemporary sociology. Although the "common philosophical position has argued that the biases of human observers . . . will always prevent any security about the conclusions the sociologist reaches if they are based on observation," Goode writes, this issue has been, and should continue to be, of little concern to the working sociologist.[13] "It is sufficient merely to note," he continues, "that most sociologists now concern themselves very little with this question. . . . Their general position is that there are no fundamental methodological or epistemological problems that cannot be solved in principle."[14] Goode justifies what I have called this second positivist postulate by proclaiming his faith in the first, in the radical separation of empirical and nonempirical dimensions: "Sociologists have been correct in adopting (along with their scientific forebears) the pragmatic position that since they are indeed developing analyses which do seem to correspond with the reality they perceive, the problems cannot be overwhelming."[15] As this latter statement indicates, Goode links these two positions to the identification of sociology with natural science, a connection that completes his articulation of the triadic foundations of the positivist persuasion. "The epistemological assumptions and canons of science in other fields," he writes, "are thought to be completely applicable to the study of social behavior."[16†]

The fourth and final postulate of the positivist persuasion continues and in a certain sense completes the intellectual thrust of the three principles that form its foundation. It posits that in a science from which "philosophical" issues have been excluded and in which, correspondingly, empirical observation is thoroughly unproblematic, questions of a theoretical or general nature can correctly be dealt with only in relation to such empirical observation. Although definitions about exactly what constitutes theory and data must, for the reasons discussed in section 1, remain fluid, there has been a continual and relentless effort in sociological discussion to reduce every theoretical whole to the sum of its more empirical, more specific parts. Three distinct manifestations of this final positivist principle can be distinguished, each referring to a different aspect of theoretical thinking in the social sciences.

First, in regard to the *formulation* of social theories, the positivist persuasion argues that the process should be one of "construction" through generalization, or induction, from observation. Perhaps the best-known argument for this point is George C. Homans' contention that sociological theory must be propositional. He describes theory as a "process of building up from the empirical to the more general," the goal of which is to produce a series of "deductive explanations inductively arrived at."[17] That this position rests, in turn, on the positivist foundations outlined above is indicated by Homans' argument, in another context, that nature is translucent to observation. "A theory of phenomena," he writes, "consists of a series of propositions, each stating a relationship between properties of nature."[18†]

But the most elaborate attempt to reduce the formation of sociological theory to an exercise in induction is Zetterberg's. He introduces his approach to sociological theory in the following way: "Systematically organized, law-like propositions about society that can be supported by evidence: this is 'theory' in the sense that this word has been used in the sciences."[19] And Zetterberg devotes the major sections of the rest of his book to developing the formal strategy by which this reduction can be achieved.[20] He elaborates first the "logical rules for induction and deduction" through which the creation of generalizing statements can be strictly tied to empirical observation, and in sections which follow he outlines the rules for confirmation and verification once the theoretical postulates have been established.[21] Although, as mentioned above, Zetterberg formally recognizes the role of concepts and definitions in sociological inquiry and differentiates himself thereby from a purely operationalist positivism, this recognition is substantively contradicted by his emphasis on the radical, "concrete" separation of concepts from data. He argues that while concepts may contribute to taxonomy and description, only propositions that have been inductively derived from observation can lead to real theoretical explanation. The sharpness of this perceived separation is demonstrated in practice by Zetterberg's insensitivity to the impact of nonempirical elements in the very examples which he chooses to illustrate his argument. For example, a number of the "multi-variate empirical generalizations" which he purportedly constructs from more specific propositional correlations are actually also informed by fundamentally incompatible general presuppositions. Furthermore, in his comments on even the most general types of competing theories, he can develop criticisms of their conceptualization only on the most strictly inductive, methodological grounds, referring rarely to their substantive content. For example, in trying to explain why "Sorokin's theory is still controversial," Zetterberg cites only the fact that "it is not entirely clear how those correlates [of Sorokin's theory] are derived from the two basic generalizations [he makes]," adding that, for this reason, "the empirical demonstrations of the correlations are not always as convincing as one might wish."[22†]

Once theories have been formulated, however, there remains a second issue posed by this final positivist postulate, that of theoretical *conflict*. In an effort to transform theoretical into empirical argument, it is maintained that if sociology is to be an empirical science then, as Catton puts it, "empirical test is the final arbiter in theoretical disputes."[23] In effect, the true theorist must turn in his dialectical tools for a new set of empirical ones. In one of the most articulate statements of this position, Arthur Stinchcombe attempts, in *Constructing Social Theories*, to set out the "logical requirements for testing ... theories against the facts."[24] Stinchcombe disparages any explicitly generalized sociological argument, contending rather that "which kind [of theory] is true of a particular phenomenon is a matter for investigation, not for debate among 'theorists.'"[25] Invoking as examples Marx, Weber, and Durkheim— "those great empirical analysts" who concerned themselves not with "theory" but with empirical "explanations"[26]—he urges that experimental logic should be substituted for argument by conceptual abstraction. The focus of theoretical argument should be the "crucial experiment," described as "a set of observations which will decide between two alternate theories."[27] And, of course, throughout his analysis, Stinchcombe premises this formal argument for theoretical reduction on the triadic foundations of the positivist position outlined above. For if experimental observations were themselves influenced by more general postulates, it would be quite impossible to accomplish the transformation of theoretical into experimental logic.[28†]

The third aspect of the final, theoretically-directed postulate of the positivist persuasion follows ineluctably from the first two. If theoretical formulation and theoretical conflict can indeed be entirely reduced to the specific, empirical side of the scientific continuum, there can be no logical basis for any structured kinds of *scientific disagreement*, for what Rolf Klima has called the nonlinear "horizontal" as opposed to the "vertical," progressive differentiation of scientific thought.[29†] According to the positivist persuasion, social scientific development is basically progressive, and differentiation is much more a product of specialization, more the result of focusing on different aspects of the empirical world, than of any more generalized, nonempirical disagreement over the same piece of observational evidence.[30] The reciprocal character of this argument should also be apparent, for in the absence of structured scientific conflict, the necessity for any kind of more general scientific debate is further undermined.

Thus formulated by its leading protagonists, this positivist persuasion in contemporary sociology has had an impoverishing effect on the sociological imagination, in both its empirical and theoretical modes. By unduly emphasizing the observational and verificational dimensions of empirical practice, the positivist impetus has severely narrowed the range of empirical analysis. Efforts at empirical generalizations increasingly remain at the level of simple correlational statements, and the fear of engaging in "speculation" inhibits the formulation of the kind of connecting links that would help counterbalance what is to some degree the inevitable atomization of scientific knowledge.

Furthermore, this attack on the generalized elements of sociological thought lends support to the notion that scientific advance depends principally on methodological innovation, for the scientific challenge is increasingly understood to be an "observational" one. There develops the ephemeral effort to achieve a pure form of observational expression. Because mathematical language appears to be stripped of all nonempirical implication—when in fact, to the contrary, it is itself a form of abstract symbolization—it comes to be seen as the preferred language of scientific discourse. One can observe the logic connecting the positivist position and the argument for quantifying empirical analysis throughout the writings of the spokesmen for the positivist persuasion referred to above. For example, with his assertion that "the purpose of the design of experiments in statistical theory is to construct crucial experiments,"[31] Stinchcombe presents quantification as the end point of his argument for the reduction of theoretical to experimental logic. And the same kind of connection is made by Goode, who after discussing some particular objections to quantitative studies is still led by the logic of his positivist commitment to the following position:

> If we assume, as sociologists have by and large, that there are no fundamental epistemological or methodological barriers to

achieving validity in the analysis of social behavior, then it must
be viewed as salutary that the energy once poured into larger
epistemological problems has been directed instead to what are
now called "methodological" problems, that is, the elaboration
and testing of particular techniques of research and statistical
analysis.[32]

Although specific developments like mathematical and formalized sociology are the most distinctive and cohesive representatives of this
movement toward equating empirical quantification with theoretical
analysis, they present only the most visible aspects of the disposition in
the sociological discipline taken as a whole.[33†] A much more widespread
methodological manifestation of the positivist persuasion, in fact, is one
that falls between quantification and the more general theoretical tendencies that I will describe below. This is the effort of a pragmatically
inspired, rough-hewn empiricism to create sociological formulations out
of whole cloth through the methodology of getting as "close to the real
world" as possible.[34†] The best deliberate legitimation of such nonquan-
titative empiricist methodology is contained in *The Discovery of
Grounded Theory*, where Glaser and Strauss argue that "theory generated . . . from a-priori assumptions" must be distinguished from "the discovery of theory from data systematically obtained from social
research."[35]

   But more significantly for the concerns of the present discussion, the
effects of empiricism extend far beyond the range of empirical analysis
itself to what has been traditionally called theoretical sociology. Not only
has the positivist persuasion greatly reduced the quantity of sociological
discussion that concerns itself directly with the more generalized elements of scientific thought, but it has to a certain unmistakable degree
affected the quality of the theoretical discussion that remains. By making
it more difficult for theoretical analysis to attain an adequate self-understanding, the positivist environment has ultimately limited the depth of
theoretical perception. In the following chapter I will elaborate on this
problem of limited theoretical perception. Here I would like to indicate
the confusion in self-understanding that positivism has generated in
even the most accomplished contemporary sociological theorists.

   In the most ambitious and successful attempt to classify the schools
of contemporary sociological theory, Walter L. Wallace introduces his
"overview" with a general analysis of the role of theory in "scientific sociology" that describes the latter as a thoroughly one-directional, inductive enterprise.[36] According to Wallace, sociological theory is simply an
"informational storehouse," the condensed "product" of individual observation which for that reason must always "lag" behind empirical
work. In a manner that is consistent with this conceptualization, the pro-

cess of sociological inquiry is described as beginning with observations, moving from there to empirical generalizations through the methodological tools of scaling and measurement, and only then advancing to the stage of theory formation, utilizing the formal rules of logic and induction.

But this conception of science provides no explanation for the very phenomenon that Wallace goes on to describe. Following his introductory analysis of the nature of sociological science, he begins his substantive analysis of sociological theories by formulating a schema of two basic cross-cutting dimensions. Two dimensions are necessary, he argues, because sociological theories differ not only in their mode of explanation but also in their vision of the phenomena-to-be-explained. Further, Wallace continues, variation in the latter dimension must inevitably be linked to basic philosophical disagreements. But if empirical data are as inviolable as Wallace has described them to be in his discussion of science as a one-directional process, this general analytic framework he has just proposed is, to say the least, highly implausible. Such a contradiction between what might be called theoretical self-consciousness and theoretical practice is revealed once again in Wallace's conclusion. After completing his substantive analysis of the empirical impact of divergent general assumptions, he attempts to squeeze this analysis back into the narrow positivist framework of his introductory discussion of the nature of science. Trying to assess the usefulness of his substantive insights, for example, Wallace suggests that the varied theoretical perspectives he has identified should be utilized eclectically to guide "the induction of theoretic conclusions from . . . empirical generalizations" according to the particular kind of phenomenon that is the focus of observation at any particular time.[37] In other words, the theoretical analysis which has been premised on the interpenetration of empirical and nonempirical elements should now be utilized according to a criterion that proposes the radical separation of observations and theoretical reconstructions.

But perhaps the best illustration of the negative impact of the positivist persuasion can be found by examining the "methodological" statement of one of the most distinguished contemporary sociological theorists, the discussion by Robert K. Merton, "On Sociological Theories of the Middle Range."[38] On the one hand, the very term "middle range" suggests a theoretical sensibility congruent with the two-directional position outlined above. If we accept an analytical approach to the relation of theory and fact, the designation "middle range" is not a statement about the focus on the empirical or nonempirical levels, but refers rather to a certain level of conceptual specificity, to a certain mix of the presuppositions, models, propositions, and correlations which, implicitly and explicitly, compose all scientific statements. In these terms, the argument

over general versus middle-range theory becomes a conflict over the allocation of scientific resources rather than an epistemological argument
over the nature of science itself. Yet this is not, I believe, how Merton's
essay has, for the most part, been interpreted. Over the last three decades, it has been regarded as a pivotal declaration of the movement away
from a concern with "generality" toward an exclusive concentration on,
and consciousness about, the more "specific" elements of sociological
thought.[39†] This interpretative paradox, moreover, can be traced to tensions within Merton's own essay, which manifests, despite its analytic
power, the extraordinary strain that the thrust toward positivism generates in theoretical thinking. For despite Merton's obvious intent, his argument conceptualizes middle-range theory in what are actually two
directly contradictory ways. By separating out these two strands of his
discussion, I will clarify the present conception of the multilayered quality of scientific thought and, at the same time, achieve a greater appreciation of the means by which that understanding is narrowed and
challenged.

In one clearly articulated strand of his argument, Merton emphasizes the generalized nonempirical aspect of middle-range theory. "Each
of these middle-range theories," he writes, "provides an *image* that gives
rise to inferences."[40] The emphasis here is clearly on abstract generalization, on the autonomy of what might be called the theoretical dimension
of middle-range formulations as distinguished from the dimension that
faces the empirical environment. "Each [middle-range] theory is more
than a mere empirical generalization—an isolated proposition sum-
marizing observed uniformities between two or more variables. A [mid-
dle-range] theory comprises a set of assumptions from which empirical
generalizations have themselves been derived."[41] Given this perspective,
it is natural that Merton views theorizing at the middle range as a distinctively two-directional process, criticizing, on the one hand, any approach that appears to be "*exclusively* committed to the exploration of a
total system" or "master conceptual scheme,"[42] and, on the other hand,
any attempt "to concentrate entirely on special theories" that produce
only "specific hypotheses."[43]

In terms of the schema set out in section 1, the implications of this
strand of Merton's argument are twofold. First, a theory located in the
middle range of the scientific continuum demands its own independent
level of analysis and must be criticized according to differentiated scientific criteria. Second, such a middle-range theory is conditioned not only
by more specific empirical generalizations but also by more general theoretical formulations. This latter implication is indicated, for example,
by Merton's counterargument against what he describes as the Marxist
"fear that [Marxist general] theory will be threatened by the role of theories of the middle range."[44] He argues, to the contrary, that "to the extent
that the general theoretical orientation provided by Marxist thought be-

comes a guide to systematic empirical research it must do so by developing intermediate special theories."[45]

By so stating that middle-range theories must be, in part, specifications and elaborations of more general formulations, Merton's analysis has effectively delineated a distinctive level of scientific analysis without making this level either exclusively privileged relative to empirical observation or exclusively dependent on inductive reasoning. This kind of subtle differentiation of levels within an overall anti-empiricist framework becomes even more sharply expressed in Merton's essay "The Bearing of Sociological Theory on Empirical Research," in which he emphasizes the impact of general "conceptual analysis" on the most specific level of scientific observation. "In research . . . our conceptual language tends to fix our perceptions and, derivatively, our thought and behavior. The concept defines the situation, and the research worker responds accordingly."[46] It is for this reason, according to Merton, that analysis at the conceptual level "provides for a *reconstruction of data*."[47]

Yet in the same classic essay on theories of the middle range, another strand of Merton's argument emerges that at almost every point is the obverse of the one just described. It is this particular analysis, when taken for the whole, that has provided such legitimation for the positivist attempt to undercut the role of the nonempirical elements in sociological formulations. Rather than acknowledging, and endorsing, the heuristic contribution of more "general" theory, Merton begins this line of reasoning by attacking such general statements as being disconnected from observation. "General theories," he writes, ". . . are too remote from particular classes of social behavior . . . to account for what is observed."[48] Instead he proposes the inductivist approach emphasized by the positivist persuasion, urging that the analysis of general elements be abandoned until "a great mass of basic observations has been accumulated."[49] In this version of his argument, Merton has accepted what are in effect the first two positivist postulates. And with his support for the position—expressed only implicitly here but more explicitly in another essay, "On the History and Systematics of Sociological Theory"[50]—that only by so eliminating any focus on nonempirical and "philosophical" concerns can sociology attain a truly scientific status, Merton has reconstructed the entire foundation of the positivist perspective on science.

It is not surprising, therefore, that one can also find in Merton's essay on middle-range theory thoroughgoing support for the fourth and final positivist proposition about the relation between "theory" and "fact." The effort to reduce general, or theoretical, argument to purely empirical concerns appears periodically throughout the essay, and the logical corollary of this position—that such an empirically based science provides no basis for fundamental, structured disagreement—is a major point to which Merton again and again returns. He contends that the division of a science into competing schools results only from the artificial imposition of generalized beliefs on empirical investigation. For example, in discussing the early period of sociology, he writes:

> The multiplicity of [general] systems, each claiming to be the genuine sociology, led naturally enough to the formulation of schools, each with its clusters of masters, disciples, epigoni. Sociology not only became differentiated from other disciplines, but it became internally differentiated. This differentiation was not in terms of specialization, as in the other sciences, but rather, as in philosophy, in terms of total systems, typically held to be internally exclusive and largely at odds.[51]

If sociology can orient itself, instead, to the level of empirically-based middle-level theories, Merton contends that the kind of horizontal differentiation and conflict that characterizes the nonempirical fields, like philosophy, will be avoided.[52] He suggests, moreover, a number of areas of sociological specialization which have accomplished this, fields in which, through the focus on formulations at the middle range, theoretical agreement has been obtained. He cites, at one point, theories of social mobility, reference groups, social stratification, authority, change, institutional interaction and anomie,[53] and, at another point, theories of racial, class, and international conflict.[54]

Yet these specialized-area middle-range theories do not, in fact, represent examples of theoretical or even empirical agreement, and the belief that they do so is directly contrary to the implications of the nonpositivist strand of Merton's own argument. For if middle-range formulations are connected not only to the empirical but also to the metaphysical side of the scientific continuum, they are bound to reflect the contention that inevitably adheres to more generalized intellectual discussion. An indication of the contradictory character of Merton's position on this issue is the fact that one of the major disputants in several of the specialized areas he has described as internally harmonious is Marxism—the same "general" position that Merton himself described in the other, nonpositivist strand of his argument as definitely informing attempts to develop empirical theories at the middle range.[55†]

Although applied at greater length in other aspects of his work, Merton's conceptualization of the "paradigm" concept in his essay on the middle range reflects the same tension. In one sense, the formal definition of paradigm analysis represents an illuminating description of the strategic options and decisions available at a distinctive analytic level of sociological thought. At the same time, however, Merton defines paradigms as mere "codifications" of previous empirical research and explicitly excludes from them any comment on the "basic set of assumptions" that inform the paradigm at the most general level.[56] It is this positivist cast of his paradigm concept that has allowed Merton to utilize it as a device for muting what are actually substantive theoretical and empirical disagreements—in his articulation of the functionalist paradigm, for example, the fundamental conflict between the perspectives of Parsons and Marx.[57†]

This examination of the writings of Wallace and Merton has demonstrated that to the degree that these important theorists have been influenced by the positivist persuasion, they not only fail to explain the nature of their own theoretical contributions but, perhaps even more strikingly, often directly contradict their own explicit analytic frameworks. It is clear that the growing positivist thrust of contemporary sociology impoverishes not only the realm of empirical inquiry but also what remains of the theoretical tradition itself.

3. THE FAILURE OF THE "HUMAN STUDIES" ALTERNATIVE TO SOCIAL SCIENTIFIC POSITIVISM

Although there have been numerous demurrals from the positivist persuasion in social science, some of the substantive arguments for which I will discuss in chapter 3, their proponents have for the most part not sought to justify themselves in terms of the philosophy of science. Moreover, the one long-standing intellectual movement which has consistently articulated a strongly antipositivist orientation to social inquiry—the "human studies" or hermeneutical critique—has usually presented itself in what is ultimately an unacceptably subjectivist manner.

Informed by various strands of nineteenth-century idealism, this alternative to positivism centers on what I have called its third postulate, the identification of social with natural science. Those who adhere to this antipositivist perspective contend that such an association does not hold: the disciplined investigation of social life—an approach identified as the "cultural" or "human" studies alternative, after Dilthey's *Geisteswissenschaft* (literally, science of spirit)—departs in a fundamental way from the science of nature. It does so, these critics argue, by virtue of its distinctive subject matter which, in contrast to physical nature, is the necessarily internal meanings that guide human action. From this initial distinction, there follows logically the negation of what are, in effect, the first two positivist postulates. It is argued that because of the wide variation and relative inaccessibility of internal meanings—because, that is, of the "nonempirical" or at least "nonphysical" aspect of the subject matter of the human studies—the universal categories and objective arguments required for prediction and explanation are impossible to achieve. Furthermore, not only is the practice of social inquiry not completely independent of such nonempirical pursuits as philosophy and literature, but this social inquiry actually will more closely resemble philosophical and literary criticism than it will the sciences of nature.

On the basis of this refutation of the foundations of the positivist persuasion, two conclusions are possible. At a minimum, it can be argued, as Dilthey did, that "understanding" rather than "explanation" should be the major goal of social inquiry, and that even those generalizations which are advanced will be of a fundamentally more tentative character than those in the natural sciences. As Dilthey wrote in his *Introduction to the Human Studies*:

> The uniformities which can be established in the field of society are in number, importance, and precision of statement far behind the laws which it has been found possible to lay down for nature on the sure foundation of relations in space and the properties of motion. . . . The social sciences are unable to guarantee such a satisfaction to the intellect. . . . The play of (to us) soulless efficient causes is here replaced by that of ideas, feelings, and motives. And there is no limit to the singularity, the wealth in the play of interaction, which is here revealed.[58]

In its more extreme form, the idealist critique declares universality and objectivity to be completely illusory and limits all social study to the analysis of single, "idiographic" events. In the contemporary period, this position has been argued by Peter Winch:

> Since ideas . . . are constantly developing and changing, and since each system of ideas, its component elements being interrelated internally, has to be understood in and for itself, the combined result . . . make[s] systems of ideas a very unsuitable subject for broad generalizations. [And since] social relations really exist only in and through the ideas which are current in society . . . it follows that social relations must be an equally unsuitable subject for generalizations and theories of the scientific sort to be formulated about them.[59]

But in either its moderate or radical version, the idealist critique leaves any attempt at formulating a "science" of society to what it regards as the pretentions of the positivist position.[60†]

Despite the significant contributions that the "human studies" position has made to the manner in which social inquiry is conducted—to the kinds of issues studied and the methodologies employed—such a subjectivist alternative to the positivist perspective on social science does not represent an adequate counterposition. Even within contemporary phenomenological and idealist traditions it is rarely practiced in its pure form.[61†] For this reason, the position has functioned, paradoxically, less as the actual foundation of a nonpositivist social inquiry than as a convenient polemical target by which the positivist position has been falsely legitimated. The argument against the "human studies" critique inevitably becomes channeled into debate over the applicability of the explanatory model of science. In terms of this polarization, the position has been almost universally supported that while many of the antipositivists' strictures may be accepted, the explanatory model must nonetheless be maintained. In the classical period of sociology, the subjectivist position received its most sophisticated critique from Max Weber, who persuasively refuted, both in logical terms and in his own scientific work, the idealist claim that interpretation rather than explanation was the only mode available to social inquiry.[62†] In the contemporary period, the most significant refutation of the human studies position has been made by Ernest Nagel, who in his analysis, "The Methodological Problems of the Social Sciences," judiciously and painstakingly demonstrates that controlled experiments in the social sciences are possible, that problems like cultural relativity and the interaction of scientific observer and scientific subject do not prevent the attainment of a certain level of precision in propositions about social causality.[63]

But although decisive in their critique of this traditional alternative to the positivist persuasion, the arguments of even such distinguished critics as Weber and Nagel obscure the central point at issue. The question taken for granted by these critics of the idealist position is the identification of natural science with a certain neutral definition of objectivity. Yet this is the very question that itself must be subjected to the most careful scrutiny, from a perspective that shares neither the radical subjectivity of the "human studies" critique nor the radical objectivity of the positivist position. While accepting the argument that the subjectivism of the "human studies" critique makes it an unacceptable alternative position, the question must then be asked whether natural science is itself related solely to empirical phenomena, whether in natural science itself there is not a "generalized" subjective element in the very perception of data.

And, in fact, when the debate over the nature of a social science shifts to this question, we find that Nagel's and Weber's arguments become much less interesting and, indeed, much less correct. For example, although Nagel, like Weber before him, moves decisively beyond the vulgar interpretations of the positivist perspective,[64] he remains in the end fundamentally committed to conceptualizing science as a one-directional process. He describes the growth of social science as a progressive, vertical development in which truth is eventually sifted out through critical experimental evaluation.[65] Nowhere in his entire discussion of the epistemological problems of the social sciences does Nagel mention the independent role of generalized theoretical elements in sociological inquiry. And the more specific chapter entitled "Explanation" relies entirely on the positivist perception of sociological theory as induction through statistical generalization. For example, in his critique of functionalism no substantive criticism of its general assumptions is offered; instead, operating purely according to the evaluative criterion of the positivist persuasion, Nagel contends that functionalism must be discarded because it is a theory that cannot be directly operationalized or "subjected to empirical control."[66]

In this brief section, I have begun to indicate how the "natural" versus "human" science debate represents an inaccurate dichotomization. In rejecting positivist objectivism, the human studies perspective tends toward a radical subjectivism that is unacceptable. Although pointing to significant weaknesses in certain aspects of the "scientific" perspective, the idealist position is ultimately retrogressive because it inhibits the search for universal criteria of evaluation, judgment, and, indeed, explanation vis-à-vis the social world. Such an unfortunate polarization is well illustrated by what Sorokin called the "illusions of operationalism." Although his criticism of the positivism of the operationalist movement elaborates important aspects of the perspective I propose in section 1, Sorokin insists on connecting this criticism to a position that denies the possibility of operationalizing altogether.[67] But to understand the illusion of the operationalist strategy is not to dismiss the utility of carrying out methodological operations aimed at testing and explanation, any more than emphasizing the autonomy and significance of the orientation to the metaphysical side of the scientific continuum implies an elimination of the orientation to the empirical world.[68†] But as long as the most self-consciously articulated alternatives to this "human studies" position remain tied to an empiricist approach to science, as do the arguments of Weber and Nagel, the rejection of the subjectivist critique of scientific objectivity must appear to lead to an acceptance of the basic tenets of the positivist persuasion.[69†] There is, however, an alternative perspective on the issue of the objectivity in science, one which shows this dilemma to be more apparent than real. I will call this alternative critique the "postpositivist" perspective on science.

4. TOWARD AN ALTERNATIVE CONCEPTION OF SCIENCE

The apparently ineluctable philosophical traverse from the rejection of the human studies alternative to the perspective of positivism is ruled by a false logic based on an underlying perception of science which both sides of the conflict share, and in which both are mistaken.[70†] It is this same false logic that governs the movement from an acceptance of what I have called the first two positivist postulates to the characterization of this acceptance, in the third postulate, as a commitment to "science" itself. It is time now to elaborate in more detail the alternative, more dialectical understanding of science that I proposed in section 1 and to which I have periodically referred since.

It is one of the major ironies of recent intellectual history that as the social sciences have moved toward the splitting of empirical from metaphysical concerns, toward the irrevocable separation of "philosophical" from observational problems, and toward the reduction of theory to fact, there has been developing a powerful movement in the philosophy and history of natural science that has become increasingly sensitive to the independent impact of the nonempirical, "generalized" aspects of scientific work.

It is possible to distinguish three ideal-typical positions as being in conflict within the history and philosophy of natural science, and although each position retains significant support there has been a gradual but distinctive shift in emphasis over the course of the last fifty years.[71†] In the 1930s and 1940s, strong support existed within these scholarly communities for the radical positivist conception of science as moving back and forth between inductive generalization and empirical verification without any independent theoretical intervention. Beginning in the 1950s, support developed for what has been called the "logical empiricist" rather than the strictly "positivist" perspective. From the present perspective, empiricism represented an important advance over radical positivism because it recognized the independent scientific contribution of theoretical elements such as conceptualization and modeling. But this "received view" remained fundamentally ambiguous and, in one sense, it strongly reinforced a central positivist contention.[72†] For while accepting the existence of "nonobservational entities," empiricism also maintains that all theoretical statements can be falsified by purely empirical, experimental procedures.

But it is the grounds on which empiricism rejected unreconstructed positivism that are significant here. Karl Popper and his followers rejected "verification" as a theoretical criterion because there would always remain the logical possibility of discovering a falsifying event. Popper then argued, however, that "falsification" could constitute such a criterion, precisely because it requires the knowledge of only one such negative case. In other words, although empiricism's rejection of the standard of verification allowed theoretical conceptualization much greater play, the rejection was in no sense based on a repudiation of the radical duality between fact and theory. By accepting the role of what has come to be called "falsificationalism," empiricism commits itself to an unproblematic perception of data as capable of being conceptualized in a relatively pure observational language. Although as one of the earliest and most formidable critics of radical positivism Popper correctly emphasized the significance of more general conceptual frameworks, he erred in assigning the decisive role of falsification to the necessity for every scientific statement to be capable of being tested by experiment. "It must be possible," Popper insisted, "for an empirical scientific system to be refuted by experience."[73†]

In a broad sense, it was this internal ambiguity that prompted the attacks against empiricism which began to gain support in the 1960s. Although such critiques appeared in the work of a variety of historians and philosophers who often sharply disagreed with one another, there did exist a widespread consensus about the necessity for fundamentally reinterpreting the positivist and empiricist perceptions of science.[74†] This third, postempiricist or "postpositivist" position became influential only in the recent period; yet its intellectual foundations were established much earlier, and it is in these earlier works that the fundamental alternatives to the postulates of the positivist persuasion are most clearly articulated.

4.1. EARLY FOUNDATIONS

The radical separation of empirical and nonempirical, which I have termed the first positivist postulate, was the epistemological issue at the center of the writings of the scientist-philosopher Michael Polanyi.[75†] In a series of books and essays written over a thirty-year period, Polanyi has argued against what he terms the "objectivist," or formalist, epistemological self-conception of science.[76] In place of the concrete distinction of positivism and empiricism, he suggests that there exists an interplay between the scientific knower and the object known. The fundamental argument that pervades Polanyi's writing is that the very intelligibility of empirical data, the very nature of what are called "observations," depends on the structuring power and the structuring framework of the scientist himself. "Into every act of knowing," he contends, "there enters a tacit and passionate contribution of the person knowing what is being known."[77]

Polanyi takes the activity which is at the center of the logic of scientific experiment, the observation of empirical regularity, and indicates how such observation would be impossible without the prior, tacit commitment of the scientist to a certain vision of that regularity. "Scientific observation," he writes, "includes an appreciation of order as contrasted to randomness."[78] And he underscores the basic character of this analytic interplay by emphasizing that even the scientific perception of a piece of data as random can be achieved only in relation to a certain kind of subjective expectation:

> [Even] the conception of events [as] being governed by chance implies a reference to orderly patterns which such events can simulate only by coincidence.[79]

You may justly speak of the improbability of particular events [only] if you recognize in them a distinctive pattern . . . and *if at the same time* you deny the reality of this pattern *and* assert instead that the events occurred at random within a wide range of possible alternatives, and were therefore much more likely to have taken a different course.[80]

Given this significance of the observer for the observed, the positivist and empiricist conception of the absolute break between empirical and nonempirical cannot be maintained. "The distinctiveness of an orderly pattern," Polanyi argues, is such that once it is considered by the scientist to be "found inherent in nature"—that is, to be a purely empirical phenomenon—it "cannot be strictly contradicted by experience."[81]

Yet at the same time, contrary to the assertions of his positivist and empiricist critics, Polanyi does not propose a radically subjectivist or idealist position—he is not, in other words, simply an antipositivist but rather a postpositivist. Committed to the epistemological distinction between the internal and external world and to the scientific ideal of universality, Polanyi conceives of scientific objectivity as emerging from the scientist's commitment to interpersonal formulations about the external world which aspire to universal validity.[82] Insofar as the tacit, personal perception of the scientist "submits to requirements acknowledged by itself as independent of itself," Polanyi contends, "it is not subjective."[83] Because "the universal [scientific standard] is constituted by being accepted as the impersonal term of this personal commitment,"[84] he continues, the otherwise subjectivist "paradox of self-set standards is eliminated, for in a [scientifically] competent mental act, the agent cannot do as he pleases, but compels himself forcibly to act as he believes he must."[85] On these grounds, Polanyi argues that the conception of science he has proposed "transcends the distinction between subjective and objective."[86†]

If Polanyi's epistemological criticism is correct, if the gap between empirical and metaphysical formulation is not concrete and scientific perception not a purely "objective" process, then we might expect the observation of scientists to be affected not only by the changing patterns in physical nature but by other, nonempirical alterations in their perceptual environment. Or, to put the issue directly in terms of the second postulate of the positivist persuasion, we might expect that specifically "philosophical" or "humanistic" issues would have a bearing on the empirical propositions of the practical scientist. And, indeed, we find support for this logical inference in another part of this "early" refutation of the positivist and empiricist perspectives on science. Appropriately, whereas the critique of the first positivist postulate involved philosophical debate, the criticism of the second has been carried out in terms of historical argument. The most important challenge to the second positivist postulate was raised by the path-breaking writings of the French historian Alexandre Koyré.

In two of his earliest and most important essays, published first in 1943 and later translated in a volume entitled *Metaphysics and Measurement*, Koyré analyzed the philosophical and cultural assumptions that underlay the revolutionary shift in the scientific understanding of the laws of motion first articulated by Galileo.[87] Koyré demonstrates how the Aristotelian perception of physical motion criticized by Galileo was imbedded in Greek cultural assumptions about the nature of social objects and cosmic order. Once the existence of this metaphysical framework has been taken into account, Koyré argues, the findings of Aristotelian physics can be understood not as the result of "unscientific" procedures, as the positivist criticism proposes, but rather as having been derived according to the objective induction from "observed" facts. According to even the most stringent contemporary methodological and experimental criteria, Koyré contends, Aristotelian physical theory was "perfectly sound"—given, once again, the more general assumptions through which the Aristotelians' scientific observations were necessarily filtered. "So sound" that, according to Koyré, "on the [cultural] basis of this physics it is utterly irrefutable."[88] Koyré points out that at the time of their formulation it was actually the Galilean proposals about inertia which were contrary to most of the scientific observations of the day. "It followed . . . with absolute necessity" from the Greek-based metaphysical framework of the period, he writes, "that the kind of motion which is postulated by inertia is utterly and perfectly impossible, and even contradictory" to observed regularity.[89] Given this situation, the "discovery" and "proof" of the new Galilean laws of motion depended not on better and more precise observations but rather on the acceptance of different ontological assumptions about the nature of objects and their relation in the cosmic order:

> The Galilean concept of motion . . . seems to us so "natural" that we even believe we have derived it from experience and observation [but to the contrary] some of the deepest and mightiest minds ever produced by mankind . . . had not to "discover," or to "establish" these simple and self-evident laws, but to work out and to build up the very framework which made these discoveries possible. They had, to begin with, to reshape and to re-form our intellect itself; to give to it a series of new concepts, to evolve a new approach to being, as a new concept of nature, a new concept of science, in other words, a new philosophy.[90†]

The impetus of these epistemological and historical critiques leads ineluctably to the refutation of the third and fourth postulates of the positivist perspective on science. Regarding the former, it may be reasoned that if empirical and nonempirical aspects of scientific work are not radically split, and if "philosophical" and "humanistic" issues do affect empirical observations, then the entire conception of science as an activity occupying only the "specific" side of the continuum of social thought must be abandoned. Scientific formulations depend, whether explicitly or implicitly, on orientations to both the metaphysical and empirical environments. When this alternative conception of science is combined with the first two counterpostulates, the foundations of the positivist persuasion have been undermined, with the result that the reductionist approach to theory—which constitutes the fourth and from the present perspective most important principle—is also called into question. If empirical generalizations cannot be based on neutral data observations, theoretical arguments cannot be "constructed" from empirical practice and reduced to the logic of experimental verification or falsification.

Drawing exactly this implication from his epistemological revisions, Polanyi asserts that the most important criterion of "scientific merit" is not absolute "accuracy" but "plausibility," a standard imbedded in the exercise of disciplined intuition that is scientific theory.[91†] Polanyi views scientific theory as the attempt at universal formalization of the scientist's personal experience of the external environment. As such, he argues, it is theories that provide the possibility for scientific objectivity, rather than data.[92] Accordingly, the positivist notion that methodological criteria like the rules of induction and experiment—utilized for either verification or falsification—achieve truly objective theorizing actually misrepresents the relation between theoretical and methodological conceptualization in science. Polanyi articulates an alternative relationship that is organized implicitly around the analytic interplay of generality and specificity.

> Specific rules of empirical inference [and] all formal rules of scientific procedures must prove ambiguous, for they will be interpreted quite differently, according to the particular conceptions about the nature of things by which the scientist is guided. . . . For within two different conceptual frameworks the same range of experience takes the shape of different facts and different evidence.[93]

Koyré's historical reformulation also leads to a challenge of the positivist perception of the role of theory in science. Because his analysis of philosophical assumptions had focused on certain historically crucial experiments, Koyré discusses the theory problem in terms of the traditional conception of the logic of scientific experiment. He argues that the experiment cannot be viewed as the starting point for the purely empirical induction of theoretical generalizations, as spokesmen for the positivist persuasion have described it. Using the analogy of language, he emphasizes instead the nonempirical, or generalized, dimension that must underlie any experimental process: "Experiment is the methodological interrogation of nature, an interrogation which presupposes and implies a language in which to formulate the questions, and a dictionary which enables us to read and to interpret the answers."[94] For this reason, theoretical argument cannot possibly be transformed into an empirical confrontation carried out in terms of experimental logic. "Obviously, the choice of the language, the decision to employ it, could not be determined by the experience which its use was to make possible. It had to come from other sources."[95†] In a conclusion which for polemical purposes exaggerates the anti-empiricist logic of his position, Koyré asserts that "experimentation is a teleological process of which the goal is determined by theory."[96†]

4.2. CONTEMPORARY ELABORATIONS

Although the basic epistemological and historical alternatives to the positivist persuasion were already established in these and other earlier works, the postpositivist writing of the 1960s and 1970s that first brought the alternative position to public prominence made important advances. By emphasizing the role of scientific "generality" per se, Polanyi and Koyré made their critique of positivism polemically powerful but analytically imprecise. Later writing began to refine this alternative position by articulating the different levels of generality and specificity in scientific thought. These developments brought the antipositivist, non-idealist position to the point where it could begin to truly reflect the complexity of scientific action, could begin, finally, to map out the particular ways in which the various elements of scientific thought are at once differentiated and interrelated.

By far the most ambitious and influential of these contemporary arguments is the one proposed by Thomas Kuhn. Although the outlines of Kuhn's work have been widely discussed, they have just as widely been misunderstood. By reexamining the arguments of Kuhn and his critics in terms of the general framework that has informed the preceding discussion, we can further clarify and differentiate the issues involved in a postpositivist conception of science.

In his description of science as a two-directional process determined by the interaction of empirical observation and a priori "paradigmatic" frameworks, Kuhn builds directly upon the earlier foundations.[97†] He advances this tradition by pushing his conception of paradigm beyond the notion of generality per se, including in his definition a number of different aspects, or levels, of scientific thought. Both these aspects of

Kuhn's work, his powerful reformulation of the general postpositivist position and his own original formulation of the paradigm concept, have aroused intense and contradictory debate. In some quarters, they have been accepted as the cornerstones of a new science; they have also been met by a body of critical scholarship which has attacked Kuhn's work as anti-intellectual and irrationalist. While the opposition to the general antipositivist thrust of Kuhn's writing can be understood simply as the response of the ingrained empiricist to any anti-objectivist proposal—as, for example, in the reactions of Popper and Watkins—the criticisms of Kuhn's particular formulation of the paradigm concept, many of which have been articulated by writers who do not share the positivist persuasion, must be more seriously considered.

In retrospect, looking back at the first edition of *The Structure of Scientific Revolutions*, published in 1962, it is clear that although Kuhn's definition of the paradigm concept as covering a range of different analytic levels constituted his great achievement, this same breadth of scope also represented the concept's greatest intellectual weakness. As Margaret Masterman first pointed out, Kuhn actually describes the "paradigmatic element" of scientific work in a variety of different ways, identifying it at various points in his discussion with general cultural assumptions, explanatory models, methodological principles, symbolic generalizations, or specific empirical examples.[98†] In terms of the framework for scientific analysis outlined in section 1, in his original paradigm concept Kuhn erred by conflating the different levels of generality of the scientific continuum. Although he succeeded in pointing to their variety and their interrelationship, he failed to stress their relative autonomy. As a result, his treatment of the impact of paradigms on scientific practice obscures two vital points. In the first place, a given piece of scientific work is not affected by each of the "paradigmatic elements" in the same way. In the second place, it appears for this reason highly likely that, contrary to the major thrust of Kuhn's argument, scientific positions can still share significant scientific commitments while sharply differing on certain others. To consider extreme cases, in the history of scientific thought scientists of similar metaphysical orientations have often diverged radically over issues on the more empirically-oriented side of the scientific continuum, such as proper models or correct propositions. Scientists have also, on occasion, agreed about empirical observations while disagreeing fundamentally about more presuppositional issues. Even in cases where both of these elements are in dispute—both specific propositions and general presuppositions—other elements might still be shared.[99†] At the methodological level, at least, there usually remain common commitments to "rationalist" notions of evidence and logic; more generally, commitments to shared disciplinary conceptions of proper scientific goals are often maintained.[100†]

If Kuhn's paradigm notion is so modified to reflect the autonomy as well as the interdependence of the components of scientific thought, his conception of the radical lack of communication among antagonistic scientific positions must also be partly revised. Periods of intellectual confrontation will indeed make scientific communication more opaque, as Kuhn has emphasized. However, the degree of this incommunicability will be contingent on the number and significance of the levels of the scientific continuum that are in dispute. Conflict over incommensurable results obtained through divergent methods and models may be partly offset by common presuppositional understandings and the acceptance of other empirical propositions that have not been challenged. Conflicting general presuppositions must be seriously repercussive, yet the crisis will be less intense if references to common models and methods remain. Similarly, the distinction Kuhn proposes between normal and revolutionary periods of science becomes less sharply demarcated. To the degree that intellectual alterations can occur independently, at different levels of the scientific continuum, there is less probability for the multilevel simultaneity of intellectual change that is the prerequisite for revolutionary scientific upheaval. Finally, the more radically relativistic aspects of Kuhn's analysis are also curtailed, for the theory would no longer necessarily present major scientific change as being promoted by two completely distinct, noncomparable paradigms. If common links exist, there remains some continuity in the application of standards of scientific judgment.[101†]

By reducing the cognitive complexity of science, Kuhn's original paradigm concept lends itself to a distortion of the intellectual contribution of each of its parts. Indeed, when the broad paradigm conceptualization has been applied to the sociological enterprise, as for example in Robert W. Friedrichs' influential *A Sociology of Sociology*, the results have revealed relatively little about the substantive issues of sociological practice. More importantly, in the effort to create an internal "paradigmatic" consistency where none in fact exists, these attempted applications have often seriously misrepresented the nature of the different elements of sociological thought. For example, deliberately adopting what he regards as Kuhn's approach to science, Friedrichs claims that from the early 1930s to the early 1960s American sociology adhered to a single paradigm, "functionalism," which he describes as a unified intellectual perspective that creates commitments ranging from the adherence to a particular philosophy of science and specific ideological and cognitive assumptions to various empirical statements and methodological perspectives. Because of his "conflationary" approach, however, Friedrichs has created a highly artificial unity, placing side by side sociological theorists—like Parsons, Homans, and Znaniecki—and sociological theories—like systems theory, game theory, and role theory—that exhibit little substantive agreement.[102†]

In a scholarly reversal that is as remarkable for its rarity as its insight, Kuhn responded to the criticisms of his work by drastically modifying his original terminology. The various elements that compose his earlier paradigm notion, he writes, are "no longer to be discussed as though they were all of a piece."[103] Instead of utilizing the single term "paradigm" to cover all the different components of scientific thought, he now recommends different terms for each analytic level.[104] Among the different kinds of a priori elements that he had included in his previous conceptualization, Kuhn now contends that the most specific empirically-oriented element, the model experiment or "exemplar," plays the most determinate role in the patterns of scientific commitment. Yet despite the much greater precision of Kuhn's later emphasis, and the fact that in most natural scientific disciplines exemplars do appear to manifest the distinctive kind of determinate power he attributes to them, this redefinition does not completely avoid the problems of his earlier analysis. Although the distortion produced by the relatively careless expansiveness of his original paradigm concept has now been eliminated, the "exemplar" utilization focuses the analyst's attention so narrowly that the greater accuracy about certain aspects of scientific action may have been attained at the cost of trivializing the study of science as a whole. By focusing attention solely on the group attachments which are the indicators of exemplar commitment at the expense of any attention to what might be called the distinctively cognitive dimension of scientific commitment, the methodology Kuhn has proposed, if utilized exclusively, threatens to have a narrowing and reductionist impact on the analysis of science.[105†]

Once again, as was the case with the original paradigm concept, this negative aspect of Kuhn's conceptual advance can be seen clearly in the attempts by sociologists to utilize the exemplar focus for illuminating the science of sociology. In *Theories and Theory Groups in Contemporary Sociology*, for example, Nicholas C. Mullins professes to explain the nature and development of sociological theory by explicitly adopting the Kuhnian emphasis on group, or organizational, analysis.[106†] The methodology Mullins develops for describing theoretical development is, in principle, completely indifferent to the actual intellectual content of sociological theory itself. "Two or more pieces of theory work are considered to be similar," he writes, "if their authors (1) Cite similar sources; (2) Are known to be colleagues or students, one of another, or all of yet another person, and (3) Are considered to be similar by themselves and others."[107] As a result of this strategy, Mullins develops, first, a description of "groups" whose members often share only the most superficial sociological commitments while disagreeing strongly on much more fundamental questions, and, second, an analysis of "theory" which fails to comprehend the basic intellectual disputes that have generated sociological conflict. In regard, for example, to the structure of theory groups, Mullins' technique of following only organizational ties leads him to describe Homans and Parsons as members of the "structural-functional" group in contrast to the "new social forecasting" school. Yet he describes the latter group as including Amatai Etzioni, whose cybernetic version of structural-functionalism actually is far closer to Parsons' work than the latter is to Homans' exchange analysis.[108†]

Whereas part of the excitement generated by Kuhn's original conceptualization of paradigm was its promise to close the distance, inevitably created by a nonpositivist perspective, between the philosophy, history, and sociology of science, on the one hand, and the cognitive issues at stake in scientific practice itself, on the other, his new terminology opens a yawning gap between these two kinds of activities. Despite their various weaknesses, one of the distinct advantages of empiricism and positivism was that they explained the causes of scientific development in terms that were consonant with the scientist's own perception of the cognitive, "scientific" issues at stake. In the postempiricist phase of analysis, where explanations of scientific development supersede the scientist's own conscious cognitive understanding, there is a great danger that this explanation will become radically reductionist and lose any real connection to the specifically scientific issues that are involved. Whether or not the extrascientific environment that influences the cognitive processes of science can be reconnected with the scientist's own perception depends on the nature of the particular postempiricist framework. As Mullins' work on sociology suggests, albeit in a somewhat truncated manner, it is now perfectly possible to conduct a "Kuhnian" analysis of scientific activity while ignoring the nature of the intellectual decisions necessary to practice it. Although in certain scientific disciplines the exemplar does represent the most effective visible determinate of scientific activity, it must be understood—as only a few "Kuhnian" analysts of science, like Warren Hagstrom, have understood[109†]—that such an exemplar is nevertheless merely a socializing conduit for the commitment to the entire range of components of scientific thought; if their effect on scientific activity is to be substantively understood, each must become the focus of analytic attention in its own right.[110†]

It is in the context of these problematic aspects of Kuhn's work that the recent formulations of Gerald Holton assume great importance. While Kuhn's later statements represent a narrowing focus on the more specific empirically-oriented segment of the scientific continuum, Holton's focus remains directed at the most general, metaphysically oriented elements of scientific thought. In a series of extensively documented historical essays on the founders of modern physics, from Kepler and Newton to Einstein and Bohr, Holton has demonstrated that even the most empirical and precise scientific formulations are shaped by very general kinds of intellectual frameworks, which in deliberate analogy to literary analysis he calls "themes." "We are lead," he writes "to introduce the recognition of the existence and even the necessity at certain stages in the growth of science, of unverifiable, unfalsifiable, and yet not-quite-arbitrary hypotheses [in order to explain] the sometimes quite flagrant neglect of 'experimental evidence' when such evidence is contrary to a given thematic commitment."[111]

Equally important, whereas Kuhn's analysis of both specific and general elements lends itself to cognitive reduction and the simplification of scientific complexity, Holton carefully acknowledges the independent contributions of those intellectual elements located at a more empirically oriented level of the scientific continuum than the one he has chosen to describe. Holton has defined nine different components of scientific thought, conceptualizing "themata" as one among three distinctively different dimensions into which these components can be divided.[112] According to his conceptualization, science consists, in part, of a "contingent plane," which he describes as "a term equivalent to operational analysis in the widest sense."[113] This plane, for didactic purposes, may be viewed as constituting an x/y axis, composed of "propositions concerning empirical matters of fact" and "analytic statements of logic" which are deductively necessary. There is, however, a third component of science, "a z-axis, perpendicular to the x- and y-axes of the contingent plane."[114] This, he writes, "is the dimension of themata, of those fundamental preconceptions of a stable and widely diffused kind that are not resolvable into or derivable from observation or analytic ratiocination."[115] In terms of this precise delineation of the different scientific domains, Holton describes positivism and empiricism as the claims "that those concepts and propositions are 'meaningless' which have zero and nearly zero components on the z dimension."[116] The concern about reductionism, or conflation, is further revealed in Holton's attempt to isolate the exact impact that scientific themata actually have. In his detailed historical, biographical, and analytic studies he has discovered certain distinctive and recurring thematic dichotomies—such as atomization/continuum, symmetry/asymmetry, and order/disorder—that structure the nature of scientific debate. He has also demonstrated much more specifically than either Kuhn or the classical writers how these thematic patterns are related to the working scientist's nonscientific philosophical and cultural environment.[117†]

Holton's work carries forward the elaboration of the postpositivist position first initiated by Kuhn. Explicitly conceiving scientific thought in terms of the kind of differentiated continuum I have described in section 1, he has advanced the necessary process of isolating the independent kinds of contributions of each of the individual analytic components. In doing so, he has begun to close the gap between the postpositivist understanding of science and the cognitive decisions involved in its actual practice.

5. THE POSTPOSITIVIST PERSUASION: REHABILITATION OF THE THEORETICAL

Despite the wide substantive disagreement as well as analytic confusion among the various advocates of a postpositivist position, there are certain basic points upon which they all agree and which present a perspective on science that is radically at odds with the one shared by the sociological protagonists of the positivist persuasion discussed in section 2.[118†] The fundamental basis of this agreement can be most effectively articulated in terms of the issue which in one form or another has preoccupied every thinker I have mentioned, namely, the relation between "theory" and "fact." According to the representatives of the postpositivist persuasion, *all scientific development is a two-tiered process, propelled as much by theoretical as by empirical argument.* I will argue for the centrality of this proposition by indicating the wide spectrum of support for four corollary principles, support for which extends from the historian and philosopher of science Imre Lakatos, who sharply emphasizes his opposition to Kuhn's alleged subjectivism, to the philosopher Paul Feyerabend, who makes a "plea for hedonism" in science, urging the rejection of formal objective criteria for the acceptance of scientific theory.[119] Although to some degree rearranged, these principles represent the alternatives to the four positivist postulates outlined above. As such they provide the justification for the generalized argument that will be conducted in the chapters which follow.

(a) All scientific data are theoretically informed. This alternative to the positivist conception of the fact/theory distinction as concrete has been most sharply articulated by the neo-Popperian Lakatos. "The problem is . . . not when we should stick to a 'theory' in the face of the 'known facts' and when the other way around," Lakatos contends, nor "what to do when theories 'clash with facts.' "[120] Theory and fact are, rather, terms of convenience, decided by the focus of scientific attention at a particular time: "Whether a proposition is a fact or a theory depends on our methodological decision. . . . The problem is which theory to consider as the interpretive one which provides the 'hard' facts and which the explanatory one which 'tentatively' explains them."[121] "Calling . . . statements 'observational,' " Lakatos insists, "is a manner of speech."[122†]

(b) Empirical commitments are not based solely on experimental evidence. On the more abstract philosophical level, this second corollary has been

supported by arguments ranging, on the one hand, from Polanyi's assertion that the principled "rejection of evidence" is the very bedrock upon
which the continuity of an empirical science depends,[123] to Lakatos'
demonstration that whether or not an experiment is actually "crucial"
for the refutation of a given commitment is a matter that can be decided
only by scientific hindsight.[124] The principle has also received extensive
historical documentation. Koyré's analysis of competing Aristotelian
and Galilean interpretations of the same "pendulum experiment" has already been discussed. In a similar manner Holton has demonstrated that
experimental evidence was relatively insignificant in the genesis of relativity theory, both in terms of his analysis of Poincaré's refusal to accept
what was apparently persuasive empirical support for relativity[125] and
in his proof that contrary to conventional scientific opinion, the empirical refutation of ether theory by the famous "Michelson experiment" actually had little effect on Einstein's original formulations.[126†] On a less
sensational level, Kuhn has provided evidence from a variety of different
scientific subfields that empirical commitments are continually maintained in spite of contrary experimental evidence.[127†]

*(c) General theoretical elaboration is normally dogmatic and horizontal
rather than skeptical and vertical.*[128†] Theoretical formulation does not
proceed, as Popper's empiricism would have it, according to the law of
"the fiercest struggle for survival,"[129] basing generalizations only on
positions which have not yet been empirically falsified and subjecting
such formulations in a completely open-minded and purely sceptical
manner to critical empirical attack. To the contrary, when a general theoretical position is confronted with contradictory empirical evidence
that cannot be ignored, it proceeds to develop ad hoc hypotheses and residual categories in order to encompass and "explain" these phenomena
without surrendering its more general formulations.[130†]

Although this understanding of the nature of scientific theorizing
has perhaps been most thoroughly elaborated and is certainly most
widely known in Kuhn's exposition of the stability and relatively uncriti-
cal character of normal as compared with revolutionary science, it has
been supported in a variety of ways by the entire spectrum of postpositivist thought. Polanyi's general references to the "circularity" of theoretical reasoning in science[131] are, for example, confirmed by Lakatos' more
specific formulations about theoretical strategy.[132] According to Lakatos,
every major natural scientific research program protects its theoretical
"hard core" through the construction of a "protective belt" of "auxiliary
hypotheses."[133] "It is this protective belt of auxiliary hypotheses which is
to bear the brunt of [empirical] test and get adjusted and readjusted, or
even completely replaced in the defense of this hardened core."[134] It is as

a result of this scientific strategy, employed in the vast majority of cases, that the fundamental theoretical assumptions of a research program become, for practical purposes, "irrefutable."[135†]

Further elaboration of this perception of theoretical strategy is provided by Stinchcombe. Any empirical falsification of a particular theoretical statement, Stinchcombe demonstrates, will produce not refutation but rather the reformulation of the same theoretical position at the next higher level of generality. "It is extremely rare," he writes, "that a refutation at a lower level involves a refutation all the way back to first principles."[136†] If such indeed is the normal condition of scientific theorizing, it is not surprising that Koyré and Butterfield conclude that the greatness of a theoretician can just as well be measured by his ability to maintain general theoretical commitments in the face of empirical anomaly as in his capacity to discard them. "Aristotelian theory came to a brilliant peak," Butterfield writes, "in the manner by which it hauled . . . exceptional [empirical] cases into the synthesis and established (at a second remove) their conformity with the stated [theoretical] rules."[137†]

(d) Fundamental shifts in scientific belief occur only when empirical changes are matched by the availability of alternative theoretical commitments. If change occurs only in the empirical environment of scientific thought, this variation either will be ignored, viewed as an inexplicable anomaly, or explained by resort to a residual category. That these options are, in fact, the only ones available is a direct consequence of the basic orientation to science that I have been emphasizing throughout: every scientific formulation is the result of pressures from two different kinds of intellectual environments. This is essentially Lakatos' point when he writes: "all that [empirical] refutation does is to enhance the problematic tension of the body of science and indicate the urgent need to revise it—in some unspecified way."[138] It is possible to resolve this tension, to create an alternative scientific commitment, only if this empirical shift occurs in the context of variation in the other, metaphysical, environment of scientific thought.[139†] But because empirical data give the appearance of being concrete rather than analytic, such significant shifts usually appear to be responses to purely experimental or empirical developments.[140†] Holton directly addresses this issue in the framework of his focus on thematic elements.

> Eventually, the basic empirical hypotheses such as heliocentricity and atomism were accepted into science because they were *regarded* as phenomenic ones [i.e., as empirical]. But is this [perception] correct? The answer is no. They remain thematic propositions, and so not directly coupled with phenomena.[141]

The reality of scientific change, in other words, belies its positivist appearance. Instead of the traditional conception of the "two-way confrontation of theories and experiment," Barbour argues that scientific shifts must be viewed as the result of a "complex confrontation of rival theories and a body of data of varying degrees of susceptibility to reinterpretation."[142] Theoretical confrontation is, therefore, just as significant a factor in creating shifts in scientific commitment as empirical confrontation. The struggle between general theoretical positions, Holton contends, is "among the most powerful energizers of [empirical] research,"[143] and it must be placed "at the heart of major changes or disputes" in the natural sciences.[144]

6. CONCLUSION: THE NEED FOR A GENERAL THEORETICAL LOGIC IN SOCIOLOGY

In evaluating the implications of Polanyi's philosophical revisions, Raymond Aron warns social scientists against "the temptation to seek absolute objectivity through empirical moderation," arguing that "to recognize the impossibility of demonstrating an axiom system . . . is not a defeat of the mind, but the recall of the mind to itself."[145]

The arguments presented in this chapter lead to the conclusion that there is a logic at work in the scientific process that has been ignored by spokesmen for the positivist persuasion in social science. Science proceeds as surely by a generalizing or "theoretical logic" as it does by the empirical logic of experiment, and the positivist decision to focus on the latter alone must ultimately prove as self-defeating as reading only one side of a double column of figures. If the nature of social science is to be properly understood, and its true potential fully achieved, the careful attention to methodological rules for induction from empirical observation must be matched by an effort to create a "theoretical methodology" that can explain the opposing movement from more general principles.

By arguing that such attention to theoretical logic is necessary not only to understand social thought better but also to practice it more effectively, I have, however, gone one step beyond the mandate of the preceding discussion. For even if we accept the argument that natural science is a two-tiered process, it is nevertheless apparent that, with certain important exceptions, scientific practice self-consciously focuses on the empirical side of the scientific continuum. Even those analysts like Kuhn and Holton who have argued most strongly for the postpositivist position are agreed that it is precisely this explicit focus on the empirical side that differentiates science from philosophy or religion.[146]† In other words, despite the acceptance of the fact that philosophical disagreement may be as crucial to scientific conflict as empirical argument, it appears that such general conflict must usually remain an implicit rather than explicit part of scientific investigation.[147†]

This cannot, however, be the case in the social sciences, in which explicit argument over general principles is a very basic part of normal scientific development. In this particular sense, there is, after all, a partial bifurcation of natural versus socially oriented inquiry, but this divergence occurs not over the possibility of adhering to explanatory, "objective" laws, as the "human studies" critique contends, but rather over which of the elements of scientific thought become the explicit focus of attention. "Generalization" and "specificity" are indeed analytic properties associated with all scientific formulations, whether in the natural or the social area, but the self-conscious focus on these properties varies from one scientific area to another.

The source of this divergence can be understood in reference to Kuhn's theory of paradigm crisis in the natural sciences. According to this argument, the general assumptions that inform a particular scientific position remain inarticulate as long as this position generates widespread agreement. But if for any one of a variety of reasons this consensus breaks down, these general background assumptions are forced into the open. In a paradigm crisis, generalized theoretical argument becomes explicit and self-conscious; there develops, in Kuhn's words, the "recourse to philosophy and to debate over fundamentals."[148]

Social science institutionalizes what is for natural science an aberration, and it does so because the intrinsic possibilities for consensus are strikingly different in the two types of concerns. For reasons related to the nature of its subject matter, disagreement at all levels of the scientific continuum is inherently much more intensive in the social sciences. Proximity of the focus of social scientific analysis to the bases of political and cultural concern in social life heightens the inevitable methodological and substantive barriers to social scientific agreement.[149†] The conditions that Kuhn associates with abnormal crisis in the natural sciences are, therefore, constant factors in the social ones. Although the severity of disagreement will vary, for example, according to the type of discipline and the nature of the historical period, these variations represent merely intensifications or moderations of a crisis that is a permanent condition of the social sciences. There are a great many two-variable correlations in sociology, and a number of general theoretical statements, but there are relatively few actual exemplars, in Kuhn's sense of the term.[150†] And this condition exists, I would argue, not because of the scientific "immaturity" of sociology but because of the nature of the sociological enterprise itself.[151†]

It is this disparity in the possibilities for consensus that explains why natural science appears to be the more "objective" effort.[152†] In the first place, although theoretical development in the natural sciences, taken over time, is no more purely progressive than development in the social sciences, at any particular point in time the greater theoretical and empirical divergence in social science makes this lack of linearity much more visible. In the second place, despite the fact that explanation in natural science is not "exact" in the positivist or empiricist sense of that term, its foundations are, indeed, more precise, for the following reason. The degree of explanatory precision that can be attained in any intellectual inquiry is directly related to the degree of explicit focus on the empirical side of the scientific continuum. In social science, because explicit intellectual attention is spread throughout the range of elements, precision is much more difficult to obtain.

For these reasons, then, I believe that the movement toward theoretical reduction and exclusively methodological precision in the social sciences not only leads to a misunderstanding of the nature of the sociological enterprise but also to a distortion of sociological practice. If empirical research alone will not invalidate more general assumptions, if the result is rather to produce a more elaborate generalizing strategy, and if this theoretical struggle is necessarily a decisive element in any major shift of social scientific commitment, then it becomes a matter of the greatest importance to make explicit the logic upon which such general debate depends. In the following chapters, I will try to define the nature of the most general element of sociological thinking and to delineate the independent contribution this generality makes to sociological analysis.

Chapter Two

THEORETICAL LOGIC IN SOCIOLOGICAL THOUGHT (1):

The Failure of Contemporary Debate to Achieve Generality

The relative poverty of theoretical discussion in sociology results from a distorted view of the scientific process, and, more particularly, of the relation between the social and natural sciences. In examining the relatively few important theoretical efforts in recent decades, from the works of Parsons and Rex to those of Gouldner and Giddens, one can see that only those thinkers who have thoroughly and explicitly broken from the positivist persuasion will even attempt an exercise in general theoretical logic.[1†] But even when this barrier is overcome, the problems that plague generalized theoretical analysis in sociology, the substantive misunderstandings that undermine its efforts at intellectual self-reflection, are by no means eliminated. It is these substantive misperceptions that this chapter will examine.[2]

One preliminary consideration must, however, first be addressed. Theoretical, generalizing analysis, as that mode was defined in the conclusion of chapter 1, can in fact focus at any point on the continuum of sociological thought; the "generalized" element emerges from isolating at any given point these aspects of a sociological formulation which derive from its orientation to the metaphysical as opposed to the observational environment.[3†] In the present work, however, the decision has been made to focus attention on the most general level of the sociological continuum, that which I have described in the preceding chapter as the level of "general presuppositions." Such a general level offers the most effective demonstration of the two-directionality of social scientific thought, its simultaneous links to both metaphysical assumptions and empirical facts. More importantly, the general framework established by commitments to such general presuppositions ramify throughout the entire continuum of sociological thought.

After the level of theoretical analysis has been specified, however, the crucial substantive question remains; we are left with the problem of defining exactly what such general presuppositions actually are. After all, most significant postpositivist theoretical discussions do, in fact, focus on what their authors consider to be the most general level of sociological thought; yet as any familiarity with these exercises will immediately indicate, the sources of theoretical contention are still very great. The contention revolves around the nature of the generalized presuppositions themselves.

There are two fundamental criteria for correctly establishing the nature of such presuppositions in social scientific argument. In the first place, they must be truly "generalized," principles so broad in scope that they cannot be subsumed by any more empirically-oriented level of the scientific continuum. They cannot be redundant, merely reformulating under the guise of formal abstraction principles which can actually be derived from other levels of analysis. Stated more positively, such presuppositions must be capable of creating a framework within which all other scientific commitments can be understood as specifications, even while the latter maintain their analytic independence. To present a simple example, syntactical rules about sentence construction are more generalized than grammatical rules covering gender agreement or verb conjugation. But possessing wide scope is not enough: a second criterion for presuppositional status is necessary. General presuppositions must, also, be truly "decisive"; they must have significant repercussions at every more specific level of sociological analysis. Such presuppositions, in other words, cannot be trivial. It is quite possible to be more generalized than other theoretical assumptions while at the same time being relatively insignificant for matters of sociological concern; presuppositions, however, must address fundamentally significant scientific problems. The resolution of these problems in any particular theory must have predictable and highly distinctive consequences at every other level of scientific thought. To continue with the example of language, although rules about punctuation are also, in some sense, more generalized than grammatical rules about gender agreement, they are clearly not as decisive as the more ramifying syntactical rules about construction.[4†] If presuppositions do so combine decisiveness with generality of scope, important theoretical consequences follow. Although the basic principles of the differentiation and autonomy that govern each level of scientific thought ensure that theorists who agree at any single level can, and usually will, disagree at other levels, the criteria of generality and decisiveness guarantee that insofar as presuppositional commitments are shared, certain clear and significant similarities will exist between arguments which may in every other respect radically diverge.

When one looks at the explicit and implicit attempts to define generalized commitments that have underlain the gradually intensifying theoretical debates of the postwar period, one finds that in most cases these two standards have not been realized. First, the levels of analysis have not attained sufficient generality of scope. For the purposes of my analysis, one can ascertain four distinctive types of reduction among the variety of specific theoretical debates. In the controversies over functionalism and systems theory, testability and precision, conflict and equilibrium, and conservatism versus radicalism the effort has been made to reduce theoretical logic to decisions, respectively, about theoretical models, methodological principles, empirical propositions, and ideological commitments. Nevertheless, a striking phenomenon that has been apparent throughout the course of these debates is that strong disagreement over each one of these issues can, in a given instance, be subsumed by unanimity at more general levels of theoretical commitment, levels of argument that are explicitly acknowledged by few of the participants in these theoretical polemics. These theoretical arguments, in other words, violate the first criterion for presuppositional status, that of generality of scope. In terms of the second principle, that of decisiveness, it is equally important that these theoretical choices are not as ramifying as their proponents contend. Drawing upon the standards proposed by the postpositivist historians and philosophers of science discussed in the preceding chapter, one can see that theoretical decisions based on these choices fail to be truly thematic because they do not define the nature of the basic elements of social life, nor do they address the question of the fundamental relationship of these elements to one another and to the natural and cosmic order.[5†] Instead, these theoretical decisions concern models for elaborating the arrangement of such general elements in more detailed patterns; methodological principles for studying such patterns; statements about the empirical result of such observation—particularly the question of whether or not such observed empirical elements are in equilibrium; and, finally, ideological values for relating these empirical statements to the enduring political conflicts of social life.

One can criticize such orientations to general logic in terms of the standards developed in the preceding chapter. In the same manner that both positivist sociology and many of the proposed postpositivist alternatives conflate and simplify the scientific enterprise, so do these efforts at constructing a general theoretical logic. By taking certain vital parts of the sociological continuum for the whole, these theoretical debates reduce the complexity of sociological thought and undermine the autonomy of the different levels of analysis upon which its intellectual integrity depends.[6]

That these efforts at clarification result in conflation can be explained partly in terms of the philosophy of science, as a failure to conceptualize properly the differentiated nature of scientific thought. Far more importantly, however, this conflation is the result of vital errors in substantive sociological reasoning. Throughout the following discussion it might be helpful to refer to figure 3, which illustrates the connection between the discussion of the scientific continuum in chapter 1 and the present analysis of conflation in contemporary theoretical debate.

1. THE REDUCTION OF GENERAL LOGIC TO POLITICAL COMMITMENT: THE DEBATE OVER IDEOLOGY

The ideological dimension of theoretical statements constitutes one aspect of their general moral relevance, that aspect which implies certain courses of distinctively political action.[7†] As such, it represents judgments about social issues that can be directly linked to traditional political classifications like left and right, radical and conservative. In the approach to theoretical logic that is ideologically reductionist, this political dimension is taken to be identical with the moral dimension as a whole and, usually, with the nonempirical dimension of sociological thought per se. It is believed, in other words, that conceptions of the fundamental elements of social life and their interrelation are established mainly by the political relevance of the scientific formulations within which they are embedded. Such an equation of general nonempirical elements and ideological statements is articulated by Mannheim in his classic essay "Conservative Thought." Mannheim first establishes the antipositivist position that social and political thought cannot simply be oriented toward empirical concerns. "If only one penetrates deeply enough," he writes, "one will find that certain philosophical assumptions lie at the basis of all political thought."[8] He then relates this nonempirical dimension directly to its ideological implications for political action: "Similarly, in any kind of philosophy a certain pattern of action and a definite approach to the world is implied."[9] In Mannheim, a nonpositivist understanding of science becomes identified completely with the reduction of scientific thought to its ideological implications.

> From our point of view, all philosophy is nothing but a deeper elaboration of a kind of action. To understand the philosophy, one has to understand the nature of the action which lies at the bottom of it. This "action" which we have in mind is a special way, peculiar to each group, of penetrating social reality, and it takes on its most tangible form in politics.[10]

Such an equation of the nonempirical "philosophical" presuppositions of sociological thought with their ideological components presents the most radical and reductionist alternative to the positivist fallacy.[11†] If the positivist vision gives scientific cognition, or observation, an all-powerful role, this alternative ideological reduction completely eliminates the independent contribution of such disciplined observation by

Figure 3

THE RELATION OF CONTEMPORARY THEORETICAL DEBATE IN SOCIOLOGY
TO THE COMPONENTS OF SCIENCE

The Continuum of Social Scientific Thought

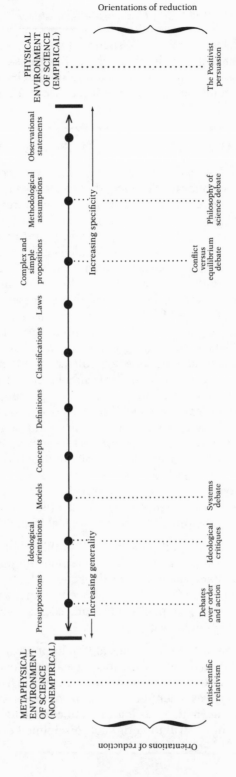

Contemporary Theoretical Debates

This diagram attempts to bring together schematically the arguments in chapters 1 and 2. The upper half is simply a recapitulation of the scientific continuum presented in chapter 1, figure 2, with one exception. I have differentiated here the category which I labeled "General presuppositions" into the two categories of "Presuppositions" and "Ideological orientations." This division is not necessary in the discussion of the natural sciences, and for this reason it would have simply complicated the discussion in chapter 1 unnecessarily.

converting knowledge into a form of action. The independent intellectual analysis of theoretical knowledge gives way, therefore, to the sociology of knowledge. The general presuppositions of science are not analyzed in terms of their intrinsic properties—evaluated, that is, for their plausibility and relevance in relation to what are proposed as universalistic intellectual criteria—but rather are judged only in terms of their social-political function. Analysis of general theoretical logic, therefore, becomes analysis of the social basis of ideas. As Mannheim himself claims in his essay "The Problem of a Sociology of Knowledge," this approach to social thought finds its historical origins in the emergence of the "unmasking turn of mind" that "does not seek to refute, negate, or call in doubt certain ideas, but rather to *disintegrate* them."[12] As such, ideological reduction rejects theoretical concerns and strives, instead, to fulfill an extratheoretical function. Indeed, Mannheim emphasizes this point. "We must pay attention," he writes, to the "distinction between 'denying the truth' of an idea, and 'determining the function' it exercises."[13]

> In denying the truth of an idea, I still presuppose it as "thesis" and thus put myself upon the same theoretical (and nothing but theoretical) basis as the one on which the idea is constituted. In casting doubt upon the "idea," I still think within the same categorical pattern as the one in which it has its being. But when I do not even raise the question (or at least when I do not make this question the burden of my argument) whether what the idea asserts is true, but consider it merely in terms of the *extra-theoretical function* it serves, then, and only then, do I achieve, an "unmasking" which in fact represents no theoretical refutation but the destruction of the practical effectiveness of these ideas.[14]

The specific types of general categories in which Mannheim articulated this ideological reduction correspond, to a certain degree at least, to the presuppositional framework of "action" and "order" which I will introduce in the following chapter—and examine in a substantively different manner. For Mannheim, theoretical conceptions that describe social action as nonrational and order as organic are inherently conservative, in contrast to what he views as the progressive nature of theories that presuppose rational action and a mechanical or individualist approach to social order. Although judgments about the specifically theoretical and more general moral ramifications of these assumptions do occasionally find their way into the analysis, such evaluations remain implicit and covert; for they cannot be Mannheim's principal concern. Primarily, the political implications of these elements are explored, their virtues as action-producing ideologies. The competition between general categories that comprises theoretical debate, in his view, relates not to any intrinsic

intellectual logic but only to details about actual social change, to alterations in class relations, geopolitical orientations, and social events. Thus,
Mannheim approaches the logic of the nonrational, organicist position in
the following manner.

> We have to show how the political and social "right-wing opposi-
> tion" not merely took up arms against the political and economic
> domination of rising capitalism, but how it opposed it intellec-
> tually too, and gathered up all those spiritual and intellectual
> factors which were in danger of suppression as the result of a
> victory for bourgeois rationalism, *even to the extent of working
> out a "counterlogic."*[15]

These particular Mannheimian categories have been preserved intact by a number of contemporary thinkers working in the sociology of
knowledge tradition. For example, in *The Fundamental Forms of Social
Thought*, Werner Stark attempts to explain theoretical variation across
the broadest possible intellectual canvas through the dichotomization of
organicism-realism and individualism-nominalism, describing basic theoretical shifts from one position to another in terms of economic cycles
of recession and inflation.[16] Writing from a much more subtle but basically similar perspective, Reinhard Bendix relates nonempirical presuppositions directly to ideological assumptions about the capacity for
individuality and autonomy, claiming that the more conservative the theory, the more it emphasizes organicism and supra-individual determinism.[17] Martindale's ambitious work, *The Nature and Types of Sociological
Theory*, although still more nuanced than either Bendix's or Stark's account, also presents a general theoretical logic organized around Mannheim's original ideological categories of organicism versus individualism.[18†]

Even when these precise classifications have been abandoned, and
the methodology for conducting a sociology of knowledge modulated
and refined, Mannheim's equation of the nonempirical and ideological
aspects of sociological thought remains. In this regard, two distinct
phases can be differentiated in American sociology since the Second
World War, corresponding to the initial period of normal theoretical conflict and the later period of intensified generalized debate. The dominant
figure in the first period, C. Wright Mills, regarded sociological theorizing as socially situated action in which conceptualization inevitably corresponds to a particular social base.[19] He tried to explain the specific
hypotheses of various sociological schools and specializations in terms of
their political and economic function for the wider society, describing,
for example, the shift from a focus on social problems to general abstract
theory as a reflection of long-run processes of bureaucratization.[20] Subsequently, Lewis Coser refined Mills' historical explanation of the social

sources of shifts in American sociology. Although also supplying other, more independent theoretical argument for his position, Coser utilized ideological reduction as his principal strategy to initiate the "conflict" debate in American sociology, a debate which I will examine in another context below.[21] In a widely read statement published ten years later, John Horton closed the circle between Coser and Mills by arguing, within an antipositivist context, that theories of deviance and social problems were determined not by empirical considerations but by social thinkers' ideological sympathy or antipathy toward conflict.[22]

The second phase of this American tradition of ideological reduction, commonly though not accurately referred to as a unique period of theoretical "crisis," was marked by the simultaneous appearance in 1970 of two books: Robert W. Friedrichs' *A Sociology of Sociology* and Alvin W. Gouldner's *The Coming Crisis of Western Sociology*. Although I have discussed the conflationary problems in Friedrichs' use of the paradigm concept in chapter 1, sec. 4.2, it is vital also to understand that this analytic confusion can be related, in turn, to his inflation of the ideological element at the expense of other nonempirical elements.[23†] For Friedrichs, the achievement of a nonpositivist position depends upon the acceptance of the role of "value judgments" in sociological theory, which are considered by him to be equivalent to ideological positions on the conservative-radical spectrum.[24] It is these judgments, he contends, that really determine theoretical disputes, for example, the debate over conflict versus equilibrium. For this reason, a significant part of Friedrichs' book is devoted to the task of locating the social roots of theoretical debate, in developments like the cold war, the development of computer technology, and the emergence of cybernetics. In a similar, though significantly more sensitive manner, Gouldner portrays sociological analysis as facing a choice between, on the one hand, the empiricist concern with validation and factuality that comprehends science as pure observation and, on the other hand, the perception of science as simply one form of political action, in which formulations are determined by ideological "domain assumptions."[25] Gouldner urges sociology to adopt the latter position, and throughout his book the argument runs from social analysis to theoretical conceptualization. For example, in the crucial chapter in Part One of *The Coming Crisis*, he tries to account for what he regards as the four central schools of Western sociological thought in terms of their contributions to the varied fortunes of the Western middle class.[26] This entire volume, in fact, may be viewed as a massive attempt to relate every major theoretical concept in sociology to some social need or utility. Encouraged by the work of Gouldner and Friedrichs as well as by a certain reading of one strand of Habermas' work, this second phase of the sociology-of-knowledge tradition culminates in the current tendency to perceive the decisions involved in theoretical logic as sufficiently described by the choice of "empirico-analytic" versus "critical" sociology.[27†]

The basic rationale for this approach to a postpositivist theoretical logic must be rejected. To portray the choice confronting generalized analysis in sociology as a choice between positivism, on one side, and determination by ideological assumption, on the other, is, quite simply, to establish a false dichotomy. The ideological dimension plays a fundamental role in every sociological statement, but at the same time the general nonempirical presuppositions that inform sociological reasoning can in no way be reduced to them. In one sense, the remainder of this chapter, and, indeed, the rest of this entire work, constitutes an argument in support of this criticism, particularly insofar as I address many of the same intellectual issues as does the "sociology of knowledge" I have described here.

But it is also possible to contest the preceding arguments more directly. By pointing to the weakness in the explanatory power of Mannheim's principal categories, one can present, in effect, "empirical" evidence for their lack of generality and decisiveness. Probably the single greatest work in this regard, explicitly dealing with the relation between political radicalism and general theoretical logic and, at the same time, covering the same historical period as Mannheim's, is Elie Halévy's *The Growth of Philosophic Radicalism*. One of the significant secondary themes in Halévy's book describes the historical location of the rationalist utilitarian tradition of middle-class democratic radicalism. Contrary to Mannheim's contention, Halévy demonstrates that the radical political tradition assumed a rationalist character only in the early nineteenth century, before which time its radicalism had been expressed in the nonrationalist, quasi-religious terminology of natural-rights theory.[28] Halévy demonstrates, moreover, that once this rationalist bourgeois tradition had become established, both antidemocratic conservatives like the early Bentham, and radical socialists, like the anarchist Godwin or the political economist Hodgkins, articulated their ideological theories in terms of a similar rationalist-utilitarian general logic.[29] Another important work that directly disputes Mannheim's central classifications, though it deals with a later period, is Robert Nisbet's *The Sociological Tradition*. Nisbet demonstrates that the organismic presuppositions developed by certain conservative thinkers became transposed, in the writings of the founders of modern sociology, into propositions often supporting an ideologically progressive perspective.[30†] More recently, this argument has been extended in an important series of revised interpretations of Durkheim's thought. Steven Lukes, Robert N. Bellah, Steven R. Marks, and J-C Filloux all emphasize, in direct though implicit opposition to the gist of Mannheim's argument, how conceptualizations of organic order and nonrational action were integral to Durkheim's ideological commitment to a liberal type of socialism.[31†]

The thrust of these alternative approaches to Mannheim's classic correlations is clear. These critics are arguing for the existence of intellectual presuppositions about the nature of fundamental social elements and their interrelation which can be differentiated from the political functions which a theory serves. The same thrust is evident in some later exercises in general theoretical logic—works by Atkinson, Jessop, Ekeh, Turner, Bershady, and Rocher—which, though implicitly oriented to the general problems Mannheim raised, are more particularly directed at the modifications of his position that have characterized the postwar American attempts at the sociology of knowledge, in both normal and crisis periods.[32] All of these theorists, many of whom are themselves committed to some form of radical ideology, focus at least in part on the same theoretical problems—for example, those of functionalism and conflict—that have been the subject of the sociology-of-knowledge tradition from Mills to Gouldner. Though often sharply divergent in other respects, what unites these writers is precisely their attempt to establish independent theoretical standards of evaluation that cannot be reduced to the traditional ideological criterion of left and right.

The theoretical logic of ideological reduction can be refuted, then, not only by pointing generally to the complexity and interrelatedness of the elements that actually constitute the sociological continuum, but also by contesting the specific explanatory arguments raised by Mannheim and his contemporary followers. The reduction can also be disputed in a third, less direct manner, by indicating the types of counterarguments which it has produced in the course of sociological debate. For if the dichotomization proposed by the ideological reduction is actually accepted, it appears that the only alternative to the complete elimination of the relative autonomy of the cognitive element in social scientific thought is the acceptance of the positivist perception of science. And, in fact, the quite legitimate opposition to ideological reduction is continually cited as justification for an illegitimate acceptance of the positivist perspective. T. B. Bottomore, for example, has made significant contributions to the redefinition of Marxist theory by implicitly separating ideological from other kinds of nonempirical considerations. Yet he apparently feels he can legitimate his independent theorizing only by denying nonempirical influences on Marx altogether, invoking, instead, what he proposes to be Marx's positivist, anti-apriori method.[33] But the construction of this false dichotomy does not simply confuse the self-understanding of thinkers who actually engage in independent theoretical reasoning; it also lends support to the positive proponents of an atheoretical, thoroughly empiricist social science. If ideological judgments are the only nonempirical assumptions available, the case for the elimination of such so-called value judgments is strengthened. One need only observe that Nagel's entire defense of the empiricist perspective on social science rests upon the equation of nonfactual judgments with political-ideological commitments.[34]

And the same justification is used by the other proponents of the positivist persuasion discussed in chapter 1—for example, by Goode and Catton.[35†]

Thus, through its conflation of the scientific continuum, the effort at ideological reduction initiates a line of theoretical reasoning that eventually circles back to undermine its own central theoretical proposition. The nonpositivist position that is most radical in its opposition to the determination of neutral observation actually facilitates, through its oversimplification, support for a positivist position. Under the guise of defending sociology against this radical ideological reduction, proponents of the positivist persuasion argue for the elimination of nonempirical presuppositions altogether. This paradox has been recognized by Habermas, who identifies as "cognitive interests" all the nonideological, supra-empirical assumptions that inform science. While arguing against the ideological reduction of science to the "objective situation of social groups," Habermas warns that in guarding against this reduction—and in defending, thereby, a degree of nonrelativist objectivity—science may become oblivious to the influence of "cognitive interests" that are actually more fundamental: "Because science must secure the objectivity of its statements, it deludes itself about the fundamental interests to which it owes not only its impetus but *the conditions of possible objectivity* themselves."[36]

If the understanding and explanation of sociological thought is ever to match the real complexity and differentiation of the scientific process, the nonempirical dimension of the sociological continuum must be opened up to influences other than the purely ideological. Employed as the principal technique of theoretical argumentation, the sociology of knowledge ultimately leads to an analysis of social rather than theoretical conflict. It also implies a thoroughgoing relativism as far as exclusively theoretical considerations are concerned. A more satisfactory approach to general logic should, to the contrary, illuminate the distinctively theoretical issues involved in sociological conflict; it should, in addition, provide criteria for choosing among them. The preceding discussion has argued for the existence and independent significance of such nonideological theoretical presuppositions, but it has not indicated what the nature of these elements might be. If one cannot simply point to the political implications of a scientific formulation to generate criteria of choice, it becomes necessary to develop a set of distinctively theoretical standards of merit and plausibility, which can, in turn, provide the basis for nonpositivist exercises in universalistic and objective evaluation. But while the justification for relativism has been undermined, such a postpositivist theoretical hierarchy has yet to be established. In the next three sections, I will examine some other recent attempts to produce evaluative criteria which, in the end, also fail to meet the fundamental criteria of generality and decisiveness.

2. THE REDUCTION OF GENERAL LOGIC TO METHODOLOGICAL CHOICE: THE DEBATE OVER POSITIVISM

I will consider the other three, nonideological, criteria commonly used to evaluate sociological theory in terms of their increasing approximation to the level of genuine presuppositions. The subject of the present section—the effort to define the most general level of theoretical logic in terms of decisions about methodological orientation—represents the least general focus of all the recent theoretical debates. As a result, it illuminates the search for general presuppositional issues only slightly more effectively than the reduction of thought to social position.

Contemporary sociology has been marked, as I suggested in chapter 1, by the ascension of the positivist persuasion, with its argument that sociological science need not include an independent theoretical component. Yet if science is, indeed, a fundamentally two-directional process, we would expect that even these positivist arguments would, inevitably, be informed by general presuppositions of their own; further, that their very success in recent sociological debate would rest on an acceptance of their particular brand of nonempirical logic. Of course, because of their own positivist self-image, such general assumptions have necessarily remained covert, for only in a thoroughly anomalous fashion could both positivism and a postpositivist attention to generalized assumptions be simultaneously expressed. Exactly such an anomolous situation is presented in the work of M. J. Mulkay, *Functionalism, Exchange and Theoretical Strategy*. Mulkay heightens the contradictions of the positivist position by contending, in the first part of his argument, that the substantive propositional content of a sociological formulation is determined by two levels of theoretical decision that are more general than direct empirical observation. He contends that theoretical development and evolution occur more because of redefinition at the general "strategic" level of analysis—defined as decisions about whether to employ "functionalism" or "exchange" perspectives—than because of changes in empirical information. Yet in the second and much more problematic part of his argument, Mulkay asserts that strategic reformulations occur because of decisions about still more general theoretical "goals," defined as commitments on the level of philosophy of science. Accordingly, Mulkay actually views the decision about whether to emphasize nonpositivist activities like concept formation or empiricist concerns like hypothetico-deduction as the major determinant of variation in sociological theory. Each step of the evolution from functionalism to exchange theory, which Mulkay presents as the theoretical sequence Pareto–Parsons–Merton–Homans–Blau, is held to have occurred solely by virtue of changing methodological decisions: each successive theorist, Mulkay believes, sought to achieve a closer fit between theoretical generalization and empirical fact.[37]

But this reduction of general theoretical logic to methodological decision has not been proposed only by sociologists of the positivist persuasion. In fact, partly in reaction to this development, there has emerged the argument which in every respect is its mirror image. We can best illustrate this approach by reference, once again, to Friedrichs' *A Sociology of Sociology*. The conflationary character of this work leads it not only to reduce theory to ideology (see sec. 1, above), but also to present simultaneously a variety of other versions of the generalized level of theoretical logic. The entire second half of Friedrichs' book tries to demonstrate that the methodological choice of empiricist-versus-nonempiricist philosophy of science necessarily leads, first, to the commitment to "priestly" (conservative) or "prophetic" (radical) ideological stances, and, second, to conceptions of the degree of empirical conflict or equilibrium.[38]

Another nonpositivistic commentator, Habermas, similarly identifies the presuppositional level with the methodological choices proposed by philosophy-of-science issues. Despite the fact that in his major methodological treatise, *Knowledge and Human Interests*, Habermas distinguishes the autonomy of methodological decision, ideological assumption, and substantive perceptions of the nature of social life, in his later writing, particularly in some essays reprinted in *Toward a Rational Society*, he indicates a persistent tendency to conflate these issues in a manner that is keyed to the overriding significance of the methodological decision.[39†] According to this understanding, the commitment to a positivist perception of science necessarily induces a thoroughly rationalist understanding of social life, which in turn is tied to the conservative acceptance of the bourgeois order. In terms of intellectual lineage, Habermas' reduction, minus its reference to the ideological component, can be traced to Parsons' *The Structure of Social Action*. Despite the fact that, considered in toto, Parsons' discussion classically differentiates the presuppositional and empirical levels of social thought—and that, later in the same work, he ascribes the problematic in Durkheim's theory to a tension between presuppositions and methodology—in part 1 Parsons clearly considers "rationalism" and "positivism" to be interchangeable terms. This is illustrated, for example, by his description of the nonindividualistic rationalist position as "radical anti-individualistic positivism." In this minor but still significant strand of the work, Parsons collapses the distinction between methodological and more generalized levels of argument, presenting rationalism as the inevitable outcome of positivism. Ultimately, he is led to the untenable position that theorists actually reject a subjectivist, irrationalist position because of a "fundamental methodological problem," claiming that in a positivist framework only material elements are visible to the scientific observer.[40†]

The most fundamental refutation of this reduction of general theoretical logic to methodological commitment derives, as did the criticism of ideological reduction, from a clear comprehension of the two-directional nature of the scientific continuum. If sociology does necessarily exhibit a multilayered quality, the decision to adopt a positivist or antipositivist methodological stance can have the effect only of decreasing or increasing theoretical self-consciousness about what is, after all, the basic structure of science itself. Theoretical decisions about levels of nonempirical commitment other than the methodological will still have to be made, if only in a covert and implicit manner.

But this nonpositivist reduction of theory to method can also be challenged in a much more direct manner by demonstrating that it does not fulfill the basic criteria established for judging the adequacy of definitions at the presuppositional level, namely, generality and decisiveness. The fact that decisions posed by the philosophy of science are not more general and inclusive than other kinds of theoretical commitments can be seen from Friedrichs' discussion. In establishing the distinctions of positivism and antipositivism, Friedrichs has purportedly identified the two most basic divisions extant in sociological theory. In his discussion of both the ideological conservatism and the empirical emphasis on equilibrium that he associates with positivism, Parsons is his primary polemical target. Yet, later in the same work, Parsons actually becomes the most cited resource for Friedrichs' discussion of the nonpositivist perspective, which is intended to imply completely different kinds of statements about ideology and equilibrium. Similarly, orthodox Marxism, which Friedrichs initially classifies as a subcategory of positivist theory, later serves also as the prime example of the conflict approach he has associated with an antipositivist methodological commitment.

The same kind of unexplained overlap between what are intended to be truly generalized theoretical divisions occurs in Habermas' work. Habermas asserts that an antipositivist position is sharply opposed to the political conservatism and utilitarianism of positivist thought. Yet such a politically traditionalist thinker as Dilthey serves as one of his primary illustrations of the postpositivist method, and Marx, the figure who sets the standard for radical ideological commitment, is sharply criticized by Habermas for his tendencies toward positivism and utilitarianism. Such confusions in both Friedrichs' and Habermas' arguments make it evident that there exist levels of theoretical commitment more general than either theorist has explicitly identified, for only such a more general level could explain the actual theoretical variation which they have identified.

The fact that methodological decisions are not sufficiently decisive is particularly evident in Mulkay's discussion. For in order adequately to justify the adoption of the exchange perspective, which is the major polemical point of his book, Mulkay is forced continually to go beyond the strict positivist criterion he has identified; he must, in addition, argue for the validity of certain substantive propositions about the role of the individual and the nature of social action. Much the same kind of implicit admission about the relative indecisiveness of the methodological criterion can also be seen in the work of Habermas, for he clearly spends as much time conducting an independent theoretical argument about the role of values in action as he does in arguing for the failure of positivist methodological perception. The methodological decision, it is clear, simply does not address what are, for both Mulkay and Habermas, the most decisive general issues in social scientific argument.

The philosophical choice about meta-methodological orientation is, indeed, a significant determinant of sociological theory. As the preceding chapter indicated, the nature of this commitment sets the parameters for any discussion of what is valuable, trivial, and obfuscating in sociological theorizing. It is, nonetheless, a decision that must be viewed as occupying a decidedly middle-range position on the continuum of sociological thought.

3. THE REDUCTION OF GENERAL LOGIC TO EMPIRICAL PROPOSITION: THE DEBATE OVER CONFLICT

The polemic over "conflict" versus "equilibrium" approaches to sociological formulations has been perhaps the most widely acknowledged theoretical debate in the recent period. As with the debates over the significance of ideological and methodological commitment, however, it is actually directed at a level of sociological analysis that is neither sufficiently generalized, nor sufficiently decisive to arbitrate successfully theoretical confrontation at the presuppositional level. The protagonists of this conflict debate have attempted, in effect, to transform propositions about an empirical condition at a given historical moment into statements claiming the most general and ramifying consequences for all sociological thought. But, in fact, such a specific description of the temporal arrangement of social elements cannot explain their fundamental nature and interrelation, the basic questions which must be addressed by any principle that aspires to truly presuppositional status. In the preceding two sections, I have first criticized the lack of generality and decisiveness of the theoretical criteria proposed, and then, subsequently, demonstrated the inability of the given classificatory scheme to explain adequately the kinds of theoretical divisions that actually have structured general debate in sociological theory. In the present section, the flow of argument seems to lend itself to a reversal of this order of critique.

When we examine the attempts over the past twenty-five years to identify general orientations and to classify theoretical works according to the designations of "conflict" and "equilibrium," we find that these efforts have produced highly inconsistent, often cross-cutting judgments. Commentators actually have associated an emphasis on what is called "conflict theory" with a variety of different general conceptual orientations. For example, Horton, following the model of Mills, declares that while "order" theory has an "adjustment" definition of deviance, conflict theory has a "growth" definition.[41] Yet Neil J. Smelser—himself a polemical target of "conflict theory"—has utilized this same distinction between adjustment and growth to differentiate among theories of social change which are both, he insists, types of "equilibrium models."[42] Coser, in contrast, considers an anti-equilibrium emphasis to be the key characteristic that identifies theoretical formulations as being concerned with social change and conflict. At the same time, he emphasizes, in direct contrast to Horton, the adjustment "functions" that such anti-equilibriating conflict performs.[43] For Ralf Dahrendorf, however, such an emphasis on the system functions of social behavior is considered the prime indicator of the very kind of static, Parsonian-style theory that Coser sees himself as refuting.[44] In still another variation on the conflict theme, Rex contends that the Millsian emphasis on conflict can be approached successfully only as a subset of a certain type of Weberian-Parsonian action theory. And to further complicate matters, not only does Rex view this theoretical orientation as different from the general assumptions that inform the approaches of both Coser and Dahrendorf, but the ideological level of his theory is cast in Marxist terms.[45†]

Such striking conceptual inconsistency inevitably manifests itself in the attempts to utilize the conflict criterion to classify different theoretical works and schools. Martindale places in his conflict school not only Marx, but also Adam Smith and Hegel, two theorists whom Marx believed with some reason, to be theoretically quite antithetical to himself.[46] Friedrichs places under the rubric of conflict theory the writings not only of Dahrendorf, Mills, Coser, and Marcuse—writers who have each, at some point, systematically attempted to exclude one another from such a designation—but also the work of theorists, such as Shils, who have been the object of almost universal opprobrium among theorists in even the most diverse types of conflict traditions.[47] The same kind of classificatory confusion pervades the later effort by Lehmann and Young to define a "conflict paradigm" for sociology. By including in this paradigm group a number of sociological theorists who have, in fact, sharply criticized one another's theoretical formulations, their attempt at classification aptly illustrates the inadequate level of generality and decisiveness provided by an exclusive reference to the conflict concept.[48†]

As this discussion begins to indicate, the identification of theoretical logic in sociology in terms of its commitment to the conflict concept pro-

duces a plethora of widely divergent accounts of the nature of generalized debate. The source of this theoretical confusion becomes clear
only when we are able to perceive what such attempts at general logic
explicitly deny. Conflict theories exist in such variety because any formulation about the degree of conflict must also involve reference to
theoretical criteria that are more general than this relatively empirically-
oriented level. Furthermore, because conflict formulations must inevitably embody such higher levels of conceptual generality, sharp theoretical
antagonism may arise between two theories that are in otherwise complete agreement on the question of conflict versus equilibrium. The attempt to identify sociological theories primarily in terms of their
commitment to conflict or equilibrium, in other words, is actually another form of theoretical conflation. And just as the problems raised by
ideological and methodological reduction were clarified only by illuminating the more general levels of analysis which they had obscured,
the same antidote must be applied to the theoretical debates over conflict. In identifying the more general theoretical criteria that are hidden
by the conflict debate, the most important of which are neither ideological nor methodological, I will, once again, be introducing subjects that
will be discussed at much greater length in the concluding section of this
chapter and in chapter 3.

The most significant of these more generalized commitments that in-
trude unacknowledged into the debate over conflict is the decision about
the relative role of coercion and value commitment in social life—the
same kind of theoretical issue that Mannheim described as the ra-
tionality/nonrationality problem. Once this additional level of debate
comes into focus, it becomes apparent that the cross-cutting references
of the different conflict approaches closely follow other, latent disagreements about these more fundamental theoretical decisions.

One distinguishable orientation within conflict theory, for example,
asserts that empirical conflict can be perceived only by identifying the
coercive, material elements in social life. Although Dahrendorf describes
himself in *Class and Class Conflict in Industrial Society* as concerned principally with the issues of conflict and equilibrium, he is actually deeply
engaged in the articulation of what he calls "coercion theory." In fact, it
is only within the framework of this more general commitment that he
considers conflict to be the preeminent factor in social life; it is generated, he argues, by the unequal access to the scarce resources of power
and authority.[49] Similarly, David Lockwood in an influential article,
"Some Remarks on 'The Social System,'" formally accepts the significance of social values, but contends that the recognition of conflict
can be incorporated into sociological theory only through an emphasis
on the "factual," Hobbesian element of analysis.[50†] And, in a parallel
manner, Horton asserts that while order theory speaks only of "cultural

integration," conflict theory delineates the "conditions of social organization."[51] In a subsequent attempt of this sort, Randall Collins defines "conflict sociology" as the tradition, initiated by Machiavelli and Hobbes, that explains "individuals' behavior . . . in terms of their self-interests in a material world of threat and violence."[52]

Although superficially similar, the conflict criticism offered by Coser actually stands in sharp contrast to the approaches of Dahrendorf, Lockwood, Horton, and Collins. For although Coser finds conflict to be just as ubiquitous empirically and argues just as strongly that this empirical insight should be the basis for generalized presuppositional argument, he identifies the conflict concept with very different kinds of presuppositional assumptions. In contrast to the approach that ties conflict to coercion, Coser interweaves questions of legitimacy and value conflict with questions of imperative control and conflict over scarce resources; he emphasizes the emotional and ideological aspects of group life along with the technical, organizational ones.[53†]

Finally, and even more confusingly, Rex's version of conflict theory contains overlapping concepts that arise from the ambiguity with which he identifies empirical conflict first with the role of value commitment, then with the role of coercion in social life. In one part of his argument, Rex appears to accept the Weberian-Parsonian approach to social action, portraying what he calls the "ruling class situation" as a hierarchical relation between two internally value-integrated social systems, a description of class conflict that is sharply at odds with the one proposed by Dahrendorf and Lockwood.[54†] In another part of his discussion, however, Rex shifts ground and identifies the perception of conflict with a perspective that emphasizes manipulation and coercion.[55†]

Only by comprehending the theoretical autonomy that exists between the more empirically-oriented decisions about degrees of social conflict and the more generalized decisions about the role of values and coercion is it possible to clarify the analytic confusion raised by the conflict polemics. For only within such a differentiated context does it become clear that, contrary to the contention of most of the participants in this debate, an emphasis on the empirical existence or probability of conflict or equilibrium is an option within *every* general theoretical orientation. Despite what has become the conventional wisdom, it is quite clear that conflict can be the major emphasis of theories that ascribe a significant social role to value commitment, as indicated not only by Coser's version of conflict theory but also by the writings of figures such as Edward Shils, Smelser, Judith Blake and Kingsley Davis, and Robin Williams.[56†] On the other hand, it is just as evident that conceptions articulating empirical equilibrium are perfectly consistent with general orientations that emphasize coercion, as illustrated, for example, by Dahrendorf's theory of the "pluralized" society.[57] It is precisely distinctions such as these that must inevitably be obscured by the reduction of general theoretical logic to propositions about conflict and equilibrium. And, indeed, the few contemporary theorists who have been able to mount successful generalized arguments are those, like Wallace, Atkinson, and Turner, who have also succeeded in recognizing the relative specificity of the conflict debate in relation to the kinds of more general issues I have described.[58†]

The second more generalized theoretical commitment that overlaps the conflict debate is the decision about the broad conceptual model within which social action of any type should be organized—for example, whether or not society is a "system" and what particular exigencies are produced by a systems commitment. Thus, Collins attempts to argue that conflict theory can be articulated only in "nominalistic" models,[59] and that "systems theory [views] the treatment of conflict as residual."[60†] Although this decision about models is less ramifying in its effects than the choice over values and coercion, it is perhaps for this very reason a level of analysis which is more often recognized by the participants in generalized theoretical debate themselves. Indeed, when the conflict/ equilibrium focus of recent debate has come under criticism, the charge has usually been that such debate ignores the more significant question of the variegated nature of the social system model within which both of these conditions must necessarily be imbedded. Disagreement over questions of conflict and equilibrium may actually be produced, it is argued, by divergence at this more fundamental level of theoretical commitment, over such questions as the particular exigencies produced by different kinds of social systems and whether any "system" organization exists at all. Similarly, the specificity of the conflict decision may allow agreement on this issue to camouflage more basic theoretical confrontation.

This kind of critique of the conflict reduction is usually made by those theorists who adhere to one or another form of "systems" conceptualization, and we can find it applied to each of the different variants of conflict theory I have described. Within the functionalist school, for example, Bert N. Adams responded to Horton's Millsian formulation of the controversy by contending that cultural integration and organizational conflict should be viewed simply as branches of "sociological functionalism"—a theoretical orientation which, he argued, should be viewed as having sui generis status.[61] From the neo-Marxist perspective, Anthony Giddens makes a similar argument against Dahrendorf's utilization of the conflict designation to distinguish Marx's theory from Parsons' and Durkheim's. Asserting that the crucial question is not the existence of conflict per se but rather the diagnosis of its particular systemic origins, Giddens reminds his readers that Marx himself envisioned equilibrium as an empirical condition in certain systemic situations.[62†] But perhaps the most striking criticism of the manner in which the conflict debate conflates the distinction between model and empirical proposition comes from Friedrichs, actually one of the foremost protagonists of the conflict approach. After having employed the conflict concept as the primary theoretical criterion throughout much of his book, Friedrichs concludes by acknowledging that " 'conflict' . . . is incapable of serving as the fundamental paradigmatic referent," adding that "many of those who have argued the case for conflict appear in fact to have retained an implicit system approach." To perceive the greater generality of the system reference, Friedrichs argues, is not to eliminate the significance of conflict, but rather to place it into greater perspective: "This is not to say that conflict becomes an illegitimate concept. But even it must be approached in fundamentally 'systemic' terms."[63]

This criticism of the conflict debate leads directly to consideration of the role of models in sociological thought. It is one thing to accept the greater generality of the systems concept. It is quite another and much more difficult task to describe the nature of its theoretical contribution.

4. THE REDUCTION OF GENERAL LOGIC TO MODEL SELECTION: THE DEBATE OVER FUNCTIONALISM

The debate over functionalist, or systems, theory takes place on perhaps the most general level of analysis addressed by recent theoretical argument in sociology. Although the critique of functionalism is implied by much of the conflict debate, for example in Dahrendorf's work, it also has been adopted as a central theoretical focus in its own right by a series of sociological theorists extending throughout the range of theoretical commitment, from Herbert Blumer and Martindale to Mulkay and Bottomore. In the logic developed by this antifunctionalist argument, these critics contend that the commitment to conceptualizing social facts in terms of a functional system represents the most ramifying of all theoretical decisions. Such a general commitment must lead, it is argued, to a reified perception of social life, a reification that manifests itself in two different ways: first, in the exclusion of the "concrete" from theoretical analysis, producing an explanatory bias that is antivoluntary, anti-interactional, and anti-institutional; second, in the perception of social units as self-regulating, implying thereby the inability to perceive social breakdown and change.[64]

When these polemics are examined closely, however, one finds that, as with the debates over ideology, methodology, and conflict, this argument about the theoretical importance of the functionalism concept is a conflationary one. To claim that this theoretical commitment represents the most general presuppositional level of sociological analysis dangerously simplifies the nature of theoretical logic. On the one hand, like

the decisions about ideology, method, and conflict, the debate over functionalism does illuminate an independent level of the sociological continuum and, indeed, a relatively significant one. In drawing attention to
the theoretical commitment to what can be understood as a certain kind
of "model," the critics of functionalism have helped make explicit what
must be considered, as Rex has cogently argued, one of the vital nonempirical reference points of scientific thought.[65] On the other hand, in accepting the systems commitment as a decision on the level of "model," it
must be recognized what such a commitment does not address. It cannot, as such, also be identified with theoretical decisions about empirical
propositions, methodological positions, or ideological values. Nor, most
importantly, can the commitment to a system model be identified with
those more generalized definitions of the fundamental elements of action and their interrelation which establish the presuppositions within
which every model must be more concretely specified. Given this basic
conceptual misperception, it is not surprising that the myriad of critiques of "functionalist" theory actually make reference to a number of
different kinds of theoretical issues. Critics as well as supporters of "systems" theory, in fact, often debate concepts quite different from those
they are proposing explicitly to discuss. Although some of these overlapping issues have already been analyzed, others must, of necessity, refer to
issues that have not yet become the central point of our theoretical focus.

The first cross-cutting issue, and perhaps one of the most confusing,
concerns the problem which I will later describe, at some length, as the
presuppositional problem of order. Although the charges that "functionalist" theory militates against the consideration of voluntarism, interaction, and institutional activity are proposed as arguments about the
degree of "freedom" allowed by a generalized theoretical position, they
can actually be no more than arguments about the freedom allowed by
one element of theory, that is, by a certain type of model. Once this clarification has been established, however, it is apparent that the issues
raised by these criticisms do not develop from the model level alone; far
more importantly, they arise from a more generalized kind of theoretical
problem, one that concerns the proper conceptualization of social order
itself. What these critics, for example Martindale or Atkinson, are actually doing is taking the systems concept as the prototype of all conceptualization of supra-individual collective organization. As such, their
criticisms derive much less from any particular attributes of the "functionalist" type of collective emphasis than from a nominalist commitment to the individual level as the proper mode of societal analysis. In
other words, such generalized arguments are directed against the role of
collectivist models per se, and "functionalism" actually represents only
one possible collective model among several others.

The second kind of criticism made against the commitment to a sys-

tem model, that it implies a reified conception of self-regulation and contains, therefore, an explanatory bias against social change, also reveals
upon closer examination a conflation of several different levels of theoretical argument. What creates the greatest problem here is the confusion of the systems issue with the debate over conflict, for the latter
focus, as we have seen, actually occupies a more empirically-oriented
position on the sociological continuum. It is, in fact, quite possible for a
theory with a functionalist commitment at the level of model to encompass a conflict commitment at the level of empirical proposition. One can
observe precisely such a combination in strands of functionalist anthropology, for example in Max Gluckman's account of "rituals of rebellion."[66] The combination is also clearly in evidence in the very
sociological writings that first drew attention to the "conflict" issue, particularly in the work of Coser, which Turner has recently described as
"conflict functionalism" to differentiate it from those other forms of conflict theory not connected to a system model.[67]

The other kind of theoretical issue raised by criticisms about the
static nature of "functionalism" conflates the commitment to a model
with a more rather than less generalized concern. The protagonists of
this critique engage in the same kind of logical confusion which I described earlier as plaguing the conflict debate.

They charge, first, that the commitment to a functional model implies a preference for explaining action in terms of values rather than
coercion and, second, that such a normative concern in turn implies an
acceptance of self-regulation and stasis rather than conflict and change.
Once the levels of theoretical argument have been properly differentiated, however, it becomes a relatively easy task to perceive the distortion
that such an attempt at simplification produces. In the first place, functionalism need not be normatively directed at all. As an independent level
of theoretical commitment it can be combined, and often is so combined,
with a rationalist, materialist perspective. One need only note, in this regard, Herbert Spencer's double commitment, in part of his work at least,
to both the functionalist model and the utilitarian conception of action. It
was just this combination of theoretical elements, in fact, that allowed
Durkheim later to split Spencer's work, accepting its functionalism on
the level of model while rejecting its utilitarianism on the more general
presuppositional level. Within the classical anthropological tradition,
sections of Malinowski's work present the most striking illustration of
combining a functionalist model with emphasis on rationalist calculation, as Cohen's analysis of functional theory has emphasized.[68†] In regard to strictly sociological writing, the neo-utilitarian emphasis in
aspects of Gouldner's earlier work on functional reciprocity and
Sztompka's synthesis of Marxism, functionalism, and exchange theory
similarly indicates the absence of any inherent relation between an em-

phasis on nonrational norms and the acceptance of a functional, system model.[69†]

The second step of this theoretical conflation, the claim that a functional theory which emphasizes values must also ignore social change, can be confronted in a similar way. Although many examples of an association between normative emphasis, functional model, and equilibrium propositions do exist, the best known being certain parts of Parsons' work, such an interrelation in no sense follows directly from the nature of general theoretical logic itself. Among many others, S. N. Eisenstadt's analysis of how internecine conflicts over legitimation contributed to the destruction of bureaucratic imperial systems represents an imposing counter-example, as do Smelser's analyses of the nonrational dimensions of social system conflict in the industrial revolution and student movements.[70†] Bob Jessop has summarized his extensive survey of such functionalist descriptions of social conflict by implicitly arguing for the very kind of separation of analytical levels that the present argument suggests. Acknowledging that "normative functionalism is concerned with power, with force, with change, with revolution," he argues, rather, that "it is the *way* in which it deals with these [i.e., 'normative' versus 'factual' approaches] that is open to criticism."[71†]

To conclude this discussion of the conflationary nature of the functionalism debate it is necessary to address a third cross-cutting argument, one which attempts to reduce analysis to still another level of theoretical analysis. Throughout both types of antifunctionalist criticism, the charges of anti-individualist bias as well as the critique about stasis, the theoretical attempt has been made to equate such allegedly "functionalist" errors with the commitment to a conservative ideological position. These attempts at ideological reduction include, for example, such elaborate sociology-of-knowledge efforts as the argument that constitutes one of the major, though submerged, polemics of Martindale's theoretical history. After locating, quite inaccurately, all of nineteenth-century "organicist" sociology in conservative political reaction, Martindale makes the claim that contemporary functionalism is simply a latter-day rendition of this earlier position.[72†] These efforts also include the less elaborated but no less reductive evaluations of "functionalist" conservatism offered by a series of critics from Mills and Irving M. Zeitlin to Gouldner and Bottomore.[73†] In demonstrating the essential misperceptions of these views, it is necessary of course to refer first to the fundamental untenability of the strategy of ideological reduction per se, as that position has been established in section 1 above. More specific refutations, however, can also be cited. Most importantly, the characteristics of functionalism that become attached to the conservative political label, namely its anti-individual and anti-change aspects, are, as the immediately preceding discussion has demonstrated, qualities not intrinsic to the choice of functional models. This independence can be no more effectively illustrated than by pointing out, as Merton and Cohen have done, that the very same ideological criticism which purports to be so antifunctional often itself implies a certain alternative conception of system and function.[74]

Only after controlling for these cross-cutting theoretical references that so distort the general logic of the functionalist debate—both those overlapping references that are more general and those that are more specific than the theoretical commitment to a particular model—is it possible accurately to perceive what the commitment to a system model actually entails. As these general characteristics have been set forth in a set of closely interrelated essays by Merton, Davis, and Goode, and more recently in important discussions by Cohen and Sztompka, "functionalism" can be understood only in relation to its polemical origins in the anthropological critique of evolutionalism. Once this frame of reference is understood, it becomes clear that the functionalist model actually implies only a few essential propositions: an acceptance of the sui generis, collective quality of social interaction; the perception of the "boundedness" of all social processes; and, within these parameters, an emphasis on the interdependent quality of all social parts.[75†] Similarly broad and differentiated definitions of the system model have been utilized by a number of other theorists to dispute the specific antifunctionalist criticisms I have described. In terms of the antivoluntarism charge, Rex has indicated, following Parsons' lead in *The Structure of Social Action*, that references to "functional purposes" need not imply hypostatization but can, instead, be viewed simply as generalizations about "the network of interlocking [means/ends] chains of action [which] may become more and more complex" as the focus of sociological analysis moves from micro to macro concerns.[76†] Employing what is a basically similar though much more formalized and elaborated conception of the differentiated contributions of the system model, Walter Buckley, in *Sociology and Modern Systems Theory*, has mounted an extensive argument about the model's compatibility with certain aspects of the more individually-oriented theories of symbolic interactionism.[77] And in regard to the charges that a system model carries an anti-change bias, Turner has recently built upon the formulations of Merton and Davis to argue that, once contemporary functionalist theory has been clearly distinguished from some of its historical antecedents, the functionalist notion of boundary maintenance, and even its more extreme formulation, "homeostasis," can be utilized without any commitment to more specific kinds of empirical outcomes, like conflict or cooperation.[78] In a parallel argument that addresses the issue of ideological conflation as well, Werner Stark demonstrates that the commitment to an "organismic" conception, broadly defined as involving the kind of general system properties noted above, is common to a wide variety of social thinkers including, for example, Marx and Weber.[79]

The adoption of a system model, therefore, does imply certain distinctive kinds of nonempirical orientations, but the important point in terms of the present argument is that qua model such "functionalism" remains, to a marked extent, distinctly open-ended. Donald N. Levine has articulated exactly this open-ended quality in criticizing the common identification of functionalism as a major sociological "paradigm."

> If one is talking about paradigms in the sense of basic theoretical orientations, then surely the term "system" is too vague and equivocal to determine problems and acceptable solutions. Scientific revolutions have occurred precisely in the shift from one *conception* of system to another. Sociologists have themselves meant many different things by the concept of system, and have used it in contradictory ways in their treatment of substantive problems.[80]

As I have tried to demonstrate, most of the more particular kinds of characteristics usually attributed to functionalism actually involve characteristics from the other levels of theoretical commitment, levels that are invoked in the process of specifying and concretizing the nature of any particular social system.

An effective demonstration of this relative indeterminacy can be found in the unintended consequences of the critical responses to the kinds of open system definitions offered by Merton and Davis. It has been argued, by friend and foe of "functionalism" alike, that these attempts at formalization have obscured the substantive implications of functionalist theory and, in so doing, actually have diluted its most distinctive theoretical contributions.[81†] Yet, in fact, these broad definitions have only succeeded in isolating what the real contributions of this type of "model" commitment actually are, as differentiated from the other kinds of theoretical commitments which, in a conflationary manner, mistakenly have been viewed as congruent with them. It is usually, in fact, precisely these other types of commitments that the critics of the broad definition of system wish to preserve, and to preserve, furthermore, without the necessity of mounting independent general arguments on their behalf. It is one of the major contributions of Wallace's classificatory scheme— whether or not the substantive contents of this scheme are entirely correct—that he places the "functionalist" category below the level of sociology's most generalized theoretical assumptions, and, further, that he insists on describing functionalism as only one subset among three distinctively "structuralist" approaches to theorizing.[82†]

But perhaps the most important indirect demonstration of the differentiated, open-ended quality of the systems commitment is the kind of confirmation that such an interpretation has received from theorists in two radically divergent intellectual traditions. In the late 1960s and 1970s, some of the most distinguished Marxist theorists and critics, on the one hand, and a number of equally significant Parsonian "functionalists," on the other, have emphasized that while Marxist and Parsonian functionalist theory differ sharply on more general "epistemological" issues, and on more specific empirical and ideological ones as well, they are similarly committed, at the model level, to the systems conceptualization. Such arguments, particularly on the functionalist side, have often, of course, utilized this commonality on the model level to underplay the other levels of theoretical divergence and to promote, thereby, a false vision of "convergence." Nonetheless, when understood in their proper context, these arguments offer significant support for the theoretical analysis I have proposed.

In terms of the Marxist critical literature, the most important writings are those of the Polish sociologist Piotr Sztompka. Throughout his work, particularly in *System and Function: Towards a Theory of Society,* Sztompka's principal concern has been to construct a "defense of functionalism" from the charges of ahistoricism and conservatism by establishing that a "fundamental affinity" exists between Marxist and functionalist approaches in their "common conceptual system-functional models of society."[83] After discussing such functional elements in Marx's writings as the emphases on organic wholeness, system and subsystem, boundary maintenance and interchange, and self-regulating feedback, Sztompka, in effect, stresses the autonomy of the model level of theoretical commitment.

> The preceding discussion concerned the *general assumptions* [of Marx's theory]. If I carried out a similar analysis of the *particular assumptions* adopted by Marx within the range of variability permitted by the general model, it would appear that as a rule his choices were opposite to those made by traditional functionalists. But, these choices were made *within the same general* framework.[84†]

In another important argument along these lines, the English historian E. J. Hobsbawm has sought to establish the same kind of differentiated commonality, marshaling extensive evidence that Marxism "implies the analysis of the structure and functioning of systems as entities maintaining themselves, in their relation both with the outside environment—nonhuman and human—and in their internal relationships."[85] Marxism is, Hobsbawm contends, one among several "structural-functional" theories of society. Equally significant, however, is the fact that this intellectual movement within Marxist thought extends beyond critical secondary argument to include attempts at general theoretical formulation and substantive sociological investigation. In what is somewhat misleadingly called the French school of "structural" Marxism, Louis Althusser, Nicos Poulantzas, and Maurice Godelier have deliberately adopted a model of the capitalist order as a functional system.[86†] Similarly, in the German "Frankfurt" school of Marxist sociology, which otherwise differs sharply from such structural Marxism on ideological and epistemological issues, Habermas has also utilized a version of the systems model, applying it most elaborately in his *Legitimation Crisis*.[87]

On the functionalist side of this theoretical dialogue, the most systematically articulated effort to establish "convergence" on this differentiated level occurs in Smelser's introductory essay to his selection of Marx's essays. In this persuasive and detailed exercise in general logic, Smelser argues that according to the "minimum definitional requirements of the concept," Marx's view "is that society is a social system."[88] The differences between functionalist and Marxist theories, Smelser argues, are not at this level of model, but rather are created by "assumptions concerning the *relations* among the different [system] structures" and by "the assumptions regarding the balance of dysfunctions and positive functions in the system."[89] In an earlier statement of essentially the same position, Charles P. Loomis points to "Marx's continuous use of the terms 'systems,' 'function,' and 'equilibrium.' "[90] And in the most recent effort of this kind, Seymour Martin Lipset has integrated a wide range of functional and Marxist approaches to social change, demonstrating that in terms of their commitments to a functional system model there is "a considerable overlap in its [i.e., the functionalist] approach with that of Marxism."[91]

Such efforts to establish the similarly systemic formulations of Marxist and functionalist theory—which, I am arguing, implicitly present the case for the open-ended and indeterminant quality of the model level of sociological analysis—have also been endorsed by important theorists who stand outside either tradition. In addition to Stinchcombe's concentrated analysis of what he calls "Marxian functionalism,"[92] there has also appeared the significant and much more extended comparative theoretical discussion by Atkinson in *Orthodox Consensus and Radical Alternative*. Rather than viewing functionalism as the fundamental line dividing Marx and Parsons, Atkinson argues that the adoption of this model actually represents the basic point of convergence between the two thinkers. He describes, for example, the "way in which Marx's range of pure types (of actor, situation, interest, class, power, state, etc.) combine into specific developmental systems of interaction":

> Such systems have lives of their own. Analysis of them proceeds
> in terms of their inner dynamism and their needs. Whilst they
> are sustained and changed by class action, that action itself is
> predetermined in terms of the logic of the system itself . . .[93]

Although, as I will indicate in a later chapter, Atkinson's general presuppositions lead him to misperceive the systems model as an antivoluntarist determinism, the proposed commonality at the model level represents one of the most successfully demonstrated points of his work.[94†]

The nonpositivist, theoretical debates which I have discussed in this chapter have provided important clarification about significant and distinct levels of theoretical commitment. At the same time, however, by their conflation of these nonempirical levels both with one another and with more generalized presuppositions, they have created an enormous amount of theoretical confusion. Most arguments about "functionalism," "conflict theory," "critical," and "nonscientific" sociology actually involve a number of different kinds of theoretical reference, both more specific and more general. In failing to perceive how their arguments have been so cross-cut, these debates have given theoretical logic a false appearance of simplicity. It is for this very reason that each of these polemics has so often been the reference point for both "convergence" and "crisis" arguments, those strategies for conducting general theoretical analysis which, from a perspective of either approval or disapproval of what they view as the theoretical consensus, have the latent purpose of blurring the boundaries of general debate in sociology.[95†] But before evaluating such issues of theoretical strategy, one must finally consider those fundamental conceptual issues in sociological thought which do constitute, by virtue of their generality and their decisiveness, the truly presuppositional level of sociological theory.

Chapter Three

THEORETICAL LOGIC IN SOCIOLOGICAL THOUGHT (2):

Toward the Restoration of Generality

Although those theoretical issues which have been the objects of recent sociological debate do present significant theoretical demarcations, they do not qualify for the status which they seek to attain: they do not illuminate the basic presuppositions that inform theoretical logic in sociology. In each debate, the issue of explicit focus either was not actually the implicit point of intellectual disagreement, or it should not have been. Under the guise of debating simply ideology or conflict, theorists are usually arguing simultaneously about quite different issues. Their explicit focus can more accurately be considered a subset of more generalized kinds of commitments, latent commitments which manifest themselves by crosscutting the explicit theoretical focus and by confusing the attempt at generalized debate. These debates, however, not only fail to attain sufficient generality of scope; the issues chosen are, just as frequently, not the most intellectually decisive. Theoretical agreements at these levels do not have implications that ramify in significant ways at every other level of sociological analysis. The issues which *are* sufficiently decisive, therefore, have been able to affect debate only in an implicit manner; they have remained "residual" to its explicit categories.[1†]

In examining these residual categories one discovers that the same kinds of implicit theoretical references continually reappear. Mannheim and his followers argue not only about ideological conservatism but also about the rationality of social life and whether societies should be studied at the individual or "organic" level. Among the protagonists of the conflict perspective, disagreement over the issue of normative values versus rationalist coercion is so intense that it fragments this supposedly unified theory group into antagonistic, competing camps. Similarly, the arguments against systems theory break down into disputes over the merits of an individualistic versus a collective and organic focus, and over the relative role of rational and normative orientations in social life. In each of these cases, the explicit theoretical focus is cross-cut by questions that are addressed to what I will describe in this chapter as problems concerning the rationality of action and the nature of social order. These problems constitute the residual categories of contemporary theoretical debate. The aim of this chapter is to define them in a positive nonresidual manner. Action and order represent the true presuppositions of sociological debate; they establish a general framework that cannot be subsumed under other kinds of theoretical dispute and, at the same time, they manifest properties that decisively affect sociological thought at every level of the intellectual continuum.

1. THE EPISTEMOLOGICAL REFERENCE FOR GENERALIZED SOCIOLOGICAL ARGUMENT

In establishing the basic reference points within which this type of generalized analysis can occur, we must finally consider those traditional, so-called philosophical issues whose scientific relevance is so mistakenly denied by those of the positivist persuasion. It is not surprising that such issues can be articulated most effectively by returning to the basic schema that served as a reference point for the postpositivist analysis of science in chapter 1. Just as the central debates over the formal structure of science can be illuminated by understanding scientific thought as a continuum stretching between metaphysical and empirical environments, this same conceptualization, reinterpreted in the broadest possible terms, can be utilized to illuminate the general substantive presuppositions of scientific theories themselves. Such a reinterpretation of that original schema will unfold through a series of redefinitions.

From the perspective of traditional epistemological concerns, a fundamental issue facing all social thought is the relation of subject and object, a problem formulated by the dichotomy of objectivism versus subjectivism. This epistemological question can, in turn, be linked to the problem of freedom versus constraint. If one defines the elements affecting human action as purely objective, as "material" or "conditional"—in terms of my earlier science schema, as oriented only to the external empirical environment—the vision of action proposed must be a determinant, exclusively constraining one. These "conditions" of action, whether material in an ontological sense or not, constitute elements of the actor's situation that he cannot control; they are objective because they function over and against his will, and if they are not material in the corporeal sense, they constrain action "as if" they were. On the other hand, if one conceives the elements impinging on action as primarily subjective, as ideal or "normative"—in terms of my earlier science schema, as oriented toward the metaphysical environment—action will be conceived not as determined by the objective environment but as voluntarily chosen by the individual actor. Only if action is conceived as oriented, in part or in whole, toward such a metaphysical environment can the subjective element of "intentionality" be preserved. To the degree that action is conceived as involving an "internal," subjective commitment, it is considered to be "voluntary." Action that is conceived as wholly "external," as determined solely by conditional constraints, contains no voluntary component at all.

Three logical possibilities can be derived from these two fundamental dichotomies, permutations which correspond to different traditions of social, and sociological, thought. Although these different traditions will be developed much more extensively in the sections which follow, it will prove useful to present them, briefly, in this introductory discussion. Quite simply, action can be conceived either as normative, as conditional, or as influenced by both types of factors. The first two conceptions are what I will call "one-dimensional" understandings of social life, corresponding in type to the one-directional versions of the scientific process described in chapter 1. The third conception I will call "multidimensional," corresponding in type to what I described as the two-directional understanding of science. The term *multidimensionality* is convenient for two reasons. First, the meaning intended here corresponds closely to its common-sense usage. Second, the term has been utilized in a wide range of technical theoretical discourse to articulate precisely the kind of synthetic conceptualization conceived here. I will explore this "dimensionality" conceptualization much more fully in subsequent sections.

This basic framework for theoretical logic can be elaborated by a process of specification. The traditional concept of the "ends" of action can be viewed as actually including two different levels of the internal, subjective reference of action, the levels of "goals" and "norms." This division is produced by the inherent tension between action's internal reference and its constraining objective conditions. Norms are the general conceptions of future expectations towards which action is directed. It is the opposition between normative ideals and conditions that generates goals. Goals are the specific ends pursued in any given act, those ideal states which are pursued with reference to particular conditions. This conception of goals necessarily leads us to the question of means and to an elaboration of action's objective components. Means are the instruments that are conceived as most effectively addressing objective conditions in pursuit of specific goals. It is this criterion of effectiveness that distinguishes means from goals: means are viewed as related primarily to the conditional environment of action, goals primarily to the ideal, or normative. In order for action to be conceived as multidimensional, for action to be seen as in part voluntary, in part determined, means and ends must be viewed as making independent contributions to a given act. As this more detailed explication makes clear, any given act must, in fact, be viewed as combining internal and external elements: every impinging condition is mediated by the actor's reference to an interpretive norm. This interpenetrating quality of the components of action suggests, indeed, that the very categories of "conditions" and "norms" must, ultimately, themselves be redefined, for they represent, in the end, relatively crude approaches to the voluntary and coercive elements of social life. These categories are, nevertheless, vital to the understanding of sociological thought, in both its classical and contemporary form.

For those at all familiar with the theoretical literature of the last forty years, it will be clear that the terminology I have presented has its intellectual roots, in a direct if distinctly qualified manner, in an earlier effort at the explication of general logic, Talcott Parsons' *The Structure of Social Action*.[2] For this reason, it is important to emphasize my belief that one of the most significant and least debatable contributions of that famous discussion is its articulation of the relationship between specifically sociological concerns and the general epistemological issues that have traditionally occupied Western thought. From Aristotle's discussion of politics and the socioreligious speculations of Augustine, to the classical economic and sociological writings of the nineteenth and early twentieth centuries, and up to the most recent contemporary theoretical debates, the elements of action and the interrelated logic of determinism and voluntarism have been basic nonempirical concerns of social thought.[3†] The pervasiveness of these themes can be illustrated by recent theoretical discussions in sociology, where arguments at every theoretical level and of every ideological stripe have focused on these action elements and their logical implications. In his proposal for conflict theory in *Key Problems of Sociological Theory*, the neo-Marxist Rex couches his argument entirely within the general conceptual rubric of Parsons' earlier work. The same vocabulary of means, ends, conditions, voluntarism, and determinism informs the major critique of systems theory offered by Atkinson in *Orthodox Consensus and Radical Alternative*, despite the fact that his individualist perspective makes him sharply critical of Parsons' actual formulations. In a less explicit but I believe no less pervasive manner, the same conceptual apparatus forms, as will be seen below, the logical backbone of Habermas' version of neo-Marxist theory, from his ideologically reductionist arguments to his critique of positivism, and of the multidimensional strand of his work as well. An essentially similar framework, this time derived explicitly from *The Structure of Social Ac-*

tion, informs the theoretical survey and middle range empirical analysis conducted in *Modern Social Theory* by Percy Cohen, whose perspective more closely follows that proposed here.

Reference to the analytic terminology of *The Structure of Social Action*, in other words, implies no necessary commitment to the specific schemas developed in Parsons' later writings—nor, of course, to his extraordinarily "Whiggish" reading of the historical direction this analytic development takes.[4†] Rather, the reference functions to establish continuity with the basic framework of theoretical reasoning utilized throughout the Western intellectual tradition. The pervasiveness of these formulations is seen clearly in the fact that the desirability of what I have described as the synthetic, multidimensional epistemological position has been expressed, in different words but in essentially the same form, by Marx as well as by Parsons. Parsons' own endorsement of this position, which basically reformulates Weber's attempted synthesis of the idealist and materialist traditions of Western thought, occurs toward the conclusion of *The Structure of Social Action* and, naturally, relates most closely to my own conceptualization of multidimensionality.

> It is impossible to have a meaningful description of an act without specifying [that] action must always be thought of as involving a state of tension between two different orders of elements, the normative and the conditional. . . . Elimination of the normative aspect of action altogether eliminates the concept of action itself. . . . Elimination of conditions, of the tension from that side, equally eliminates action and results in idealistic emanationism. Thus conditions may be conceived at one pole, ends and normative rules at the other, means and [voluntary] effort as the connecting links between them.[5]

This epistemological commitment to multidimensionality occurs despite the fact that, for reasons connected to an idealist strain in his sociological work, Parsons calls the perspective he has described the "voluntarist theory of action." The same basic epistemological perspective, fueled by the same intention to interweave the forces generating internal subjective freedom and external material constraint, is forcefully expressed in the young Marx's first critical "Thesis" on Feuerbach's materialism.

> The main shortcoming of all materialism up to now (including that of Feuerbach) is that the object, the reality, . . . is conceived only in the form of the *object*, . . . not as sensuous human activity, *practice* [praxis], not subjectively. Hence, the *active* side was developed abstractly in opposition to materialism by idealism, which naturally does not know the real sensuous activity as such. . . . [Feuerbach] therefore does not apprehend the significance of the "revolutionary," practical-critical activity.[6†]

Despite the fact that Marx himself somewhat misleadingly describes this alternative position as the "true materialism," the notion of "praxis" is a thoroughly synthetic epistemological concept that expresses, in only somewhat different words, the same logic as Parsons' definition.

An essay by a leading Marxist sociologist, T. B. Bottomore, further demonstrates how these otherwise competing theoretical frameworks are oriented toward similar logical reference points. Attempting to characterize the contributions of that part of recent Marxist literature which emphasizes Marx's earlier concept of praxis, Bottomore writes that by emphasizing "much more strongly the role of cultural and intellectual factors—of 'consciousness,'" this literature "can be regarded as formulating a 'voluntaristic' theory of action rather than a theory of 'economic determinism.'"[7] Whether or not Bottomore's evaluation of the success of this theoretical effort is accurate, and I will argue in volume 2 that it is not, to establish this judgment he has relied on the same general epistemological logic—the interconnection between the dichotomies of ideal/material and voluntarist/determinist—as that formalized by Parsons in his earlier work.

Before proceeding to determine precisely how this general framework informs the actual presuppositional questions of sociological theory, it is necessary to make explicit a point that only has been hinted at thus far. In their strictly epistemological form, the problematic "one-dimensional" understandings described above were largely transcended by the social thinkers who will be the subjects of the interpretive analysis that occupies the other volumes of this work. I have just described this resolution in the writings of Marx and Parsons. Weber, too, explicitly stated his commitment to a view that simultaneously emphasized subjectivity and its external material context, at least for all human action that extended beyond the status of what Weber pejoratively described as behavior.[8] And throughout Durkheim's analysis of the role of normative ideals, he never ceased to eschew subjectivity in its traditional idealist ✓ form, emphasizing the "social" basis of norms in the interaction between concrete individuals and groups.[9] For none of these thinkers, except in clearly anomalous instances, was the dialectical epistemological position ever in doubt; it has only come to seem so in certain vulgarized presentations by their followers and interpreters. Indeed, it was the resolution of these epistemological complexities by the classical sociologists that has made the problem of knowledge qua knowledge no longer a problematic one for most of today's sophisticated sociological thinkers.

If these issues are in fact so settled, one may justifiably inquire how they can still be viewed as shaping the problematic presuppositional decisions that fragment generalized sociological debate. The answer depends on a distinction between the strictly epistemological, abstract side of these issues and their manifestation in sociological thought. When one moves from the epistemological perception of action abstractly considered to the specific consideration of action in society as studied in what are today called the social sciences, the concepts of subjectivity, objectivity, voluntarism, and determinism take on a character that is different from the meaning of these concepts in what is conceived to be strictly philosophical debate. In terms of their social, or sociological relevance, the implications of these epistemological commitments are altered in two ways. In the first place, instead of taking the individual as the unit of analysis, the question of the nature of action must take into account the fact of the social interrelationship of a plurality of individual actors. Second, in terms of evaluating the nature of action itself, the problem of freedom and constraint becomes not merely a question of acknowledging the independent existence of internal motivation per se but rather an issue of the nature of that subjective factor itself.

The sociological relevance of these modulations of traditional epistemological issues can, therefore, be formulated as the answers to two fundamental questions. First, in terms of the subjectivity that is now explicitly recognized, the question becomes one of the particular nature of norms and motivation, what I will call the "problem of action." Regarding the second complicating factor, the different unit of analysis in sociological analysis necessitated by the interaction of a plurality of individual actors, the question which now affects the resolution of the freedom/determinism issue concerns the manner in which these actors are interrelated, what I will call the "problem of order." In answering these questions, the problems that have been overcome in their purely epistemological form—subjectivity and objectivity, freedom and determinism—return in a distinctively social guise as the problems of "sociological materialism" and "sociological idealism."[10] So fundamental is this distinction between the epistemological and sociological version of these questions that the failure to separate them leads ineluctably to basic misunderstandings of the nature of generalized sociological logic. Without acknowledging this separation, for example, it is impossible to recognize that Marx's and Weber's acceptance of a praxis perspective need not imply a rejection of sociological determinism, nor, conversely, need Durkheim's acceptance of the social basis of human action prevent an equally one-sided commitment to sociological voluntarism.

But to enter into such discussion is to get ahead of the argument and to begin evaluating issues that have not yet been sufficiently defined. At this point, only the basic foundations for generalized argument have been laid. From Koyré and Polanyi to Kuhn and Holton, the postpositivist persuasion has sought to define the nonempirical issues that are most critical to general scientific practice. The problems of action and order meet this challenge for the practice of social science. In elaborating these presuppositional questions, I will be describing how general perceptions of the nature of basic elements and their interrelationship to one another and to the natural and cosmic orders inform even the most specific kinds of empirical social scientific propositions. This elaboration will contribute to the construction of a "theoretical methodology," or theoretical logic, for the social sciences.

2. THE GENERALIZED PROBLEM OF ACTION

The problem of action, first proposed as an explicit focus for theoretical argument by Weber and subsequently emphasized by Parsons, directs attention to the nature of action's subjective component, or, more specifically, to the nature of the relationship between means and ends. Given the reductionism of recent theoretical debate, it is not surprising that this suggested focus has consistently been perceived, by its proponents and critics alike, not as signaling generalized theoretical issues which all sociological effort must address, but rather as representing particular questions raised by certain theoretical schools. The manner in which Weber's references to action have been accorded this dubious honor of "misplaced concreteness" is illustrated, for example, by Martindale's discussions. Martindale presents what he calls Weber's "action theory" as based on a nominalist individualism and a distinctively qualified subjectivism, features in contrast with other traditions such as functionalism, formalism, and conflict theory.[11] An individualistic strand of sociological theorizing informed by British "action philosophy"—as seen, for example, in works by Hollis, Dawe, and Giddens—takes much the same particularistic stance, contrasting their own emphasis on "action" with that of others on "behavior."[12†] Ironically, the origins of this mistaken approach to action can be traced in part to a reaction against the manner in which the Weberian conception was developed by Parsons, for despite Parsons' contributions to explicating the general status of the means/ends problem, his work has also manifested a strong cross-cutting tendency to present the "action frame of reference" as identified solely with his own particular theoretical system.[13] It is in relation to Parsons' work, of course, that the action concept has received its most intensive particularizing interpretation. In his well-known survey discussion of contemporary theory, for example, Wallace considers the focus on action to be one particular type among thirteen different theoretical approaches he investigates.[14] Whitney Pope presents the same kind of truncated conception of action in a discussion of Durkheim's work. He argues that Durkheim's "social realism" and "objectivism" make the problem of Durkheim's conception of action irrelevant because such emphases prevent Durkheim from making explicit reference to what Pope calls the nominalist problem of action, the problem of the individual's manipulation of means and ends.[15]

Contrary to these arguments, I would maintain that the nature of action should be viewed as a generic, truly generalized, question. Every social theory, as Rex has argued, must contain an implicit conception of the "hypothetical actor," and, as such, every theory commits itself to a certain conception of motivation, to a particular perception of the manner in which actors relate means and ends. Emphasizing the nonempirical status of the action issue, Rex puts the matter in the following way: "The 'hypothetical actor' is a theoretical construction and statements about his motivation have empirical implications."[16] The same position, interrelating conceptions of action with views of the means/ends relationship and according to both a generalized, nonempirical status, has been more elaborately stated by Alfred Schutz. Schutz argues that the "postulate of subjective interpretation" must be considered basic to all attempts at understanding social phenomena. "We cannot understand them [social phenomena] otherwise than within the scheme of human motives, human means and ends, human planning—in short—within the categories of human action."[17†]

2.1. THE PRESUPPOSITION OF RATIONALITY: "INSTRUMENTAL" ACTION AND THE REDUCTION OF ENDS TO MEANS

The central question that every social theory addresses in defining the nature of action is whether or not—or to what degree—action is rational.[18†] The centrality of this issue has made the question of what kinds of means/ends relations are rational and nonrational one of the most vexed issues in Western social thought. To minimize the possibilities for confusion about a concept that will be so crucial in the following pages, I will first present the approach to the rational/nonrational dichotomy which will be utilized here. In the section which follows, I will indicate the relation between this understanding and other approaches which have received significant attention in the Western intellectual tradition and in sociological theory.

The approach to action which, I believe, plays a truly presuppositional role in sociological theory is the decision about whether, and to what degree, action is rational in the instrumental calculative sense. In terms of the epistemological framework presented above, to presuppose that action is instrumentally rational is to assume that action is guided by ends of pure efficiency. In terms of the more differentiated terminology of goals and norms, it assumes that goals are calculated to achieve broader normative purposes in the most efficient manner possible, given constraining external conditions. Because any relation of goals to norms that is not efficiently rational is disregarded, goals can be viewed as performing a function similar to means. Ideally oriented goals are, in effect, reduced to materially oriented means, and more general norms as such become irrelevant: action is viewed as a continuous effort at economizing, calculating, and, indeed, "rationalizing."

The effective reduction of ends to means that results from this perception of action as instrumentally rational was succinctly articulated by Hume—from whom, despite his own criticisms of this perspective, one of the major strands of the rationalist tradition in social thought, utilitarianism, was later derived. In the *Inquiry Concerning the Principles of Morals*, Hume describes the reduction in the following manner:

> Ask a man why he uses exercise; he will answer because he desires to keep his health. If you then enquire, why he desires health, he will readily reply, because sickness is painful. If you push your inquiries further and desire a reason, why he hates pain, it is impossible he can ever give any. *This is an ultimate end, and is never referred to by any other object.*[19]

In the instrumentally rationalist perception, the explanation for one means (e.g., exercise) becomes, not an end, but merely another means (e.g., health), and what might be called the ultimate means—in this case, the avoidance of pain—replaces any conception of truly noninstrumental, ultimate ends. Employing a similar though more hedonistically rational perception, Bentham's famous opening proposition in his *Introduction to the Principles of Morals and Legislation* makes even more explicit the subordination of normative moral standards to instrumental calculation.

> Nature has placed mankind under the governance of two sovereign masters, pain and pleasure. It is for them alone to point out what we *ought* to do, as well as to determine what we shall do. On the one hand the *standard of right and wrong*, on the other the chain of causes and effects, are fastened to their throne. . . . The principle of utility recognizes this subjection, and assumes it for the foundation of that system.[20†]

Given this effective reduction of ends to means and the elimination of ideal reference, one can describe instrumental rationality as being guided only by "technical" concerns as compared with substantive moral ones.[21†] Such a notion of mere technicality, I believe, aptly characterizes the fateful implications of such a rationalistic instrumental perspective. For despite the political activism associated with the rationalist tradition in Western social thought, the instrumentalization of action which it implies threatens to eliminate from theoretical understanding the intellectual foundations upon which any conception of individual self-assertion must rest. It does so by effectively ignoring the internal subjective reference of action which, if intentionality is to be preserved and a pure determinism prevented, must counterbalance reference to the influence of objective conditions. By thus eliminating the active internal component, the logic of technical rationality leads theory to portray action as simply an adaptation to material conditions rather than as a multidimensional alternation of freedom and constraint. Parsons' analysis of the implications of utilitarian thought in *The Structure of Social Action* remains the classic description of the inherent connection between such rationalist commitment and elimination of the voluntary component, despite the fact that the analysis blurs the distinction between action and social order.[22†] In the most important subsequent formulation of this rationality problem, Habermas has described the instrumentalist perspective on rationality in a closely parallel manner, as the "purposive-rational organization of means or adaptive behavior" according to which internal subjective knowledge becomes "a mere instrument of an organism's adaptation to a changing environment."[23]

I have deliberately defined this instrumental perception of rational action abstractly, in order to stress that it represents a commitment on the level of general logic itself. As such, it is independent of the particular kind of theory in which it is imbedded. In fact, the rationalist orientation occurs in theories which are ostensibly committed to ends other than those of simple "efficiency"; indeed, in few theories is such a merely technical orientation explicitly betrayed. This is clear even if we limit ourselves to those theories most typically associated with the instrumentally rationalist tradition. Economism, utilitarianism, hedonism, behaviorism, Darwinism, Machiavellianism—all refer to certain substantive and quite varied kinds of general guiding norms: money, power, survival, pleasure and pain. It might be assumed, therefore, that the view of action in these theories is not simply technical, that they actually perceive action as oriented toward differentiated ideal ends and not simply to objective conditions. This inference would, however, be thoroughly misleading, for what is really significant in these theories is their implicit view of the means/ends relation, not the substantive nature of the general norm they formally propose. What such theories have in common is their conception of action as exclusively guided by calculations of efficiency in the pursuit of general norms. As a result, they view the more immediate goals of action as the sole product of a technical evaluation of external conditions rather than as being related also to substantive considerations induced by ideal commitments. Despite the differences in longer-range ends, in other words, each theory reduces goals to the status of means. Since action is determined by calculations of efficiency vis-à-vis external conditions, the particular content of the ostensibly guiding norms becomes irrelevant.[24†]

Perhaps the best illustration of the presuppositional common denominator shared by all instrumentalist theories is presented by contemporary "exchange theory," which has sought to establish the theoretical hegemony of the "rational actor." Its proponents argue that action of any sort can be evaluated from the perspective of efficient calculation, that beneath any substantive normative commitment the real motivating factor is the desire on the actor's part to maximize utility. Thus Homans, basing himself on a combination of the economic-utilitarian, behaviorist, and hedonistic traditions, tries to develop a theory of "social exchange" that covers both "tangible and intangible" goods.[25] Peter Blau carries that effort further, contending that economically instrumental behavior should be considered only as a special case of the general phenomenon of exchange that governs all areas of social life, from psychology to politics to morality.[26†]

No survey of the different theories which specify a general rationalist commitment would be complete without reference to the problem of scientism. The tradition in social thought which views scientific action from the kind of positivist perspective outlined in chapter 1 must be understood as a variant of the instrumentally rational perspective.[27†] For, according to positivist belief, science relates only to the material, "empirical" environment and is not therefore dependent on the internal normative commitments of the acting scientist. Furthermore, scientism is frequently associated with the other forms of instrumentalist thought, an association arising from the belief that only such a completely technical and objective approach to knowledge is capable of supplying the kind of calculated goals upon which these other instrumentally rationalist theories depend. A distinction must, however, be sharply made between scientistic rationalist views of science and science itself, a distinction that some of the most vigorous critics of positivism have often ignored. Habermas, for example, despite his sophisticated methodological understanding, continually misperceives contemporary science as being identical with knowledge that is merely "technical."[28] Similarly, for the British anthropologist J. H. M. Beattie, to view human action as empirical is to reduce it to a purely utilitarian status.[29] To the contrary, I believe that to criticize positivism as instrumentalist can lead to an appreciation of the nonrational elements in science; properly understood, science itself gives the lie to conceptions of action which presuppose instrumental rationality.[30†]

2.2. THE PRESUPPOSITION OF NONRATIONALITY: "NORMATIVE" ACTION AND THE RELATIVE AUTONOMY OF ENDS

In defining the nature of action, of course, theories do not have to presuppose instrumental rationality. There is an alternative presupposition which also has deep roots in Western intellectual history—I need only cite Plato's discussion of mimesis or Augustine's emphasis on *caritas* over *cupiditas*.[31] Nevertheless, it is a highly significant fact that throughout Western intellectual development only the instrumental-rationalist approach to action has been explicitly articulated and formally labeled as an abstract theoretical category, that is, as *"rationalist* theory." The alternative tradition has no such clearly identifiable label. This asymmetry occurred because the pioneering developments in self-conscious social theory—"modern thought"—emerged from polemics against the limitations of religious thinking about the nature of social life. As part of the task of differentiating a mode of analytic thinking not so religiously oriented, the definition of rationality became an explicit theoretical focus. This is not to say that there have not been a number of particular theoretical attempts emphasizing an orientation other than the rational, but rather that the general orientation of these theories has not been formulated on the same level of abstraction as the rationality concept. For want of such a parallel usage—and also to forestall any confusion between the very general level of analysis intended here and the kinds of more specific, empirically oriented theories of anti-instrumental action which are described in following sections—I will indicate this alternative orientation to technical action by a regrettably awkward term: nonrationality.

Because of the historical asymmetry, any attempt to develop an abstract definition of the nonrational approach to action must have recourse to the comparative language of negation, for this type of action can be approached only in terms of what instrumental rationality is not. Yet this method need not be a completely negative one; in a very real sense, there was implicit reference to an independent notion of nonrational behavior throughout the discussion of rationality itself.

In action conceived to be nonrational the actor's goals are not considered to have been chosen as the most efficient possible path for the realization of more general norms in the face of extant conditions. They are, rather, viewed as produced not only by the nature of these conditions but by the substantive ideal contents of the norms themselves. Norms, therefore, do not appear to be exhausted by the actor's reliance on instrumental calculation, nor do his goals appear effectively to be reduced to the status of means. Because the ideal reference is so explicitly preserved, action does not take on a purely technical quality. Accordingly, the internal voluntary aspect of human action is maintained and a purely determinist perspective prevented. By explicitly drawing attention to the noninstrumental dimensions of action, to norms that do not qualify as technically rational ones, the nonrational perspective on action emphasizes rather than minimizes the subjective element in the multidimensional epistemological framework and the commitment to freedom that this element implies.

As an issue on the level of general logic, then, nonrationality presents an abstract presuppositional orientation in relation to which every social theory must take a position. Yet, on a more substantive level, this presupposition has been concretized in a variety of different ways in the history of social thought. As was the case with the varieties of the rationalist tradition examined above, the particular theories that articulate nonrational orientations have usually emphasized certain aspects of the orientation over others. It is possible, in fact, to view the different strands of the nonrationalist tradition as focusing on different elements of the epistemological framework of action.

Certain aspects of the tradition have manifest their commitment to a nonrational perspective primarily in terms of where they locate social causation, emphasizing what they view as the greater significance of the "internal" realm of human experience. This approach particularly characterizes phenomenological writing—for example, George Herbert Mead's famous critique of Watson's behaviorism. "Watson explained the whole field of inner experience in terms of external behavior," Mead writes, as if "the experience of the individual [could be understood] without bringing in the observation of an inner experience, a consciousness as such."[32] According to the general logic I have described, such scientific observation of the internal aspects of behavior would be possible only through the adoption of a nonrational perspective. This is precisely the commitment that underlay Mead's own formulation of "social behaviorism," which he described as "behavioristic in the sense of starting off with observable activity . . . but . . . not behavioristic in the sense of ignoring the inner experience of the individual—the inner phase of that process or activity."[33]

Whereas Mead's phenomenological approach emphasizes the location of the determining elements, another strand of the nonrational tradition emphasizes the quality of the element that allows such an internal reference: its nonmaterial status.[34†] While Mead's emphasis on nonrationality characterizes the contemporary sociological school of symbolic interactionism, this second method of articulating nonrationality underlies a significant strand of anthropological writing on mythical thought and ritual behavior. For example, in *Purity and Danger* the British anthropologist Mary Douglas emphasizes the "fictive, abstract" character of ritual behavior, asserting that it has "no fixed material point of reference." The same concentration on what are termed the "symbolic" as opposed to "real" or "factual" determinants of action identifies the strand of anthropological writing stretching from Robertson Smith's classical work on totemism and Mauss' on gift exchange to the writings of Douglas' contemporary, Victor Turner, on the transcendent, invisible foundations of social structure.[35†] Elvin Hatch has characterized the theoretical debate over the "image of man," by which he means this conflict between rationality and nonrationality, as the primary point of generalized division in the history of the anthropological discipline;[36] Marshall Sahlins has similarly demonstrated the decisive impact of the conflict between "culture and practical reason" on historical and contemporary anthropological thought.[37]

In still other substantive approaches to nonrational action, theoretical efforts have focused not on the location or quality of the nonrational causal elements but on the character of the voluntary action that they preserve. The pervasiveness of "emotion" over "reason" in human affairs, for example, emphasizes the significance of intuitive, expressive modes of perception in contrast to the calculating and cognitive. Such emphases are most common in psychological approaches to nonrationality, particularly in the depth psychology of Freud and his followers which posits the affective basis of intellectual processes. This same manner of formulating the contrast between nonrational and rational corresponds to the classical/romantic, realist/surrealist division that runs through literary and artistic debate. As Hughes has pointed out in regard to the early twentieth century, shifts in the general orientation of such humanistic approaches to action usually correspond to the disposition of generalized debate in social thought.[38]

The other basic approach to the voluntarism engendered by nonrationality defines itself not in terms of the expressiveness of human action but in terms of its ethical quality. Kant and such neo-Kantians as the French social philosopher Charles Renouvier dichotomize the instrumentally-rational emphasis on physical, purely worldly considerations and what they consider to be the independent and equally valid reality of metaphysical and religious orientation: they contrast purely utilitarian concerns with inherent moral sensibility, and self-interest with the capacity for altruism.[39] The same general view of intentionality appears also in the writings of nineteenth-century conservative thinkers, particularly in their conception of the moral community as formed by the intersection of religious and traditional action.[40†]

Despite their great value in illuminating the nature of nonrational commitment, these substantive approaches to the nonrational remain only partly satisfactory from the theoretical perspective proposed here. In part because they emphasize only certain elements of action over others—internal versus external, ideal versus material, voluntary versus determined—these attempts produce definitions of rationality and nonrationality that are overly specific, that partly obscure the logic of the generalized distinctions presented here. These definitions, in fact, are taken up in the discussion of competing approaches to nonrationality in section 2.3 which follows. The few theoretical discussions of nonrationality that do attain sufficient generality and abstraction, and which do not, therefore, increase the possibilities for theoretical confusion, are the same discussions—by Parsons and Habermas—that contain the most satisfactory formulations of the rationality issue. Parsons presents the nonrational alternative to utilitarian rationality simply as "normative action," and ascribes to it the general properties of voluntarism and internality that I have described.[41] Habermas' similar attempt to achieve abstraction as a means of facilitating theoretical synthesis is more direct, if less systematic. At different points in his writing, he establishes the alternative to technical rationality in terms of the following dichotomies: communication/manipulation, transcendent/empirical, symbolic/factual, moral/technical, expressive/cognitive, traditional/instrumental, and interactive/purposive.[42] These definitions cover each of the substantive versions of nonrationality I have discussed. Further, Habermas develops these approaches within the general rubric of the technical/normative dichotomy. For this reason, his treatment clearly corresponds to the generalized, abstract definition of nonrationality presented here.

Finally, in analyzing the nonrational approach, it is important to recognize that this approach, also, has its "radical" form. When considered as the exclusive focus of action, nonrationality produces the effective reduction of action to one of its dimensions. In such a purely nonrationalist orientation, while the external conditional elements of action are not explicitly denied, they are ignored in a de facto way. Accordingly, theoretical attention shifts to the actor's subjective assertion of normative commitments, focusing on the internal elements of action at the expense of the external impingements that inevitably prevent such norms from being fully realized. The result is that instead of a general vision that conceives action as containing a voluntary aspect, action appears to be purely voluntary. Such a shift toward an exclusively nonrational emphasis, manifest in many of the substantive theoretical approaches to nonrationality that have been discussed above, paves the way for sociological idealism as surely as rationalist theory ushers in sociological materialism. The full significance of these decisions about the nature of action can be perceived, however, only by integrating them with the issue of order, the other crucial commitment whose logic governs general theoretical argument.

2.3. OTHER APPROACHES TO RATIONALITY AND THE PROBLEM OF THEORETICAL REDUCTION

As one of the central conceptions in Western thought, the concept of rationality has, for important ideological and empirical as well as for generalized theoretical reasons, come to convey a variety of meanings. Because the dichotomy of rational/nonrational has such importance for all that follows, how others have drawn the distinction must be considered, as must the problem of how such frequently overlapping versions compare with the one presented here. Only after this comparison can the relationship between decisions about action's rationality and the second generalized issue—the problem of order—be fully explored.

In conducting a comparison of different approaches to the rationality issue, it is necessary to develop a framework within which they can all be included. Despite the great variation, all such approaches can, I believe, be classified according to two distinctive types of theoretical strategies. Some view rationality as adhering to action simply from the fact of means/ends calculation per se; others allow rationality only to a subset of all means/ends acts, those which pursue a particular kind of end.

2.3.1. Rationality as Means/Ends Calculation

Whereas from the multidimensional perspective advanced here, all action, both rational and nonrational, inherently involves the weighing of means and ends, norms and conditions, there is a persistent strand of social theory that envisions the possibility of a purely unreflexive action in which there exists no intentionality or purposive end-orientation. This possibility implies the reduction of action to what is viewed as pure "habit" or as purely spontaneous affect. Significantly, such action is usually designated by the pejorative label of "irrational" rather than by the more neutral term *nonrational*. In contrast to such irrational habits, all action which involves means/ends manipulation is considered to be "rational." It is this very approach to the action question that informs the categories employed by the substantive approaches to nonrationality described in the preceding section. It is because of their overly broad approach to rationality that their more presuppositional relevance—the fact that they actually reveal alternatives to instrumental rationality—has so often been obscured. In discussing this problem, I will examine each of these intellectual traditions in turn.

In the phenomenological tradition, instead of identifying the internal reference as indicating a nonrational orientation, one of its most important theorists, Alfred Schutz, asserts that such action should actually be called rational. The reason for this designation is that Schutz equates rationality with the ability to calculate means/ends as such. Action is rational as long as it appears reasonable according to common sense—as long as, in Schutz's words, it is consistent with the behavior of the "healthy, adult, and wide-awake human being."[43]

The same approach to rationality affects the anthropological debate over the nature of symbolism in "primitive" ritual and thought. In reaction against Lévy-Bruhl's early contention about its prelogical and magical qualities, anthropologists from Evans-Pritchard and Beattie to Jarvie and Agassi have argued that such activity, whether or not it has a symbolic status, should be described as rational because it is as "logical" and "realistic" from the actor's perspective as modern thinking. A good illustration of this identification of rationality with the means/ends calculation per se is the polemical statement of Jarvie and Agassi, who argue against identifying ritual action as nonlogical and assert that, to the contrary, it exhibits purpose and calculation. "Let us attribute rationality to an action," they write, "if there is a goal to which it is directed."[44] Similarly, Keith Dixon has recently proposed a sociological approach to rationality which basically adheres to the same position as that of the anthropologists.

> Typically rational action is conceived of as an actor's realistic perception of the means whereby to attain his ends. I am said to act rationally if, in the pursuit of my wants and desires, I employ the appropriate steps towards achieving them. . . . [To argue that action is irrational is] to argue that wholly inappropriate and incoherent means are being pursued to reach certain selected ends . . .[45]

The general perception appears in the psychoanalytic tradition as well. Freud does not characterize as nonrational the voluntarism vis-à-vis objective conditions which is established by his emphasis on the emotional sources of action. Instead, he uses the term *irrational* and refers, thereby, only to those aspects of action that are so overloaded with unregulated affect as to proceed from what he calls primary rather than secondary process.[46] Similarly, Heinz Hartmann, perhaps the preeminent contemporary psychoanalytic theorist, equates rationality simply with "purposive action," with behavior that "attain[s] a given aim [i.e., goal] as a consequence of being calculated to reach it."[47]

This same approach also cross-cuts the fourth, neo-Kantian strand of the nonrational tradition. Indeed, it has created continual confusion within the thought of Max Weber, the most important contributor to a sophisticated understanding of the action issue within the classical sociological tradition. For example, although Weber effectively articulates the instrumental/normative distinction in his discussions of the four specific types of social action, he also organizes these types in two more general categories designated as rational and nonrational—on the basis of whether the calculation of means and ends is involved. Because "traditional" and "affective" actions are purely "reactive," according to Weber, they cannot be labeled rational.[48]

Finally, it is interesting to observe that this approach has also undermined the theoretical self-consciousness of thinkers in the instrumentally-rationalist tradition itself. For example, despite the fact that James Coleman's work fits squarely within the basically utilitarian movement of exchange theory, he portrays the instrumentally rational understanding of action that informs his work as identical with the means/ends schema per se. Introducing his conceptualization in the most universal terms, Coleman writes that "there is one general approach to theory that has been used most widely in both common-sense and formal approaches to the society," and he offers a specific definition that does not go beyond the elementary notion of action qua action: "This is the approach that treats the acting individual as a purposive agent acting with some goals or purposes in mind . . ."[49] In other words, while actually recommending the very particular kind of means/end rationality of exchange theory, Coleman identifies it with means/ends manipulation in general.

From the perspective I have developed in the preceding sections, the problem with all of these approaches to rationality is that they are not sufficiently generalized: they do not provide the necessary criteria to differentiate basic theoretical issues. As a result, they essentially leave unanswered what for general theoretical discussion is actually the most significant intellectual question, for in such generalized analysis the important consideration is not that means and ends are interrelated but that they can be interrelated in essentially different ways. Depending on the nature of the end, or norm, means and ends may or may not be calculated in a purely technical, efficient manner. By extending the label of rationality to virtually all action that is not purely instinctual or automatic, the broad definitions leave the nature of normative regulation unexplained and the critical question of the voluntarism of action unexamined.

Each of the approaches discussed suffers from this lack of explanatory power. Schutz, for example, writes that "the choice of action is rational if the actor selects from among all means within his reach the one most appropriate for realizing the intended end."[50] But the question remains: What are these normative standards of "appropriate" action that the actor so employs? For this, Schutz can provide no criterion; according to his definition, in different situations the most self-interested economic actor and the most other-worldly religious one can appear to be acting within the dictates of "rational" sense.[51] This weakness in the phenomenological approach to rationality is revealed even more clearly in Atkinson's assertion that all human action will be seen as rational if it is approached in terms of the "logic of the situation."

> All action, whilst not necessarily proceeding in accordance with the laws of classical logic, can be regarded as being within the bounds of reason and common sense when judged from the point of view of the actors involved. There is a logic that any actor gives to his action in each situation even though that action be vague and unarticulated.[52]

Such inattentiveness to the different types of standards which can guide such "rational" action reflects the phenomenologist's inattentiveness to the variable impact of collective, supra-individual forces. For example, in the extremely revealing exchange of letters between Parsons and Schutz that occurred after the publication of Parsons' *Structure of Social Action*, Schutz insisted that an outside, scientific observer could not differentiate between rational and nonrational action, arguing that from the point of view of the actor almost all action appears rational. In part this represented a methodological caveat, but more generally it reveals a strong idealist strain, and Schutz argued, in fact, that scientific sociology should be concerned primarily with subjective motives. He connected his insistence on the typical rationality of action with the argument that *any* forces which develop from outside the individual actor, whether cultural or material, were "objective" in that they were not creations of the actor himself. From this, he concluded that motives could be severed from norms, that voluntarism depended not upon the differential impact of norms, but on this dissociated subjectivity, on the fact of consciousness per se.[53] To avoid this extreme subjectivity, to explain the difference between motives which retain subjectivity and those which do not, it is necessary to differentiate the "situation" into parts with distinctive properties—into metaphysical and material environments. The broad definition of rationality will then be more sharply differentiated, for "rationality" and "nonrationality" can then be judged according to the influence of one type of situational element vis-à-vis the other.

The same criticism applies to symbolic anthropology as to phenomenology. For once one accepts the fact that "primitive" actors are indeed goal-directed, the task remains to understand the general logic of their action. How else can one comprehend the tremendous debate waged within the ranks of those anthropologists who themselves agree on the broad definition of rationality? After rejecting the "prelogical" status of ritual, they still must decide whether that ritual is oriented to political, economic, or cultural-symbolic exigencies—questions which will decide the degree to which any particular ritual is voluntarily enacted. Thus Beattie writes that while he has "never at all disputed the self-evident fact that people practice magic because they want results," he has doubted this fact's ultimate significance. This insight "is the beginning, not the end, of . . . analysis," he contends, and "it is only *after* [this] that the interesting problems in the analysis of ritual thought and action arise.[54] It is only at this point, in other words, that the problem of distinguishing between rational and nonrational *kinds* of purposive action begins, and along with it the possibility of determining the relation of ritual action to external conditions.

In psychoanalytic thought, too, the definition of rationality in terms of the means/ends schema has, by obfuscating the technical/normative distinction, created certain fundamental theoretical confusions. Psycho-logical rationality has often been mistakenly identified with instrumen-tal utilitarian action, a connection that not only seriously reduces the concept's applicability but also misrepresents the relationship between such ego-rationality and voluntary control. This error even finds its way into the most distinguished exercises in psychoanalytic social theory, as, for example, when Gerald Platt and Fred Weinstein identify unconscious primary process with nonrational normative action, and conscious, sec-ondary process with instrumental, utilitarian rationality, as in their early, theoretical chapters in *The Wish to Be Free*.[55†] This identification has con-tributed to the difficulty that psychoanalytic theory has had in coming to terms with the symbolic aspect of conscious action. Because the term ir-rational is applied only to the aspects of symbolism associated with neu-rosis or with affectively-loaded primary process, all secondary process or conscious thought must be called rational and, by implication, non-symbolic. Yet if secondary process is not symbolic, conscious action would appear to be reduced to the merely technical and adaptive. It is revealing of Hartmann's distinction as a theorist that he implicitly ac-knowledges this terminological morass: he suggests that the obsessive and deterministic quality of utilitarian action does not actually qualify as purposive, secondary process.[56] Yet in arguing that utilitarian action is psychologically irrational, Hartmann exposes the difficulties that the broad rationality usage has created for the task of incorporating psycho-analytic theory into the history of generalized theoretical debate. For utilitarianism is, of course, the very prototype of the rationalist mode.

　　In Weber's work on rationality one finds, indeed, the forceful re-pudiation of this broad approach, even though he himself has employed it. If Weber had utilized only his broad definition of rationality as means/ends calculation, he would not have been able to differentiate between the passive and merely technical rationality of the bureaucrat and the value-inspired, voluntaristic rationality of the Puritan. Instead, Weber acknowledges the lack of generality and decisiveness in his general def-inition of rationality by creating within it two subtypes, *Wertrationalität*, which is value oriented, and *Zweckrationalität*, which includes—though is not coextensive with—utilitarian rationality as defined here.[57] Because of Weber's ambiguity on this point, his differentiation of the rationality concept has often gone unnoticed. When it is ignored, the inadequacy of such a nondifferentiated approach becomes strikingly apparent. For ex-ample, following correctly the logic of Weber's nondifferentiated defini-tion, Rex identifies rationality with "purposive" action, contrasting it, as Weber does, with nonreflexive "affectual" behavior. But this approach to rationality does not distinguish between specifically instrumental and goal-oriented action as such. Rex is led, therefore, to insist that to focus on the purposive rationality of action is to examine how people function "as means or conditions of the act[s]" of others.[58] In this way, Rex ends up equating purely technical interests with ends in general. Faithfully following one strand of Weber's approach, he has justified a thoroughly utilitarian, and deterministic, conception of social life.[59†]

Finally, the unfortunate consequences of this broad approach to rationality are nowhere more clearly seen than in the rationalist tradition itself. If identifying the use of the means/ends schema with rationality effectively eliminates explicit recognition of the difference between instrumental and nonrational normative action, then the characteristics we have identified with the latter, namely, voluntarism and intentionality, will appear as equally applicable to the former. This false identification occurs time and time again throughout the rationalist tradition; it is one of the primary theoretical "camouflages" for the antivoluntarist implications of what is in actuality an exclusively instrumentalist position.[60] The ultimate conclusion of this line of reasoning also demonstrates its ultimate futility. Within the context of the instrumentally rationalist tradition, accepting the nondifferentiated rationality usage renders the very concept of rationality a meaningless theoretical distinction. This is, in fact, exactly the argument proposed by the economic theorist von Mises in *Human Action*. Although he defines action broadly as intentional means/ends activity, he assumes that the concept's applicability to social science is strictly limited to utilitarian calculation. On this basis, he concludes, quite naturally, that since "human action is always rational" the "term 'rational act' is therefore pleonastic and must be rejected as such."[61]

I have criticized these theoretical attempts according to the standard of presuppositional "generality" developed in the theoretical arguments of the preceding chapter. I have done so in order to indicate that the problem is not that they are "incorrect" but that they attempt to raise to the most generalized theoretical level conceptions of rationality that are actually grounded at more specific empirically-oriented levels of analysis. This can be demonstrated in two ways. In the first place, the broad definition usually reflects an implicit effort to identify presuppositional rationality with ideological or political rationality, with the Enlightenment tradition which Mannheim identifies with individualism, self-assertion, and abstraction. Accordingly, irrationality—which indicates, so these theorists believe, unreflective habit and instinct—is connected to the conservative and Romantic ideological traditions that emphasize passivity and the absorption of the individual in tradition or uncontrolled affect. But to the degree that rationality is so ideologically defined, the broadness of its application is undermined in the same manner as Mannheim undermined it in his effort at ideological reduction (see ch. 2, sec. 1, above). Because of this reduction, general theoretical argument cannot recognize the *presuppositionally* nonrational aspects of *ideologically* rational behavior—the degree to which action that is rational in some political, ideological sense depends on reference to internal, ideal factors.

The other reductionist aspect of the broad definition of rationality rests upon formulations that belong to the level not of ideology but of empirical propositions. In this case, the error resides in attempting to transpose empirical characterizations to the most generalized, theoretical level of analysis. Thus, Schutz's reference to rationality as common sense derives not from a conception of the basic, presuppositional alternatives of action but from his more detailed empirical reconstruction of the cultural components of common sense as one of the principal "phenomenological worlds" that compose reality.[62] Similarly, the anthropological debate over the nature of symbolic action is not actually a generalized argument, but refers, at least in part, to much more elaborate causal propositions about the interrelation of ritual and social structure. The psychoanalytic formulations, in their turn, actually rest, in part, on empirically oriented notions about psychic health and illness. Finally, Weber's distinction between habitual and affective action and other rational types builds upon his empirical theory about the direction of historical change.

2.3.2 Rationality as the Achievement of Particular Ends

The second possible alternative perspective on rational action defines rationality not as means/ends calculation per se but as the pursuit of a particular kind of end.

A number of different conceptions of this normative criterion of rationality have been advanced.[63†] Action can, for example, be regarded as rational only if it adheres to the standards of scientific truth, a criterion usually proposed by thinkers who identify themselves with the scientific tradition in social thought. Brian Wilson, for example, the British sociologist of religion, defines the classical problem of attaining a "rational [social] ethic" as equivalent to the problem of whether or not "social regulation" is guided by "the findings of scientific social inquiry." This possibility in turn depends, according to Wilson, on the nature of "the limitations of rational procedures of inquiry and understanding,"[64] that is, on the possibilities for establishing the objectivity of social science. Reinhard Bendix, in his essay "Embattled Reason," applies a similarly scientific normative standard. Setting rationality as the central determinant of ethical obligation, Bendix writes that "we are bound to make . . . some estimate of what men are and what they are capable of becoming." He then defines this capability as synonymous with the ability to act in terms of scientific truth: "Reason refers to our estimate of the role of knowledge in human affairs."[65]

This conception of rationality as the pursuit of scientific truth is also at the heart of a distinction articulated by Jarvie and Agassi. They claim that to ask whether action is goal directed—whether it is "rational" in contrast to the "irrationality" of Lévy-Bruhl—actually poses only the weak version of the rationality question. Rationality in the strong sense is achieved only when action is directed to a goal that is true according to strict scientific standards.[66] This definition of the rational/irrational issue in terms of the normative criterion of scientific truth also appears among the classical generation of sociologists, particularly in the work of Pareto. Taken in its entirety, Pareto's discussion of the nature of logical action cross-cuts other approaches to the question—for example, in the close correlation that can be drawn between his irrational "residues" and the psychological tradition's emphasis on emotionalism or irrationalism. Nonetheless, his principal criterion for judging rationality stands entirely outside the process of means/ends calculation per se: action is rational to the degree it is guided by the normative criterion of experimental truth.[67†]

Although it does fall within the positivist intellectual tradition as broadly conceived, this approach to rationality as scientific truth must not be confused with the scientistic approach to rationality, which reduces action to scientifically-guided efficient calculations about the nature of the material environment. The failure to understand the distinction between "rationality" as a normative standard, albeit a purely scientific one, and "rationality" as pure nonnormative instrumentalism leads to certain basic misconceptions. For example, in a criticism of Parsons' antipositivist polemic in *The Structure of Social Action*, Jere Cohen takes issue with what he views as Parsons' claim that a scientific approach to action leads to pure determinism. He contrasts this with Durkheim's conception that the adoption of the scientific perspective brings an enlargement of human freedom.[68] In fact, Parsons actually criticized only the normless, materialistic perspective on science, the scientistic, positivistic perspective that views it as equivalent to utilitarianism. Further, he made this criticism precisely in order to emphasize that science can be linked to freedom only by viewing it as a normative activity of the type that Durkheim described. Cohen could not perceive this argument because he failed to make the distinction proposed here, between science as a means to an instrumental end (the view which Parsons actually criticized) and science conceived as a normative end in itself (the view Durkheim, and Parsons, upheld). This same confusion seriously limits the scope of Habermas' work, for Habermas equates the application of scientific standards in industrial society with the normless condition of the scientistic perception of scientific practice as technical rationality.

The second way of regarding rationality as a particular normative criterion upholds other, nonscientific, humanitarian and moral standards. The best-known formulation along these lines is the conception of "substantive rationality" developed by Weber in his discussions of law, religion, and economy which was later elaborated by Mannheim. For Weber, substantive rationality in economic action, for example, involves not simply the manipulation of ends and means but also an orientation toward some "particular given ends" which "judge the outcome of economic action" according to some more ultimate standard.[69] While according to certain strands of Weber's discussion this ultimate normative standard can be of any particular type, in Mannheim substantive rationality can be achieved only to the degree that these ends allow individuals to "act intelligently in a given situation on the basis of one's own insight."[70†] Another version of this substantive approach to rationality— which, though strikingly different in content, derives from the same German classical philosophic tradition of Kant, Hegel, and Marx—has been developed by writers within the neo-Marxist Frankfurt school. Their conception of the nonscientific moral and humanistic standards of "substantive reason" resembles Weber's and Mannheim's but is limited to a still more particular type of normative standard. As defined by Marcuse, "reason" presents a moral criterion that criticizes the ideals of the capitalist historical period from the radical Romantic perspective of the potentially universalistic reconciliation of subject and object. In *Reason and Revolution*, he attempts to demonstrate that this approach to substantive rationality represents the restoration of the unity of subject and object, the same reconciliation, Marcuse believes, that underlay the critical aspects of Hegel's thought. "Reason," he writes, "is motivated by the need to 'restore the totality.' "[71] A somewhat different version of this neo-Marxist Frankfurt school approach to substantive rationality has been developed by Habermas in the strand of his work concerned with "emancipatory reason." Habermas disagrees with Marcuse's more romantic emphasis and formulates a normative standard that is a hybrid of scientific, Freudian, and classical democratic criteria.[72]

The first classification of rationality as simply the use of the means/ends schema proved unsatisfactory because it does not sufficiently differentiate the kinds of conflicts that permeate the most generalized level of theoretical logic. This failure, I argued, resulted from the erroneous attempt to generalize theoretical points made at more specific ideological and empirical levels of analysis. In evaluating the different versions of this second approach to the rationality concept, my basic criticism remains the same. As in the first approach, these efforts to define rationality as a substantive normative quality do not attain the necessary generality because they attempt to convert distinctively ideological properties into presuppositional ones. But in contrast to the first approach, here the attempts at ideological reduction are usually entirely self-conscious. For this reason, they manifest themselves in definitions of rationality that are overly specific and differentiating rather than not sufficiently so.

Every social theory, of course, must evaluate action in terms of some standard of scientific accuracy and in terms of some substantive moral goal. The very possibility of making such ideal judgments, however, depends on the prior existence of a certain more general orientation. To argue for differentiating some norms as morally superior to others is to accept the prior presuppositional assumption that action is a normatively regulated phenomenon, that it is not purely instrumental and conditionally determined. This brings us to a fundamental point: the different kinds of particular normative standards proposed by these thinkers as "rational" standards can be seen as different substantive versions of what I have described, more abstractly, as the general category of "nonrational" action. In fact, it is precisely for this reason that presupposing exclusively instrumental rationality has such ramifying effects. Without presupposing the existence of nonrational action, it is impossible to formulate the possibilities for voluntarism upon which all ideological arguments for increased freedom depend. In other theoretical efforts, oriented more directly to the logic of ideological concerns, I have developed this position in terms of the distinction between "formal" and "substantive" voluntarism.[73] On the level of general theoretical logic, insofar as the presupposition of nonrationality is accepted, voluntarism can be defined as a formal—epistemological or structural—property of action. Whether or not action is also voluntary in the substantive, contingent sense defined by various progressive ideological traditions depends on the nature of the empirical constraints on action at a given historical moment. In other words, the formal capacity for normative action is a necessary prerequisite for achieving freedom in the substantive ideological sense; it is not a sufficient one.

The only truly presuppositional version of the rational/nonrational dichotomy falls within the second of the two possible approaches discussed: it evaluates rationality according to the achievement of a specific type of normative standard, one of pure efficiency. I have argued, therefore, that when this normative standard is considered to be the exclusive ideal reference of action, subjective references appear to be superceded by purely external considerations. In relation to this presuppositional definition, the present discussion has attempted to demonstrate two interrelated points. Once the different approaches to rationality are understood, it is apparent that the approach proposed here need not necessarily eliminate the others; but it is equally clear that it cannot be reduced to them. I have contended, moreover, that not only does this particular rational/nonrational dichotomy represent a distinctively differentiated level of social analysis but that it formulates one of the two most generalized and decisive questions in theoretical argument. It is to the other, equally important question that the discussion now turns.

3. THE GENERALIZED PROBLEM OF ORDER

Earlier in this chapter, I introduced two conceptual innovations to designate the sociological relevance of the traditional epistemological issues of subjectivity and objectivity, freedom and determinism. These two reformulations establish the basic presuppositional questions for sociological theory. First, the question about the simple existence of the subjective element is superceded. This existence is now assumed: the crucial question becomes that of determining the nature of its particular normative components. The implications of this normative issue for freedom and constraint cannot be fully assessed, however, without addressing a second fundamental question. Because social science must deal with a plurality of individuals, the problem of action must be complemented by the problem of order. Every social theory inherently combines an answer to the problem of action with an answer to the question of how a plurality of such actions become interrelated and ordered.

As Kuhn once suggested while pointing out the similarities between postpositivist philosophy of science and Wittgensteinian philosophy of language, comparative theoretical argument involves problems of "translation" between different sets of nonempirical scientific "languages." As we have seen, precisely such communications problems have greatly confused discussions about the rationality of action. Though less dramatic, a similar ambiguity surrounds the concept of order. It too must be clarified before the translation necessary for generalized theoretical argument can begin.[74†]

3.1. THE CONFLATIONARY DIMENSIONS OF CURRENT APPROACHES TO ORDER: EMPIRICAL, IDEOLOGICAL, AND PRESUPPOSITIONAL REDUCTION

Broadly speaking, the approaches to order that pose problems for generalized theoretical debate represent overly particularistic conceptions. What is needed instead is a thoroughly generic conceptualization. For, in abstract terms, these particularist approaches erroneously combine theoretical reductions of the type I have discussed in the sections on action with a bias toward one presuppositional perspective on action over another.

The first and most basic problem occurs because of what is described in chapter 2 as the reductive influence of the "conflict debate." Both critics and proponents of the theoretical utility of the order concept have incorrectly identified the presuppositional issue of order with empirical propositions emphasizing social tranquility and the absence of struggle. This problematic position is often overlaid by a second one, arising from an ideological interpretation of the order issue that associates its use with the reaction against the French Revolution during the nineteenth century by those conservative political intellectuals espousing the "restoration" of traditional social arrangements. The third particularist usage associates this conservative, Burkian emphasis on the causal significance of tradition and religion with an organicist perspective as Mannheim defined it. Because of this association, simply to address the problem of order appears to involve a presuppositional emphasis on the nonrationality of action.

This mixture of theoretical reduction and presuppositional bias has created a situation in which social theorists apparently can argue for or against theoretical recognition of "the problem of order," making evaluations about its empirical incidence, its political desirability, and the more general commitments it implies. Addressing himself to presuppositional issues, Shils demonstrates the theoretical centrality of the order concept by pointing to the pervasiveness of common belief in sacred tradition within even the most modern societies.[75] Eisenstadt addresses himself to the empirical level, arguing that only by explicit reference to the problem of order can political sociology recognize the need for normative harmony that exists alongside even the most intensive political strife.[76] Parsons' work too, despite its singular contributions to the formulation of a more generic conceptualization, includes one line of argument that equates theoretical attention to order with the focus on nonrational norms and social equilibrium.

Despite their position on the other side of this conflict debate, theorists like Dahrendorf and Lockwood adopt a basically similar perspective on the nature of the order question because, in arguing that an emphasis on conflict, materialist epistemology, and progressive ideology produces on "anti-order" position, they are also working with a particularist definition.[77] This misleading approach to the order concept is, in fact, so imbedded in sociological debate that even those who deny the usefulness of the concept altogether do so only after adopting a reductionist interpretation of it. Giddens, for example, pejoratively labels the vary existence of the "problem of order" one of the great "myths" in the history of social thought, and attempts to demonstrate that such a distinguished theorist as Durkheim rarely concerned himself with the issue. Yet, significantly, Giddens can make this argument only after he has denied the generalized status of the order issue, identifying it via each of the three levels of reduction we have noted: empirical stability versus change; cultural versus institutional causation; and conservative versus socialist ideology.[78] The sequence of reductionist associations, then, are usually the following: when order is emphasized, conservatism, equilibrium, and idealism follow; when order is not emphasized, there follow radicalism, conflict, and materialism. I would argue, however, that these two sequences are not theoretically inevitable even if they sometimes empirically occur.[79†]

The point is not that these different approaches to order are simply incorrect, for they do utilize the concept to point to real empirical, ideological, and presuppositional facts of social life. The problem is, rather, that the reduction of order to any one particular version eliminates its usefulness in generalized theoretical argument. If the concept is to achieve that general potential, to become capable of expressing the logic of truly generalized decisions, it is necessary to break through particularist definitions that present order as a theoretical path that may or may not be taken. The problem of order is the problem of how individual units, of whatever motivation, are arranged in nonrandom social patterns. Defined in such a generic manner, as the neutral problem of "arrangement" or "pattern," it is clear that every social theory must address the order question. Every theory must adopt a solution to the order problem just as it must also address the problem of action and motivation.

Although this generic approach has rarely been explicitly articulated in general theoretical argument, it has been pointed to implicitly by a number of more substantive theoretical efforts in a variety of intellectual traditions and disciplines. Since, for the kinds of overlapping ideological and empirical reasons I have described, "order" is more often referred to within the nonrationalist tradition of social thought, it is here that we also find the most frequent generic usage. Michael Polanyi, for example, formulates his postpositivist philosophy of science by asserting, as we have seen, that the scientific actor relies on an internal, a priori sense of the pattern of external empirical events. When he articulates this position by writing that "scientific observation includes an appreciation of order as contrasted to randomness," he is employing the order concept, within the context of his normative emphasis, in a fully generalized manner, differentiating it entirely from any specific vision of its scientific content.[80†] Within normatively oriented anthropology, Mary Douglas uses the order concept in much the same way to indicate the drive for consistency and integrity in cultural patterns, regardless of whether the particular pattern happens to produce conflict or harmony or whether it is radical or conservative. In her study of hygiene taboos, for example, she emphasizes the generic aspect of order by using it to define both conformity and rebellion. "The definition of dirt as matter out of place . . . implies two conditions: a set of ordered relations and a contravention of that order [because dirt] is the by product of a systematic ordering and classification of matter, insofar as ordering involves rejecting inappropriate elements."[81†]

This distinction between the generalized and more empirically oriented approaches to order is perhaps most decisively stated by David Little in his monograph *Religion, Order, and Law*, which can be viewed as a sociological version of the normative approaches to the problem. Little first establishes the generality of the order question by defining it as concerned with those "rules and patterns" that produce a "reasonably . . . coherent and consistent character of human action," identifying the existence of order with "structured action" as such.[82] Although his nonrational perspective reveals itself in his emphasis on religion as the cause of this order, his subsequent analysis views religious order as a source for both a conservative ideological emphasis on social harmony, as in the case of Anglicanism, and a radical ideological emphasis on social conflict, as in Calvinism.[83] Finally, although the rationalist tradition in social theory does not usually accept the validity of the order question in an explicit way, the notion of order as the material basis of social arrangements, differentiated from particular political or economic "orders" as such, has also been utilized on occasion. This has nowhere been more effectively illustrated than in Weber's discussions of patrimonial, feudal, and bureaucratic authority as different methods for the imposition of "order" by leadership groups.[84†]

Only by adopting such a generic understanding is it possible even to approach the level of generality necessary to explain the basic divisions in sociological thought. A major reason for the unusually wide explanatory scope of Percy Cohen's *Modern Social Theory* is, for example, that although the author formally defines order in a reductionist way as stability versus change, he actually utilizes these different approaches to empirical equilibrium to indicate the more general presuppositional frameworks of sociological analysis.[85†] Similarly, in a more recent work of theoretical interpretation, Jonathan Turner introduces his analysis by defining the order problem as parallel with that of "institutionalization," or "the conditions under which different social processes and patterns of social organization are likely to occur."[86] By utilizing such a generalized understanding, Turner frees his subsequent analysis from the kinds of theoretical confusions that have arisen from the common identification of order with particular types of empirical, ideological and presuppositional commitment.

Order is, then, a problem generic to all social theory, a question which, though interrelated with, must still be viewed as analytically distinct from the problem of action. Two basic conceptual distinctions will be elaborated in the following discussion. First, borrowing the language introduced by Peter Ekeh's important discussion in *Social Exchange Theory: The Two Traditions*,[87†] one may describe the order question as informed either by an "individual" or "collective" level of analysis.

Second, both these levels in turn can be understood as cross-cut by commitments which connect them to the epistemologically related questions
of rationality and nonrationality. I will describe the combinations that
result by the concepts of "external order" and "internal order."

3.2. THE INDIVIDUALIST PRESUPPOSITION IN ITS
INSTRUMENTAL AND NORMATIVE FORMS: SOCIAL ORDER
AS RESIDUAL CATEGORY

Approaches to social order that remain rooted at the individual level
do not simply ignore the contextual social arrangements that are supra-
individual. This would be an impossible feat in theories that profess to
explain society. Rather, such theories explain social arrangements in any
given historical moment as built up principally through the actions of
the individuals in that particular interaction. Arrangements established
prior to the individual activity in that particular moment are not considered as significant foci of study. Theorists either will not acknowledge
such a priori elements or else will regard them only as parameters in relation to which actors have an ultimate discretion. Accordingly, theoretical attention shifts to the individual actors themselves. Such an
individualist approach to the order question can combine with both instrumentally rational and normative, nonrational understandings of action; in fact, the individualist approach constitutes a subset within all of
the substantive versions of instrumental and normative theory described
in the preceding section.

In the instrumentalist tradition, the classical individualist position
was articulated by the Lockean strand of nineteenth-century utilitarian
economic and political theory. Economic institutions and legal arrangements were understood simply as multiplications of one-to-one interactions. Individualist strands also appear in nineteenth-century social
Darwinism, emanating first from Malthus, and in Realpolitik theories of
political order, though both of these traditions involve more collectivist
conceptualizations as well. In contemporary sociological thought, rationalist individualism has a variety of spokesmen. In his exchange theory, Homans emphasizes that he is interested only in reward and
punishment as it develops within face-to-face interactions; he denies the
legitimacy of third-party mediation, whether normative or institutional.
Theoretical analysis, Homans contends, must focus at the level of "the
person."[88] Certain political sociologists are also committed to formulating their rationalist assumptions in an individualistic way. Coleman, for
example, introduces his notion of collective decision-making in the following manner: "I will start with an image of man as wholly free [and]
not constrained"; and the order eventually constructed by Coleman's actors is truly Lockean.[89†] In the neo-utilitarian strands of Erving

Goffman's writings, the individual is similarly described as a self-constituting atom, distanced, as a "self," from social controls. Again, the focus naturally shifts in Goffman's work to the presentation of this self and its vicissitudes.[90]

Because of the clear relation between the emphasis in nonrational theory on subjectivity and the element of volition emphasized by an individualist approach, it is not surprising that more individualistic theory is actually written within a normative than an instrumentalist framework. Emphasizing the individualistic rather than the "generalized" aspects of Mead's analysis of self/other activity, symbolic interactionism focuses primarily on the self-created aspects of situations. Although Herbert Blumer allows that the "organization of a human society is the framework inside of which social action takes place," he emphasizes that this organization "is not the determinant of that action." On the basis of this distinction, he can then argue that all "such organization and changes in it" must be viewed as the sole "product of the activity of [individual] acting units."[91]† The existentialist position is in this respect nearly identical. While Sartre formally argues in *Search for a Method* that individuals have freedom only within collective structures as they are constituted by Marxian theory, he implicitly asserts that a viable social theory must focus on the level of free individual action as such.[92] Similarly, in the phenomenological tradition, Atkinson has proposed that collective social arrangements be perceived as "kaleidoscope" rather than as "structure."[93] He insists that the only viable level of order is the individual; sociological analysis must be reoriented to the "resilience, uniqueness, and passion of the individual" and the "permanently escalating intended and unintended consequences of [individual] interaction."[94] Still another version of nonrationalist thought, classical psychoanalytic social theory, approaches social analysis only through the personality of the individual actor.[95]

In historical terms, the origins of theoretical individualism undoubtedly lay in the desire to make the conception of order compatible with the theorists' own ideological commitments to voluntarism and freedom. Such a relationship can be seen, for example, in the clear connection between English Puritanism and nineteenth-century utilitarian theory.[96]† In theoretical terms, however, this correlation is not legitimate; it rests on a radical misunderstanding of the nature of the individual and, therefore, of the very basis for such ideologically valued freedom. Individuals need not be atomized in order to be free. A thorough analytic discussion of this point, and a direct, "positive" critique of the individualist position, will have to wait for the section on normative collective order below. At the present stage of the argument, I can support this position only indirectly, by presenting "negative" evidence which demonstrates the internal inconsistencies of an individualist approach.

The inadequacy of an individualist understanding of order is indicated by the fact that every one of the theories I have just cited has been forced at one point or another by the logic of its empirical or ideological position to try to incorporate a collectivist emphasis. Yet, given their overriding individualist presuppositions, they have been able to broach this level of collective arrangements only in the most truncated manner. They can do so only by smuggling in ad hoc, residual categories that implicitly contradict the thrust of their central analysis. The classic analysis of this problem is Halévy's devastating critique, in *The Growth of Philosophic Radicalism*, of individualistic utilitarianism. Halévy proved that these theorists could explain collective economic and political arrangements only by postulating two "eminently paradoxical" facts, propositions which were, implicitly, strikingly at variance with their individualist assumptions. First, the utilitarians proposed the principle Halévy calls the "fusion of interests." By citing this principle, they were able to "solve" the order problem by arguing that "the identification of personal and general interest is spontaneously performed within each individual conscience by feelings of sympathy which interest us directly in the happiness of our neighbor." The second such residual postulate they employed Halévy calls the thesis of the "natural identity of interests." It posits that collective order is achieved because "the various egoisms harmonize of their own accord and automatically bring about the good of the species."[97†] In other words, only by fairly implausible means could the utilitarians address the problem of collective order while ostensibly remaining within an individualist framework.[98†]

Within the contemporary tradition of rationalist individualism, it is clear that Homans allows individual exchange to be mediated by the "distributive justice" principle because of the need to balance the purely individualist thrust of the rest of his exchange theory. Yet the supra-individual source of this collectivist concept is left unexplained. Either it is considered simply as another product of the individual calculation of investment, costs, and rewards,[99] or it is referred to collective categories that according to Homans' explicit logic do not even exist.[100†] Similarly, Coleman acknowledges that the collective order he describes as emergent from individual decisions actually depends on the prior acceptance of constitutional "rules of the game," yet the origins and status of such rules remain completely unexplained.[101] Finally, in such a work as *Asylums*, Goffman explodes the individualist assumptions of interactionism from within, for his major theoretical point depends not simply on the results of individual negotiation, but also on a strong conception of the overarching dimensions of social systems. Yet *Asylums* contains no systematic explanation for such collective phenomena; rather, Goffman attempts to explain the characteristics of his "total institutions" by resorting to an individualist hypothesis about the self-interested actions of individual psychiatric and administrative personnel.[102]

The same kind of contradiction surfaces in the normative tradition of individualist theory. Sartre, for example, alongside his individualist emphasis, stresses the completely objective and determinate character of certain supra-individual economic factors, such as class position. It is because this represents an ambiguous and uneasy compromise between individual and collectivist approaches to the order problem and not a resolution of it that Sartre's "progressive-regressive" method has proved so resistant to systematization, and must ultimately be regarded as an ineffective reworking of the Marxian problem.[103†] In Freud's psycho-analytic writing on collective social phenomena, we can find similar conflict on the presuppositional level. Overtly, *Group Psychology and the Analysis of the Ego* concerns the internal, individual roots of those collective arrangements Freud calls "groups." Yet Freud admits in the course of his discussion that this psychoanalytic theory explains only "pathological" group phenomena. For "normal" collective processes, he refers to McDougall's analysis of "organized groups," thereby introducing notions about group continuity through time, group complexity and self-consciousness, and the role of tradition and social conflict. The relation between such collective factors and the individual anxiety at the root of group pathology are left completely unexplained; they must remain so given their necessarily residual status in Freud's primarily individualistic theory.[104]

Alfred Schutz's phenomenological efforts similarly reveal the fundamental inadequacy of the individualist approach, though his attempted incorporation of the collective element is, at least in terms of theoretical logic, somewhat more successful than the others. Although Schutz, like Atkinson, concentrates primarily on processes at the individual level, he also employs the notion of phenomenological "worlds." Phenomena like common sense, religion, and science, according to his view, embody cultural definitions of collective reality that actually supersede any attempt at individual definition.[105] Schutz speaks of "the same undivided and common environment, which we may call 'our environment,' " and affirms: "The world of the We is not private to either of us, but is our world, the one common intersubjective world which is right there in front of us"; yet the presuppositional tension remains, for he adds the contradictory claim that "It is only from the face-to-face relationship, from the common lived experience in the We, that the intersubjective world can be constituted."[106†] Only by recognizing this tension is it possible to understand why Berger and Luckmann, in further extending Schutz's phenomenological approach, have to rely on theoretical traditions whose principal presuppositions were so widely divergent from the major thrust of his own,[107] or why, in Garfinkle's ethnomethodology, the nominalist emphasis on individual "construction" is periodically punctuated with the affirmation—"in principle"—of order in a more collectivist sense.[108†]

In the pages which follow, the individualist understanding of social order, in either its instrumental or normative form, will not be of central concern. For the theorists who form the principal focus of this work, such individualism functions mainly as a point of departure. For the classical founders of sociology, the basic question is not how social arrangements are constructed from individual negotiation; it is, rather, how social theories which do accept the sui generis collective character of social arrangements can retain a conception of individual freedom and voluntarism. This, as will be seen, is a quite different issue.

3.3. THE COLLECTIVIST PRESUPPOSITION IN ITS RATIONALIST FORM: COERCIVE ORDER AND THE ELIMINATION OF FREEDOM

The first great secular theorist of the collectivist rational mode was Thomas Hobbes. Elie Halévy first recognized Hobbes' distinctive significance for the order issue in *The Growth of Philosophic Radicalism*, and Talcott Parsons subsequently elaborated Halévy's perception in *The Structure of Social Action*. Hobbes' legacy was transmitted through such Enlightenment thinkers as Helvétius and Beccaria and achieved, perhaps, its culmination in Bentham's political theories. The Hobbesian view has continued to exert a significant influence in the modern social scientific tradition.[109†]

By not only acknowledging but actually conceptualizing the role of the objective conditions that impinge on individual action, these Hobbesian theorists made great and permanent theoretical advances. By formulating a "collective" order, they moved beyond the obfuscating artifices, residual categories, and theoretical ambiguities that necessarily plague individualist attempts at theorizing about rational action. Within the parameters set by the rationalist tradition, they moved from the wishful assumption which Halévy calls the "natural identity of interests" postulate to the reality of the notion of the "artificial identity of interests." Hobbes knew that insofar as action is instrumental a notion of purely individual interaction would, logically, lead to a description of chaos—in our terms random, nonpatterned action—a description that, in fact, does not reflect social life as it actually exists.

> And therefore if any two men desire the same thing, which neverthelesse they cannot both enjoy, they become enemies; and in the way to their End, (which is principally their owne conservation, and sometimes their delectation only), endeavour to destroy, or subdue one another.[110†]

According to Hobbes, the individualist assumption is, therefore, an untenable one. Hobbes' alternative theoretical construct, the ordering power of the sovereign, may thus be seen as the prototype of supra-individual collective force. In characterizing this accomplishment, Halévy simultaneously draws attention to its assumptions about the rationality of action: "Hobbes has based a complete system . . . on the doctrine of utility. . . . It is the threat of punishment inflicted by the sovereign which establishes the connection between interest and duty."[111] The Hobbesian solution to the presuppositional problem of order was later conceptualized, albeit in different empirical and ideological terms, in the highly influential political theories of Bentham. As Halévy again emphasized, Bentham's theory of government was thoroughly rationalistic.[112†] Simultaneously, it was just as thoroughly collectivist. In his polemics against natural rights theory, Bentham assumed that his instrumental perspective on action was inherently intertwined with his acceptance of the principle of collective order. As Halévy appropriately interprets Bentham's thinking on the order issue:

> A right only ceases to be a mere fiction and becomes a real right when it is sanctioned by force; the right of force is real. . . . The State . . . is a machine so well constructed that every individual, taken individually, cannot for one instant escape the control of all the individuals taken collectively.[113†]

As this last passage indicates, however, such clarification of the order issue was achieved only at a certain cost: the element of voluntarism was eliminated from social explanation. Here we can finally connect our earlier analysis of the deficiencies of a purely rationalist orientation to action with this second presuppositional problem of order. For an unusual paradox inevitably affects any social scientific understanding of the rationalist position. In its individualist form, rationalism can be, and often is, associated with a voluntaristic emphasis—not only on the presuppositional level but also in terms of empirical description of action and ideological stance. One need simply cite in this regard the theories of Locke or Adam Smith, or, more immediately, the writings of Homans or Coleman. What happens in such an association is that the misplaced emphasis on the individual has obscured the anti-individualist implications of the rationalist approach. The deficiencies of the rationalist perspective become apparent only after the establishment of a more satisfactory collectivist position on the order issue.

Although collectivist approaches to the ordering of rational action often continue formally to acknowledge the role of individual subjective intention, their conception of norms as exclusively instrumental inevitably shifts the true focus of analytic attention to the individual's "conditional" environment. The result is an anti-voluntaristic, deterministic analysis. In terms of this general theoretical logic, the substantive empirical focus of any particular theory is unimportant. Whether instrumental collectivist analysis is directed toward the explanation of economic, political, demographic, legal, religious, ecological, or psychological life, each of these spheres will be explained in terms of means and conditions, not in terms of goals or norms. Collective order is reduced to the external, objective elements of action. Despite the recognition of subjectivity and intentionality on the purely epistemological level, such "sociological materialism" allows no explanatory role to society's ideal, normative elements, unless, of course, they are themselves conceived in an external, purely conditional way, i.e., transformed from normative into quasi-material elements.[114†] If an instrumentally collectivist position is adopted, then, "motivation" as an explicit explanatory concern drops out of sociological theory, and the voluntary component of action disappears.

The theoretical logic of this problem was first outlined, once again, by Halévy, although his focus on explicitly political implications partly obscured the full range of the presuppositional issues involved. Halévy applauds the collectivist achievements of Bentham, particularly the articulation of the "artificial identity of interest" concept; yet he simultaneously condemns it as a "despotic principle."[115†] In fact, the major, if rarely articulated, theme of Halévy's great work is devoted to illuminating in more directly political terms what I have called the central paradox of rationalist collectivist theory. He demonstrates that it was partly in order to create a politically more democratic and reformist social theory that the philosophic radicals of the Benthamite tradition transformed individualistic utilitarianism into a collectivist theory, for only a collectivist theory could create the more egalitarian "artificial identity" of interests such egalitarian reformers desired. Yet in the very act of formulating this revision, these reformers eliminated from their theory the basic democratic notions of freedom and voluntarism. Bentham's goal of creating social justice through collectivist principles was, Halévy writes, "to place each of the members of the political society in social conditions such that his own interest shall coincide with the general interest."[116] Yet Bentham had to work toward this goal within the strictures of an instrumental rationalism, according to which "all professions of disinterestedness and of purity of intentions must be taken as so many lies."[117] For this reason, even the differences between dictators and democrats could be explained only in external, materialist, and deterministic terms. For example, Bentham compares the political leaders Washington and Bonaparte in the following manner:

> The only reason Washington did not act in America as Bonaparte acted in France, must be sought not in a difference of motives, which were egoistic in both cases, but in the difference of political conditions.[118]

By undermining the normative basis of disinterest and altruism, and eschewing the very concept of "motivation," the presuppositions of Bentham's theory undercut the presuppositional foundations of the very democratic society it espoused in ideological and empirical terms.[119†]

Forty years after the publication of Halévy's work, Parsons reformulated his basic insight by focusing more directly on the presuppositional issue of order. In terms of the framework presented here, Parsons' famous "utilitarian dilemma" concerns the cost of moving from the individual to the collective level within the rationalist tradition.

> Positivistic [i.e. rationalist] thought is caught in the "utilitarian dilemma." That is, either the active agency of the actor in the choice of ends is an independent factor in action, and the end element must be random; or the objectionable implication of the randomness of ends is denied, but their independence disappears and they are assimilated to the conditions of the situation, that is to elements analyzable in terms of nonsubjective categories . . . [120†]

Parsons describes the two substantive variations of this collectivist, antisubjective position as "radical rationalistic positivism" and "radical antiintellectualistic positivism."[121†]

The theoretical logic of rationalist collectivism inheres in the process of theorizing itself, regardless of the conscious intentions of the theorist and his commitments at any other level of the scientific continuum. Within contemporary theoretical debate, this fact can perhaps be seen most clearly in John Rex's well-known attempt to produce a theory of social conflict. Although Rex expresses his commitment to an "action" approach that emphasizes individual intentionality and to an integrated perspective on order that emphasizes both material power and norms, he can accomplish neither goal because he approaches collective explanation in an exclusively rationalist context.[122†] The reduction of action to interest leads Rex to reduce collective order to external coercion. He describes society as facing only two options: an orderless state of internal war, in which the allocation of power is completely unresolved, or a condition in which order is achieved as the result of one social group's asserting its superior force so that "each side recognized that compliance to a certain degree was more profitable than a continuance of the conflict."[123] Rex subsequently recommends that three types of order should be the central focus of sociological analysis. Yet these actually are only variants of one more general type: the approach to collective order that eliminates any normative component. Thus, given his presuppositional position, Rex can describe each of these three types only as group alignments that result from "conflicts over access to the *means* of life."[124]

Rex's "ruling class situation," "revolutionary situation," and "truce situation" simply represent different balances of coercive social force.[125]

Finally, although sociological materialism eliminates the independent impact of subjective elements, it need not necessarily do so in the direct manner of Bentham, Hobbes, or Rex. There exist at least three strategies by which the existence of norms can be both acknowledged and simultaneously relegated to thoroughly epiphenomenal status. First, norms can be viewed as contrived simply to serve or to oppose material power. As such, the actual relation of means and ends is reversed: ends come to be viewed as means manipulated to serve the ends of adaptation to material conditions. Mills follows this presuppositional strategy in *The Sociological Imagination* when he endorses the significance of "normative structures" but argues that this significance can be discovered only in terms of their "use to justify or to oppose the arrangement of power and the position within this arrangement of the powerful."[126] Given what he views as the actual, effective cause of normative action, it is not surprising that in this work Mills never develops an independent analysis of the role of subjective elements and instead proceeds to construct an argument that is ultimately antisubjective and reductionist.

A second strategy for the indirect elimination of subjectivity is to describe every action that is not rational, which deviates from the norm of instrumental rationality, as an "error." Since a nonrational norm as such cannot be envisioned, this anomalous action must somehow be made consistent with a rationalist perspective on motivation. To characterize it as an error meets this challenge via the technique of ad hoc explanation. This residual quality is apparent in a discussion by the economist von Mises. "It is a fact," von Mises admits, "that human reason is not infallible and that man very often errs in selecting and applying means." Nevertheless, even this case remains rational, he contends, if understood as an action that while "connected to the end sought" simply "falls short of expectation": "It is contrary to purpose, but it is rational, i.e., the outcome of a reasonable—although faulty—deliberation and an attempt—although an ineffectual attempt—to attain a definite goal."[127†] Explaining nonrational action as error also will ultimately push theoretical argument back into a purely conditional, materialist logic. For if one persists in trying to locate a cause for such "mistaken" behavior—to eliminate thereby the theoretical embarrassment of this residual category—one must conclude that such action can be produced only by factors unknown to the actor. As Parsons describes the problem, the scientific observer must "get behind" the actor's subjective experience of his situation to find the processes that operated without the actor's knowledge of what was "really" happening.[128] Inevitably, a higher order of determining conditions is established, separated from the immediate action level of ends-means-norms-conditions. In this way, individuals can still be described as acting rationally toward the conditions of their immediate situation, but there now exists a second level of external conditions outside the reach of human insight and, therefore, human rationality.

A third kind of indirect strategy for rational reduction acknowledges the role of normative, ideal elements but claims that the very voluntarism induced by such elements proves they have individualistic rather than collectivist status. As such, the only elements which remain to determine action on the level of collective order are the material ones. In his widely read article "Structural Effects," Blau provides an excellent illustration of just such an approach. "Internal" processes like value commitments must, Blau writes, be psychological rather than social. They therefore address only the individual level, not the collective level of "social structure." Why must this be so? Blau argues that, by definition, social structure can refer only to collective arrangements based on the "fear of sanctions"—in our terms, on external, conditional variables.[129†] Gianfranco Poggi similarly explains the normative approach to order in a negative manner. It results, he writes, either from an inability to perceive order in a fully collective manner or as the reflection of an empirical situation that exhibits unusually high levels of individualism and atomism.[130]

Whether direct or indirect, the impact of sociological materialism remains the same, the reduction of action to determination by conditions and the consequent elimination of the voluntary from social life.

3.4. THE COLLECTIVIST PRESUPPOSITION IN ITS NORMATIVE FORM

It is the great paradox of the rationalist position that its ideological and presuppositional commitments can be in such stark opposition to one another. Often associated ideologically with the reformist and radical movements of liberalism and socialism, on the most general level of theoretical logic the rationalist approach to collective order must of necessity eliminate the element of individual freedom.[131†] To maintain the voluntary, intentional quality of action it is necessary to relate social order, in part or in whole, to the normative, nonrational elements of action. In doing so, we create a conception of collective *internal* order. Although proponents of the external collectivist position deny its validity, such a perspective does indeed provide an additional, or alternative, method for explaining the collective basis of social patterns.

3.4.1. Social Constraint and the Preservation of Voluntarism

It should be clear from our previous discussion of action how voluntarism is maintained through conceptualizing action in a nonrational manner. Because an actor's norms are conceived as producing more than a reliance on instrumental calculation, the specific ends, or goals, of action are not effectively reduced to the status of means. By thus preserving the ideal, normative element, the voluntarism associated with the internal reference of action remains intact. But how can such a normative emphasis also indicate the basis of collective order?

Again, we must refer to basic epistemological issues and their impact on freedom and determinism. Because norms are not material, the same norm can be conceived as interconnecting two or more individuals. Such an interconnection creates collective patterns. Habermas effectively describes this ordering function of the normative component by contrasting the results of rational-purposive action with the kind of ordered relationship produced by nonrational norms, describing the "binding consensual norms which define reciprocal expectations about behavior and which must be understood and recognized by at least two acting subjects."[132] Rational collectivist conceptions explain order by describing how conditional forces pattern behavior through external sanctions; nonrational collectivist conceptions explain order by describing how subjective normative forces pattern behavior through internal commitments. It is because the sources of order are internal rather than external that voluntarism is maintained. Once again, as Habermas articulates this crucial fact, although interaction is mediated by "an intersubjectively valid employment of symbols," a normative "medium in which meanings are shared," the voluntary element is actually enhanced, not denied. It is true that "on the foundation of intersubjectivity" individuals "identify with one another ... as homogeneous subjects," but "at the same time ... in [such] communication individuals ... also keep a distance from one another and assert against each the inalienable identity of their egos."[133] To arrange normative action collectively is in no way to negate the voluntary reference given by its subjective epistemological status.[134†]

3.4.2. Voluntarism, Constraint and the Reification of the Free Will Concept

The notion that collective ordering, if internal, need not eliminate individual freedom is fundamental to an understanding of the logic of social theory. It is not, however, a notion immediately apparent to common sense, nor is it a position that appears at first glance to agree with certain widely held philosophical notions about the basis of freedom. For these reasons, it remains a controversial and widely misunderstood issue in contemporary debate. It is possible to view opposition to the complementarity of internal order and voluntarism as coalescing around two different kinds of critiques, each of which corresponds to a different approach to action. In the rationalist tradition, it is believed that internal commitments cannot provide a solution to the order problem precisely because of their subjective status. If such commitments are not "really real," they cannot possess any sanctioning power. Ideally-directed action is thus seen as completely random, as free in the purest sense.

The other type of opposition comes from within the normative tradition itself and is, therefore, much more significant for the present argument. According to this criticism, shared internal commitments provide, in a sense, too much order rather than too little. While acknowledging, in opposition to the materialist position, the legitimacy of normative structures, this view regards them as antithetical to the realization of voluntarism. Such a criticism is based on what I believe to be a fundamental error in general theoretical reasoning, an error that colors every attempt to move from individualist to collectivist conceptions of order regardless of the nature of action involved. The belief that collective order and individual voluntarism are incompatible derives, ultimately, from a purely antideterministic understanding of the relation between free will and action.[135†] Yet from a modified, neo-Kantian position, free will is not irreconcilable with an acceptance of some form of determinism.[136†] The notion of collective order actually need never deny free will in an individual case: it can and usually does refer to the probability that individuals will act in a patterned fashion, not to the certainty that any specific individual will so act. As such, it can accept a notion of determinism compatible with the widest possible latitude for any given individual. To believe otherwise is to adopt a reified conception of individual freedom.

Because on the empirical level the notion of collective order implies the existence of scientifically predictable patterned behavior, it is understandable that these critics also insist upon the essential incompatibility of a belief in free will and commitment to the scientific analysis of social life. Yet a similar response can be made to this second critique. As Nagel has perhaps demonstrated most persuasively, determinism in social science implies only probability, not the predictability of any particular action.[137†] Scientific determinism locates the patterns, and perhaps the origins, of collective order. Neither the success of the scientific method nor the existence of the phenomena it discovers depends on an elimination of the unpredictability that, "in the last instance," inheres in any individual act.

If, however, an hypostasized conception of free will is accepted, then supra-individual determination will indeed be seen as eliminating voluntarism. When this reified notion is faithfully adhered to, no collective order can be acknowledged by a social theory which is committed also to encompass individual freedom. In fact, this is exactly the misconception that underlies the individualist theories of social order I described earlier.[138†] For these individualistic theorists, if collective action is to be voluntary, no supra-individual force can impinge on it.

In one of the most significant examples of this approach, Atkinson insists that individual actors are free only to the degree that theory describes them as acting completely "without constraint."[139†] In the symbolic interactionist tradition, Blumer continually equates the postulate of order at the supra-individual level with a denial of the individual freedom to act; in the terminology developed by Mead, Blumer holds, in effect, that only through the "I" of present action, rather than the "me" of past associations, can a voluntaristic component be described. Goffman, too, can visualize freedom as occurring only outside the normative context—on the level of role, in terms of the notion of "role distance."[140] According to ethnomethodology, at least as interpreted by Thomas P. Wilson, sociological "paradigms" that emphasize "normative" pressures describe action as "rule-governed" and as antivoluntary; ethnomethodology, in contrast, views action not as rule governed but as "interpretive" because it postulates action as originating in the action of the individual rather than the norm. Similarly, in the existentialist tradition, a large part of Sartre's criticism of Marxism proceeds from this erroneous equation of supra-individual determination with an antivoluntary position.[141]

This same problem even limits the self-consciousness of theorists who are strong adherents to the collectivist tradition. In the Weberian tradition, for example, Bendix relates an emphasis on supra-individual order to determinism and the suppression of individual autonomy.[142†] A similar nominalist bias permeates the Weberianism of Martindale's discussion of the nature and types of sociological theory.[143] And in the neo-Marxist tradition, Alain Tourraine identifies normatively governed activity as unfree and conformistic; activity can only become creative, voluntary "action" if it is originated by the individual actor himself.[144†]

Parsons offers a useful shorthand way of conceptualizing this reification problem by characterizing it as a confusion of "concrete" and "analytic" conceptions of the individual.[145] It is possible, according to Parsons, to conceive of the individual in a purely "concrete" manner. In common-sense terms, we see before us such a concrete individual—the living, breathing, visible person, the same individual the scientist can observe according to the positivist, materialist perception of science. Those analysts who reify the free will concept, who view collective order as necessarily antivoluntarist, do so by viewing the individual only in this way. Of course, in such a purely empiricist sense, the concrete individual actually is free, for he is indeed physically separated from other persons and from social controls. In Parsons' terminology, this perspective produces an image of individuals as "discrete" rather than as "interpenetrated." For discrete individuals, no supra-individual normative order is possible. A good example of such a misperception of the individual as concrete is Atkinson's claim that the individual actor is "irreducible" and "self-contained."[146] However, when the individual person is viewed "analytically" rather than concretely, we can see that he is not in fact a "black box," but rather incorporates a range of normative, social forces. Although in purely physical terms these elements are invisible, they exist nevertheless: what appears in concrete terms to be a discrete, self-contained individual is actually an actor interpenetrated with other actors by virtue of shared norms. Once we perceive this concrete/analytic distinction, we can see that no empirical individual is actually free of collective constraint in the radical sense proposed by individualist theory. At the same time, this fact in no way denies an element of nondeterminism and unpredictability in considering the action of any particular individual.[147†]

Only by making this distinction between analytic and concrete perspectives on the individual and by not reifying the concept of free will does it become apparent that supra-individual collective order is not, in itself, antithetical to the maintenance of voluntarism. And only then can a further distinction, one crucial to understanding the extant divisions in sociological theory, be made. It is the particular *nature* of social determinism, not simply that determinism itself, that decides the fate of voluntarism. For example, the European intellectual and artistic generation of the 1890s accomplished their critique of rational mechanistic determinism, according to Hughes, by recovering an understanding of how subjective patterns shape social process. Yet they sought to restore this conception in order to develop a stronger argument for the voluntary, autonomous character of social action.[148] In his important work *The Structure of Freedom*, the political philosopher Christian Bay explicitly addresses the problem of freedom in terms of the particular nature of social and psychological restraints, not in terms of whether or not such restraints actually exist. "Something important was missing," Bay writes, "in the individualistic self concept of the empiricists." They "tend[ed] to overlook the important process of *identification* as a process affecting the very constitution of the self."[149]

> What the empiricists tended to overlook [in their approach to freedom] is that the individual as a social being demands restraints, if this word is taken in a wide sense. . . . Life in groups and in society implies and necessitates many kinds of restraints on the individual, but they are not all perceived as restraints. Some are internalized . . .[150†]

Without making this distinction between internal and external restraints on individual action, it is impossible to recognize the vast differences between normative and instrumental approaches to collective order.[151†] For this very reason, in their theoretical critiques neither the ethnomethodologist Wilson nor the symbolic interactionist Blumer makes any effort to distinguish between different kinds of collective order. For them, one has sufficient grounds for criticizing a theory as antivoluntarist if one can demonstrate that the theory is directed at the supra-individual level per se. Given the logic of their presuppositional position, whether this collective element is material or ideal is not significant.[152†] Similarly, Atkinson devotes more than half of his study to establishing the parallel commitments of Marx, Weber, and Parsons to a collectivist conception of order, which he calls the "orthodox consensus." He does not attempt to distinguish the great differences in their approaches to such order because, from the perspective of his individualist version of phenomenology, the collectivist approach in itself makes any voluntary commitment impossible. It is the contrary contention of the present work that precisely such distinctions must be made in order to discern the full scope of general argument in social theory.[153†]

Because the hope for combining collective order and individual voluntarism lies within the normative, rather than the rationalist tradition, I have particularly emphasized how the ability of nonrationalist theory to accept a collective level of analysis has been undermined by a *misplaced* concern about individualism. However, as I mentioned at the beginning of this discussion, the individualism problem must be viewed as generic to the presuppositional level of order itself: it is also relevant to the rationalist tradition of social thought. Its impact on this tradition, however, is not perhaps immediately discernable. In rationalist theory, the impact of the reified free will notion is curiously reinforced by the anti-individualist impetus of its collectivism formulation. Underlying both notions is the idea that individuals are free only to the extent that no supra-individual forces impinge on them. In rationalist collectivist terms, it is precisely such forces, in their external and conditional form, which create social order. In individualist terms, it is such collective forces, material or ideal, that inhibit the realization of individual freedom. The two perspectives, therefore, share an important middle ground. In other words, the rationalist notion that collective order can be attained only through determination by external conditions coincides perfectly with the reified conception of the individual as completely discrete and self-contained. After all, the only way that collective forces can impinge on such a discrete individual is from without.[154†] This insight further illuminates the paradox described above, that while theorists in the rationalist collectivist tradition are often the most intent on establishing the realm of freedom, for reasons of presuppositional logic they are bound to eliminate voluntarism from their theories. We will find that every social theory which addresses collective order from an exclusively rationalist orientation also manifests a confusion of the analytic and concrete perspectives on the individual.

In the preceding discussion I have emphasized the broad, generic quality of the individualism problem in order to clarify the possibilities for a theory to be simultaneously voluntarist and collectivist. But it is necessary also to remain sensitive to the theoretical boundaries of this voluntarism. Because the problem of order represents one of the two most basic, presuppositional questions any social theory can address, it has significant implications for formulations at the other levels of the scientific continuum—for example, for ideological commitments and empirical propositions. Yet presuppositional voluntarism does not in any sense necessitate voluntarism in terms of these more specific commitments. To say that the presuppositions of a theoretical vision retain a voluntaristic orientation does not mean that the theory will find that "freedom reigns," in the popular sense of that phrase. It does not mean that the theory will find that Christian, socialist, or democratic ethics are fulfilled, that the weak are cared for and the strong morally responsible. These are questions that can be decided only by specifying these general presuppositions in terms of a particular ideological framework and an analysis of extant empirical conditions. As was noted earlier, in the analysis of nonrational action, voluntarism at the most general presuppositional level should be considered a structural or "formal" property of action. All action must be viewed as motivated, in part, by internal subjective volition as opposed to purely external, coercive control. Orthodox religious action, for example, presents a case of action that is voluntary in this sense. Whether or not such action can also be considered free and voluntary in a more substantive sense depends on further ideological and empirical considerations. Thus, orthodox religious practice would not be considered free activity by critics within secular traditions or by theologians of heretical persuasions.

An internal conception of order, then, is necessary to establish freedom in a substantive sense; it is not, however, sufficient. The mistaken assumption that presuppositional voluntarism automatically implies the realization of ideological freedom is a problem of theoretical conflation that affects both critics and proponents of the nonrationalist collective position. This confusion is, for example, one of the primary errors of theoretical logic involved in Gouldner's characterization of Parsons' voluntaristic theory as inherently conservative. He wrongly assumes that because Parsons speaks of voluntarism he must also view the citizens of a capitalist industrial society as free in an ideological and empirical sense. That Parsons does in fact often make such an assumption is not the point: he need not, and it is impossible to reason directly from his presuppositional assumptions to his ideological position.[155†] On the other side of the debate about normative order, similar conflationary lapses affect the writings of Habermas. He conceives contemporary industrial societies, both capitalist and socialist, as antivoluntary because, according to his empirical perspective, they both institutionalize exclusively instrumental action. This is a perfectly legitimate combination of different theoretical levels. At the same time, however, Habermas assumes, illegitimately, that insofar as action can become normatively directed—can become, in his terms, "interaction" rather than "work"—it will become more voluntary and liberating, approximating the goals of socialist humanism. It is, indeed, among proponents of the nonrationalist collective tradition that this problem has the most unfortunate implications, for it is often a corrolary of what I have termed "sociological idealism."

3.4.3. Voluntary Order and the Problem of Sociological Idealism

If a materialist orientation dominates theory, internal order will appear to be no order at all, and the order that is constructed will eliminate voluntarism altogether. If a reified conception of the individual dominates theory, the possibility for reconciling voluntarism and order will be denied in principle. Yet even if both of these debilitating problems are overcome, the resolution of the order problem may still not be satisfactory. The internal collective "solution" can take the form of sociological idealism. The problem in this case is that voluntarism is thought to be complete. Sociological idealism is not idealism in its pure epistemological form; rather, as I emphasized earlier, it is a version of the epistemological problem fitted to a sophisticated, socially directed explanation of social life. The existence of the conditional environment of action is acknowledged, the determinism associated with the externality of the "means" element formally recognized. Actual theoretical attention is devoted, however, exclusively to the normative, internal aspects of collective order. The conflict between internal and external dimensions of social life is effectively eliminated. Instead of voluntarism being an element of action, with determinism being another, action becomes, in effect, simply voluntary. Empirically, sociological idealism will focus either on those institutions concerned primarily with internal order— the family, the church, tradition—or will define other institutions—the economy, the state—in terms only of their ideal components; in either case, emphasis is on the shared, common properties of actor and environment.

Marx's critique of Hegel's idealism in his early writings remains a classic description of the problems I have just presented even though his later and more famous definitions of idealism are overly inclusive.[156†] Marx appreciates Hegel's depiction of the interaction between subject and object, a conceptualization that, mediated by Feuerbach, formed the basis of Marx's own synthetic approach to epistemological "praxis." However, Marx objects that this insight is immediately reduced in Hegel's writing to a truncated, one-dimensional formulation. The external, objective dimension is not treated as a conditional restraint on action but as, in effect, an extension of the subjectivity of the actor: "The object appears as an entity of thought," "the object is only *objectified* self-consciousness."[157] The multidimensional epistemological perspective is reduced to an approach that emphasizes only internal processes: "Man is regarded as a non-objective, spiritual being. . . . Real Man and real nature become mere predicates."[158] The result, as Marx sees it, is a purely voluntaristic conception of order, according to which the individual no longer must grapple with the frustrating reality of external conditions.[159] Marx views Hegel's empirical focus on ideas alone or on the purely subjective aspects of other institutions, like the state, as produced by this presuppositional position. "Hegel begins," Marx asserts, "from the absolute and fixed abstraction; i.e., in ordinary language, from religion and theology."[160]

Such is the abstract logic of the sociologically idealist position. It has, of course, appeared in a variety of substantive forms. In theology, for instance, internal collective order as manifest through divine will has often been considered the sole force capable of motivating action toward salvation; the external impediments to faith could remain, in this case, only an implicit focus of theological speculation.[161]† Early nineteenth-century conservative and Romantic thinkers were equally one-sided in their secular vision of the collective order. Writers like Burke and Maistre emphasized principally the role of religion and tradition, despite the fact that they viewed the continued existence of such social forces as historically precarious.

Sociological idealism recurs throughout contemporary social thought. It permeates, for example, Nisbet's major work, *The Sociological Tradition*, seriously undercutting his central argument.[162] On the one hand, Nisbet explicitly acknowledges the importance of the polar tension between instrumental and normative and, indeed, implicitly structures his entire book around it. The conditional side of this tension is, however, rarely examined in an explicit way, for Nisbet makes the claim that the origins of sociology as a distinctive discipline lay only in its emphasis on the nonrationalist alternatives to rationalist, Enlightenment orientations. Once this subjectivist position is established, Nisbet goes on to describe the emphasis on such concepts as community, authority, and status as, in effect, theoretical alternatives to conceptions of association, power, and class. As a characterization of the presuppositional positions that informed the origins of sociology, this account ignores the tremendous significance of the rationalist tradition, particulary in its collectivist version. Specifically, it allows Nisbet to ignore Marx and the rationalist aspects of Weber's work.

The same kind of problem, though less markedly, mars Parsons presentation of the emerging sociological tradition in *The Structure of Social*

Action. As I indicated earlier in this chapter, Parsons presents an action schema that is fully multidimensional; he also presents the order concept as a fully generalized, "generic" usage. Yet if one looks more closely at Parsons' treatment, one sees that he views instrumental collective order not as a coequal dimension throughout all sociological analysis but rather as a necessary historical stopping-point on the road to normative collectivist theory. As I will demonstrate at length in volume 4, in a significant part of Parsons' account the problem of order, generally conceived, is reduced to the particular problem of normative interpenetration. Correspondingly, to the degree that this reduction occurs, Parsons' analysis of the problems of maintaining a voluntarist position are transformed from a forthright and basically successful critique of exclusively utilitarian collectivism to an ad hoc and unsuccessful argument that defines the "voluntarist theory of action" in an exclusively normative sense. One can, finally, observe a similar and less ambiguous idealist reduction in the writings of Shils. In his formulations about center and periphery not only is social order defined in an exclusively normative sense, but the roots of the voluntaristic activities that Shils describes as antagonistic to that order—secessions, revolutions, rebellions—are themselves seen as motivated by primarily normative, "chiliastic" concerns.[163] The point here is not that Shils' analyses do not illuminate significant aspects of empirical reality, for they do so and often brilliantly. The point is rather that because of a sociologically idealist presuppositional perspective, they illuminate this reality in a partial manner, one that effectively eliminates the material conditions that impinge on social action.

In the two chapters preceding, I developed an argument for reclaiming the generalized aspects of social scientific debate. I held that this task could be accomplished by going beyond the positivist reduction of theory to fact, and beyond the conflationary acceptance of a standard for generalized argument that is not genuinely presuppositional. In this chapter, the social scientific problems that are truly generalized, that are neither positivistic nor conflationary, have been identified. But these fundamental questions—attention to which constitutes the cornerstone of "theoretical logic"—occupy a position on the scientific continuum more removed from the empirical environment than any other. Is theoretical logic, then, irrevocably subjectivist? If so, the search for presuppositional questions has opened a Pandora's box. I will try to close this box in the concluding chapter, which follows.

Chapter Four

THEORETICAL LOGIC AS OBJECTIVE ARGUMENT

There are indeed vast possibilities for relativism in any nonpositivist position, and Thomas Kuhn, its best-known proponent, has a disquieting penchant for emphasizing them. "When paradigms enter, as they must, into a debate about paradigm choice," he warns, "their role is necessarily circular."[1] It is true that if one accepts a nonpositivist perspective, it must be acknowledged that one's objection to other positions rests upon assumptions that, to some degree, have been accepted without objective proof in the empirical sense. Given this situation, I must agree with Kuhn's contention that "those who refuse to step into the circle" may not find my arguments "logically or even probabilistically compelling."[2] Just as no empirical argument can be made without presuppositions, no theoretical argument can be conducted without first "translating" competing positions into a theoretical language whose presuppositions are complementary with one's own. [3†] Popper is wrong: generalized frameworks cannot be discussed critically if by critical discussion one means the subjection of them to the traditional tests of empiricism.[4] For metaphysics can no more be eliminated from science than the nonrational element can be eliminated from action in general. The positivist persuasion, in its insistence on empiricist standards of objectivity, merely obfuscates this irreversible fact.

Yet to give up the positivist persuasion and recognize the theoretical a priori is not necessarily to abandon the search for objectivity and rational intellectual standards. This, of course, is the relativistic recourse of the more radically-antiscientific idealist critiques of positivism. One may, however, continue to pursue objectivity as a goal: one must simply face more directly the actual context within which such objectivity can be sustained. This involves, above all, the development of postpositivist standards of rational knowledge. One must rationalize the methodology of theoretical argument, objectifying the standards according to which it is conducted, if the intention is to discuss general frameworks critically without simply referring to the empirical world. Instead of relying simply upon deductive reasoning and empirical proof, one must establish objectivity, as Habermas argues, "by means of the justification of a choice of standards."[5]

> The approval of a procedure or the acceptance of a scientific norm can be supported or weakened by argument; it can at least be rationally assessed. And this is precisely the task of critical theoretical thought . . . [6]

Universalistic standards can be achieved without the false support of positivism if they are applied in a consistent, disciplined manner in relation to explicit, fully generalized criteria. Such criteria are precisely what I have sought to provide in the preceding presuppositional arguments about action and order. I will present the case for their universalistic status by formulating three basic requirements for achieving objectivity in a nonempiricist context.[7†]

1. OBJECTIVE EVALUATION THROUGH UNIVERSAL REFERENCE: THE "STRUCTURAL" STATUS OF ACTION AND ORDER

A rational comparison of theories must refer to issues which are universally addressed. Such universality is crucial, for it is a necessary, though not sufficient, assurance that theoretical argument will be conducted on common ground. As they have been defined here, the problems of action and order meet this requirement. No matter what its particular genre, social theory must provide an answer to the questions of action and order along one of several pathways I have described. In turn, every social theory can be evaluated on the basis of the particular paths it has chosen to take. I mentioned earlier that the particular presuppositional positions of a theory are related to lower levels of the scientific continuum as a language's rules about sentence structure are related to its rules about tense or gender. We might describe the universality of the presuppositional questions by continuing this analogy as follows: the generic categories of action and order are related to any particular presuppositional positions as the structures of Chomsky's generative grammar are related to the syntax of any particular language.[8] Generative grammar, according to Chomsky, provides the basic patterns of organization, the basic structures within which all particular languages must be articulated. In this sense, action and order constitute the "structural" properties of social theory. They are not, as such, the elements of any particular theory. They cannot be eliminated from one theory or another, nor are they subject to change depending on the historical circumstances.[9†] As the most general basis of social scientific cognition, they represent the categories that Habermas calls for but does not provide, those which can "establish the specific viewpoints from which we can apprehend reality as such in any way whatsoever."[10†] These deep structural problems of action and order produce a logic discernible in every sociological theory, regardless of more specific ideological, empirical, or methodological considerations.

2. OBJECTIVE EVALUATION THROUGH SYNTHETIC STANDARDS: THE SCOPE AND MUTUAL AUTONOMY OF ACTION AND ORDER

Simple reference to the existence of certain universal problems does not in itself establish objectivity. The specific solutions to these problems must also be defined in a manner that is widely accepted. Since nonpositivist arguments about generalized logic ultimately rest not upon "automatic" processes of proof but upon contingent processes of persuasion, objectivity can occur only to the degree there is agreement among the contending parties that their disputes shall be judged according to the same higher standard. It is precisely his belief in the impossibility of such agreement that pushes Kuhn toward relativism. "The premises and values shared by the two parties to a debate over paradigms," he writes, simply "are not sufficiently extensive."[11] From this situation there follows the "incompleteness of logical contact" that leads disputing parties to "inevitably talk through each other."[12] Clearly, communication failure must be considered an inherent problem from a nonpositivist perspective. But given a more differentiated understanding of science than Kuhn's paradigm concept provides, it need not always produce as radical a schism as he envisions. Certainly, every effort at formulating a general logic should seek to overcome the obstacle of distorted communication.

In order to so rationalize general argument and to bring it one step closer to nonempirical standards of objectivity, evaluative criteria must be expansive and inclusive. They must attempt to draw upon the full range of theoretical options presented by competing theories and to elaborate standards for evaluation that synthesize, as much as possible, the distinctive qualities embodied by each. Only then will one increase that consensus about evaluative standards which alone can diminish the "incompleteness of logical contact." Such standards can never be neutral, but if their scope has been broadly gauged they can still approach a certain impartiality. For they will be able to stand outside the particular intellectual experiences of the theories they judge. [13][†]

The presuppositional problems of action and order were formulated according to the criteria of generality and decisiveness set out in chapter 2; they are designed, in other words, to achieve exactly such an expansive and synthetic scope. Being insufficiently general and ramifying, the other attempts at generalized argument which I examined not only failed to acheive presuppositional status but failed also to meet the standards required for increased objectivity. The arguments about conflict, system, method, and ideology seize upon particular problems and attempt, through a process of theoretical conflation, to present them as universalistic criteria according to which all theories can be judged. Yet, as was seen in that earlier discussion, such criteria do not contribute to the consensus which attempts at objective theoretical argument must strive to sustain; on the contrary, agreement over these principles masks conflict at a more general level, conflict which, within the confines of the framework proposed, cannot be explained. In their failure to illuminate this most general level, these arguments necessarily distort the theoretical conflicts which they do perceive. Thus, although on their distinctive levels each clarifies a smaller or larger area of sociological thought, in relation to the standards for postpositivist objectivity they are distinctly biased, reinforcing a theoretical relativism. These generalized arguments, then, are particularistic; they cannot stand outside the experience of the social theories they attempt to judge.

In the course of those preceding discussions, the presuppositional definitions of order and action were reached by disclosing this lack of generality. I examined the theoretical conflicts which they left unexplained and in each case identified certain common themes—the problem of whether action was normative or instrumental, the conflict over whether it was organized by individual or collective structure. From their very inception, in other words, the issues of action and order were conceived because they were more expansive in "scope": they promised, from the beginning, to provide grounds for more consensual general evaluation. In chapter 3, my approach to action and order was compared with a variety of others. In each case, I tried to demonstrate that other definitions can be regarded as distinctive subsets of my own. As defined here, these presuppositions are broad enough to encompass each of the other approaches considered. To adopt any other definition would be to treat the concepts of action and order in a reductionist way, to tie them to more particularized references that would be less widely applicable.

Yet the problem of establishing universalistic standards has still not been completely resolved, for even among those theories which accept the general approach I have outlined, the possibilities for conflation remain. Before proceeding to evaluate the third requirement for objective general argument, I must examine a final strategy by which the general status of presuppositional argument can be reduced to a particularistic form.

In the discussions thus far it has been demonstrated that reference to the problems of action and order is central to the theoretical vocabulary of social science. I have criticized various theorists for their particular positions on these presuppositional questions—for errors of sociological idealism and materialism—but have not tried to evaluate their approaches to presuppositional argument as such. If that is done, a striking fact appears: in almost every case where such one-dimensional thinking occurs, the mutual autonomy of the presuppositional decisions about action and order has been denied. Instead of acknowledging that these decisions are made independently of one another, they are presented as inherently interconnected, as if a position on one question automatically determines a position on the other. This is merely a different form of the kind of conflationary error I have so often discussed before. In this instance, however, instead of identifying different levels of the scientific continuum with one another, the conflation reduces one presuppositional question to the other.

For the most part, it is the problem of action that is subordinated to the problem of order. For example, in the rationalist tradition, Blau argues, as has been seen, for an antipsychological, "social" approach to sanctions—in my terms, for a collectivist approach to order. Yet by presenting these sanctions as effective only because they rely on "external fear," he is ignoring the autonomy of decisions about the nature of action. He assumes that collective order necessarily implies instrumental action; yet such order can also clearly be achieved by another, less instrumental path.[14]

The same conflationary strategy can be seen in Coleman's work on "collective decisions," which presents itself as primarily engaged in a polemic against Homans' individualistic approach. Yet the problem of order is certainly not the only fundamental issue that informs Coleman's theory, for the collective level need not be approached only by the rational calculus of aggregated interest he describes. It can be presented in this way only by camouflaging, as Coleman does, the autonomy of the action question, the possibility that collective decisions can be brought about through nonrational norms.[15†] Homans' own work carries the same camouflage; he simply uses it to defend an individualist rather than collectivist approach. Homans claims to be primarily concerned with "bringing men back in," in contrast, most pointedly, with the collectivist approach of functional theory. Yet in doing so, he smuggles in his utilitarian approach to the problem of action.

A good illustration of this strategy is Homans' conclusion to his critique of Smelser's book on the Industrial Revolution. While purportedly

criticizing only Smelser's organicist, or collective, approach to order, he
has also systematically introduced his own rationalist understanding of
motivation: "Let us ... confess that most of the men in question,"
Homans writes in reference to Smelser's workers and capitalists, "were
concerned with their own profits. Let us bring men back in, *and let us put
some blood in them.*"[16] In other words, contrary to his overt polemical
focus on order, Homans is not concerned with the individual per se, but
only with the individual who engages in a particular type of action—that
which is profit-seeking and instrumental.

This presuppositional conflation is not confined, however, only to instrumental theorizing. Theorists continually present themselves as concerned simply with the problem of restoring an emphasis on the
collective "whole" over and against the atomistic emphasis on the individual, while in reality they effect this restoration by emphasizing normative collective structures alone. Ekeh, for example, describes the
antagonism between Lévi-Strauss and Homans as a contest between the
collectivist and individualist traditions. Yet although this presuppositional division certainly does exist, there surely is another issue involved
in this debate—namely, the opposition between the normative emphasis
of Lévi-Strauss, derived from the Durkheimian tradition, and Homans'
utilitarian approach to action, derived from classical economics and behaviorism. Although Ekeh continually refers to this conflict in fact, he
cannot recognize it in theory because he does not acknowledge action as
an independent presuppositional decision.[17] The same reasoning informs Nisbet's account of the origins of the sociological tradition, in
which he argues, in effect, that the only way that classical sociologists
could overcome the individualism which he takes to be at the heart of
liberal Enlightenment theory was to emphasize moral and cultural cohe-
sion.[18] Similarly, in Shils' writing, theoretical appreciation for the whole
is identified with an emphasis on such primarily normative issues as the
relation between charisma, center, and periphery. Shils himself vacillates in his self-conscious justification for this emphasis, arguing both
that the whole can be discovered only through such a subjective focus
and, more reasonably, that his own emphasis on this dimension derives
from an attempt to balance the rationalism of modern Western
thought.[19] Habermas, in contrast, conflates action and order by con-
centrating exclusively on the problem of action and ignoring the autonomy of the order question. He opposes instrumentalist theorizing by
presenting the alternative—nonrational behavior—as necessarily reciprocal and cooperative.[20] Nonrational action can, however, easily be
conceived as individualistic and competitive.

Surely the most striking illustration of such conflation within the
presuppositional level itself can be found by comparing the great early
works of Halévy and Parsons. Placed side by side, their arguments com-

pose a sort of intellectual fugue. Because of their presuppositional concern with action and order, they are clearly part of the same intellectual whole; yet they present lines of analysis that are as much counterpoint as harmony. Despite its political overlay and its specific focus on a particular school of thought, Halévy's analysis in *The Growth of Philosophic Radicalism* represents perhaps the major twentieth-century treatment of the individualist/collectivist problem in social theory. Yet according to Halévy's argument, the only alternative to the individualism of "natural identity of interest theory" was the "artificial identity" approach, whose lineage he traces from Hobbes to Bentham and the elder Mill. In proposing this as the only alternative, Halévy has eliminated the autonomy of the action question, for he has assumed that collective order can be achieved only through rationalistic means. Given this conflation, it is not surprising that in order to avoid such a coercive approach to theoretical explanation and to provide for a countervailing voluntary emphasis, Halévy can only recommend that social theory return to a more individualistic level of analysis.[21†]

In *The Structure of Social Action*, Parsons implicitly addresses this very weakness in Halévy's theoretical logic, arguing that the level of collective order can indeed be attained through a normative emphasis. The problem is that in doing so Parsons tends simply to turn Halévy on his head. Instead of presenting normative theory simply as a "voluntaristic" approach to the problem of collective order, there is a strong tendency for Parsons to present it as the only collective approach per se. Instead of arguing about the particular quality of the rationalist solution to collective order, then, he describes it as providing no solution at all. In other words, Parsons often argues that to describe collective order is, at the same time, to describe normative action. He has conflated the two presuppositional questions of social thought, reducing the action problem, ironically, to an epiphenominal status.

Throughout my analysis in these chapters, I have criticized not only such substantive attempts at theoretical argument, but also a range of general classificatory schemes. For this reason, one should take note of this conflationary problem in a number of classificatory works that otherwise develop analyses similar to the one employed here. In their introductory essay to *Contemporary Analytic Theory*, David E. Apter and Charles F. Andrain, for example, define the notion of "choice," a concept that clearly corresponds to the action problem, as the "core problem of all social science theory."[22] They then describe three "dimensions" in which human choices are made—normative, structural, and behavioral—and do so in a manner that just as clearly relates them to what I have described as the criterion of order. Normative and structural dimensions emphasize, in their words, "external," that is, collective, influences on the individual, while the behavioral dimension allows for "individual" selection. Apter and Andrain then utilize these three dimensions as their principal classificatory device, describing the major dichotomization in social thought as that between externalist and individualist approaches. But their argument obscures the crucial distinctions that differentiate among different types of individual and collectivist theory, that can determine, for example, whether a theory is voluntary or coercive in its collectivist, "external" form. This problem arises because decisions about the nature of action have not been represented by distinctive classificatory criteria. The dimensions of "choice" cannot, in fact, be expressed only through the categories of individualist versus externalist; choice involves decisions about the rationality and nonrationality of action that cross-cut these decisions about the order problem.[23†]

A similar failure to differentiate these presuppositional issues undercuts Werner Stark's somewhat less nuanced classification in *The Fundamental Forms of Social Thought*. On the basis of the traditional realist/ nominalist distinction, Stark proposes that theory can be understood as either "organicist" or "mechanical." As such, these distinctions correspond, respectively, to our collectivist-versus-individualist options for defining social order. As Stark's argument develops, however, it becomes apparent that he is also utilizing these categories to make another distinction.[24†] On the one hand, he describes theorists of the mechanical, purportedly individualist, variety as also rationalistic, presenting Bentham as a prototypical figure among other classical economists and social Darwinists. On the other hand, Aquinas and Radcliffe-Brown, who greatly emphasize the normative element, rank among the prototypical organicists, as do Marx and Spencer. As Stark tries to squeeze all theoretical conflict into his two major categories, his classification becomes increasingly arbitrary and confusing. For Bentham is not simply a rationalist, but also a collectivist, a fact that violates mechanism's principal criterion; and Marx and Spencer, on the other hand, are not simply collectivists, but also rationalists, facts which violate the definition of the organicist category. Stark, like so many other analysts of social theory, has tried to say too much with too little. His principal categories are derived from an analysis of different approaches to the order problem. To classify accurately the theories he has described, however, he would have to allow for conflict over the nature of action as well. He would, in other words, have to differentiate the two basic presuppositional questions rather than conflating them. Mechanical and organic can describe division over the order question, or conceivably over the action question, but they cannot describe theoretical division over both at the same time.[25†]

While it is true that generalized argument in sociology can never achieve permanent consensus, the formulation of evaluative standards should seek, by their expansive and synthetic scope, to extend common ground rather than to diminish it.[26†] If objectivity is to be sustained, the kind of presuppositional conflation I have described must be avoided at all costs. It is not, of course, difficult to understand the motivations for such conflation: it represents an attempt to present theoretical options in a manner that makes the theorist's own presuppositional position appear to have been a necessary, indeed inevitable, choice. If collectivist order can indeed be achieved only through exclusively normative constraints, then clearly such a normative position must be adopted. If, on the other hand, normative constraints can have only an individualistic and psychological status, then an exclusive focus on material constraints must obviously be accepted if theory is to achieve a collectivist emphasis. By so preventing evaluative standards from standing over and against the range of their own particular theoretical experience, such conflation institutionalizes theoretical bias.[27†] This bias, however, is not the result of "subjective" elements intruding on the scientific argument. To the contrary, conflation blocks the possibility for objectivity by minimizing the extent of subjective choice involved in theoretical analysis.

By narrowing the range of presuppositional choice, such conflationary arguments lose their flexibility, and along with it their ability to explain empirical variation in social theory. Within the instrumental tradition, Homans must ignore the emphasis in Smelser's work on psychological and religious issues, for according to his conflationary framework the individualism he finds in Smelser must by definition exhibit also a utilitarian thrust. Further, Homans' analysis must leave completely unrecognized the tremendous range of variation within the nonrationalist individualist tradition. Similarly, Blau depicts Durkheim's theory of social control as based on fear, and thereby radically distorts Durkheim's approach to social sanction. By thus assuming that collective order must be rational and external, Blau cannot account for the myriad theories that describe how constraint is maintained through conscious and unconscious volition. Even Halévy commits this rationalist error. He cannot recognize the normative aspects of certain parts of nineteenth-century radical thought, explaining Thomas Hodgkins' anarchist economic theory, for example, simply in terms of Hodgkins' adherence to the individualist belief in a natural identity of interest. For Halévy, the appreciation for collective order that underlies radicalism can only occur within a rationalist context.[28†]

On the normative side, presuppositional conflation results in a similar loss of explanatory power. Neither Nisbet nor Shils can approach rationalist theory in anything but a negative way; it simply is not, for them, a solution to the problem of order. Yet by not recognizing collective order in its instrumentalist guise, they must ignore the tremendous variation within the rationalist tradition, the kinds of variation, for example, upon which Halévy builds his entire work. Given this blind spot, Nisbet and, in part, Parsons cannot help but distort the history of sociological thought, relegating rationalists like Bentham and Marx, along with the equally instrumental segments of Weber, to the mists of intellectual prehistory.

On both sides of the debate, then, the costs of this presuppositional conflation have been great, exacerbating the mutual distrust and distorted communication that characterize generalized argument. To consider a single case, Parsons' conflationary definition in *The Structure of Social Action* has itself generated a spiraling misunderstanding of the order concept that continues to the present day. This misunderstanding has confused attempts at reconciliation and polemic alike.

One can develop more objective standards for nonempirical argument only if one acknowledges the autonomy of each presuppositional issue. Decisions about action and order are the most fundamental issues that confront any social theory: the positions taken in regard to them structure each theory's most general logic. Only if we recognize that they represent truly independent choices can we recognize the range of permutations that this general logic actually implies. Commitments to rational or nonrational action are not necessarily congruent with, or antagonistic to, commitments to any specific approach to social order. Theories that accept collective or individual order can differ over conceptions of action; indeed, this will later be described as the primary source of antagonism between Durkheim and Marx. Likewise, theories sharply at odds over order can still agree about approaches to action, even to the extent of seeking to combine a normative theory of action with an approach to order as an external force. It is, in fact, precisely by seeking to postulate such an unlikely combination that I will later explain the paradox of one strand of Durkheim's early work.[29†]

Finally, since conflating order and action often camouflages hidden commitments to sociological idealism and materialism, the development of an alternative, multidimensional perspective depends upon recognizing the autonomy of both these decisions. The need to articulate fully such a multidimensional position constitutes, in fact, the third and final requirement for objective evaluation.

3. OBJECTIVE EVALUATION THROUGH EXPLICIT HIERARCHICAL JUDGMENT: THE NEED FOR A MULTIDIMENSIONAL APPROACH TO ACTION AND ORDER

For generalized argument to approach objectivity, then, it must evaluate universal, structural properties of action and order according to standards that are expansive and synthetic in scope. But meeting these criteria is not sufficient. If they are to satisfy the requirements of postpositivist universalism, the judgments produced by such standards must also be capable of disciplined and consistent application. Only by making completely explicit the intellectual and moral implications of these standards can this goal be achieved. For only when the theoretical hierarchy produced by a given set of generalized criteria is made explicit can these standards be responsibly applied beyond the particular cases within which they were originally formulated.

The preceding discussion of order and action has sought throughout to achieve this goal of objectivity. The ramifications of each presuppositional position have been clearly delineated, as has the theoretical logic by which such ramifications proceed. In addition, the discussion has consistently upheld the hierarchical standard of "multidimensionality" implied by these judgments. For only through articulating a multidimensional framework can theory avoid the kinds of repercussions that undermine the epistemological framework of action. In this final section, I will present this hierarchical standard in a more precise fashion.

If theory is individualistic, the problem of order becomes a residual category. One must therefore discount individualism as a viable option for a truly social theory—despite the fact that it often reveals fundamentally important aspects of actual empirical process.[30] One is left with two sets of fundamental presuppositional dichotomies: social theory can be normative or instrumental in its approach to action, and it can conceptualize the collective arrangement of this action in an internal or external manner. These are the presuppositional "dilemmas" that every nonindividualistic social theory must face. They are dilemmas in the truest sense of the word, for I have argued that in each case neither of the two options, taken by itself, is a viable one. To choose either pole of the dilemma pushes theory into one-dimensionality, in either the sociologically materialist or idealist direction. What is the alternative? If neither pole of the dilemma can be taken separately, both must be taken together. Instead of breaking the dilemma down and choosing one pole over another, the dilemma itself must be transcended. This option represents what Hegel called a "concrete" rather than "abstract" negation. If opposition to a position is abstract, it simply negates it; if opposition is concrete, it not only negates the position but also incorporates some of its significant points. Applying this dialectical notion to theoretical logic, I propose that action should be conceived not as either instrumental or normative, but as both. Furthermore, this action should be conceived as ordered both through internal and external structures. Only such a dialectical criticism of the presuppositional dilemma enables us to conceive of social theory in a multidimensional way, and multidimensionality is the standard by which I propose to evaluate theoretical logic.

This presuppositional choice cannot be demonstrated simply by evoking the structure of empirical reality, although such reference plays an important role; neither can it be derived by a process of purely cognitive reasoning, although cognition and logic are most certainly involved. The choice is, like all social action, also guided by moral commitments and moral preferences. In Habermas' terms, the standard of multidimensionality rests not simply on "technical" kinds of cognitive interest but upon "practical-cognitive interest" as well. It attempts not just to disclose reality but also to preserve and extend the relevance of a particular interpretation of it.[31†] A multidimensional perspective encompasses the voluntary striving for ideals without which human society would be bankrupt indeed, and does this without emphasizing individualization to the point of foregoing the communality and mutual identification without which such striving becomes a hollow shell. But multidimensionality preserves also the reality of the external conditions that impinge on action. It recognizes in them both the barriers that so often prevent the realization of human ideals and also the concrete opportunities for their actualization.

Although a multidimensional commitment has (an elective affinity with a certain moral stance, the position it represents is more general than that of a specifically political ideology. In fact, a general presuppositional position can inform a range of different ideological judgments, just as it can also encompass a number of different conceptual frameworks, models, empirical propositions, and methodological frameworks. In part, it is precisely because a particular presuppositional choice involves an attempt to effectuate certain general moral values that the presuppositional level of science influences conceptions at every other, more specific level of the scientific continuum, including the level of ideology.

We will see in the volumes which follow that a multidimensional position has been rejected, in part or in whole, by every major theoretical tradition. At the same time, every tradition has also, at one time or another, accepted it as its primary theoretical goal. The term itself, in fact, continually recurs in the programmatic criticism of social thinkers who represent the widest possible range of orientations and specialities. On the broadest level, the term has been utilized to prescribe the proper understanding of science itself. Holton, for example, criticizes the tendency to focus on empirical components as the projection from an x-y-z space to the x-y plane, a movement that reduces the "three-dimensional," multiplaned conceptualization of science he has proposed.[32] Within a narrower focus, Mannheim employs similar terminology to propose a framework for social science in the age of postwar reconstruction. Theory is "one-dimensional," Mannheim writes, if different social spheres are treated as completely separated from one another: "This one-dimensional pattern is turned into a multidimensional one when at the highest stage of development the separate spheres such as politics, economics, etc., which were formerly thought to be closed circles, are seen to interact upon each other and lead to a multidimensional structure."[33] Even the goals of such a specialized branch of social thought as "Frankfurt school" Marxism have been described in a similar way. As Martin Jay, the major historian of the school, formulates their vision:

> The relationship between the totality and its moments was reciprocal. Vulgar Marxists had been mistaken in seeking a reductionist derivation of superstructural, cultural spheres, from their substructural, socio-economic base. [But] culture [the Frankfurt school Marxists argued] was never epiphenomenal, although it was never fully autonomous. Its relationship to the material substructure of society was multidimensional.[34]

On a less grand scale, the same terminology has been the vehicle for programmatic criticism in a number of empirically specialized fields of sociological discourse. In cultural sociology, Geertz calls for an approach to ideology that interweaves social, psychological, and symbolic analysis, concluding that "a theoretical framework adequate to the analysis of such three-dimensional processes is . . . a task but barely begun."[35] Evaluating the status of contemporary political sociology, Lipset asserts that only by recognizing the autonomy of religious commitment can the relation between social class and political action be correctly perceived as a "multi-dimensional problem."[36] In political anthropology, Abner Cohen entitles his sweeping call for a revitalizing focus on the interrelation of symbols and power, *Two Dimensional Man*.[37] And in stratification theory, Bernard Barber describes as "multi-dimensional analysis" his formulation of two sets of interconnecting variables: concern with religious purity, knowledge, ethnicity and community status, on the one hand, and wealth, power, and occupationally generated prestige on the other.[38]

As a generic term, "multidimensionality" thus provides an effective standard by which to evaluate presuppositional argument. In applying this critical standard, my purpose is to overcome the debilitating dualism of one-dimensional thought, in both its sociologically idealist and materialist forms. In doing so, I seek to create an understanding of conditional and normative elements as distinctive parts of any approach to action and order, and to trace the interplay between them. In order to do so, the sense that such divisions actually exist in a concrete form must be revised. I will propose, instead, that they be treated—much as the two environments of science—as analytic divisions that can be elaborated within any concrete action or social unit. The goal of the present volume has been to argue for the importance of a presuppositional position of multidimensionality; the ambition of the volumes which follow is to discover how this synthetic position can actually be articulated.

The problems of action and order are the "switchmen" that determine the tracks along which social theories must proceed. In the subsequent volumes of this work, I will explore the logic of this "cybernetic control" in the most powerful social theories of our day. I will examine the classical antinomies of social thought, the classical attempt at synthesis, and the major contemporary effort to reconstruct the classical tradition of sociology along more multidimensional lines. I will trace back the most important limitations and achievements of this theorizing to the effects of these "epistemological" switchmen. In the course of this ensuing discussion I will develop a theoretical logic for sociology, demonstrating that if social theory is an art, it is a creative act that is bound to certain extraordinarily exacting though often invisible rules.[39] If I have clarified the nature of these theoretical "rules" and their relation to structures at other levels of social scientific thought, then I will have accomplished the more limited aims of the present volume.

Notes

CHAPTER ONE

1. My formulation is in opposition to the dominant tradition in the twentieth-century philosophy of science, as first presented by the Vienna Circle in the 1920s. Neither the philosophers of the Vienna Circle, nor the logical empiricists who followed, showed any substantive interest in what I am calling metaphysically oriented statements. For my disagreements with these positions, see the discussion later in this chapter.

The diagrammatic conceptualization of science as a two-directional continuum which follows in the text and is elaborated in figure 2 and figure 3 (ch. 2), has been inspired by three sources: Talcott Parsons' concept of the "cybernetic hierarchy of control," as articulated, e.g., in *Societies: Evolutionary and Comparative Perspectives* (Englewood Cliffs, N.J., 1966), pp. 28–29, and, with specific reference to science, his Introduction to "Culture and the Social System," in Parsons, Edward Shils, Kaspar D. Naegele, and Jesse R. Pitts, eds., *Theories of Society* (New York, 1961), pp. 964–965; Neil J. Smelser's discussion, "Levels of Specificity of the Components of Social Action," in *Theory of Collective Behavior* (New York, 1962), pp. 42–45; and Arthur Stinchcombe's analysis, "Levels of Generality in Social Theory," in *Constructing Social Theories* (New York, 1968), pp. 47–63.

This conceptualization also relies, in a more general way, on the "multidimensional" theory of action and order which I will present in ch. 3. The epistemological basis of this theory can be traced back to the early writings of both Marx and Parsons and, of course, many others; it implies a dialectical conception of the interaction of subject and object that attempts to transcend the idealism/materialism dichotomy.

In terms of the philosophy of science, this conception bears a strong general resemblance to the visions of science presented by R. G. Collingwood in *Metaphysics* (London, 1940), especially chs. 4, "On Presupposing," and 5, "The Science of Absolute Presuppositions," and by Stephen Toulmin in *The Philosophy of Science* (London, 1953).

2. In a complementary kind of descriptive attempt, though made from a somewhat different perspective, Calvin J. Larson has presented five commonly accepted approaches to organizing the components of sociology, from the "hunch-hypothesis-theorem-postulate" conception of scientific generalization and the "proposition-axiom-law" schema to the "model-paradigm" sequence (*Major Themes in Sociological Theory* [New York, 1975], p. 5). These formulations can, I think, be regarded as shorter, partial continuums of the general type I have suggested. Toulmin's taxonomy of "laws, hypotheses, and principles" (*Philosophy of Science*, pp. 77–85) presents an early example of the kind of conception I have in mind. Toulmin writes, e.g., about the "hierarchy" and "stratified language" of science (p. 80).

3. Talcott Parsons, *The Structure of Social Action* (New York, [1937] 1968), pp. 27–42, 728–731; John Rex, *Key Problems in Sociological Theory* (London, 1961), pp. 60–61.

4. Hans Zetterberg, *On Theory and Verification in Sociology*, 3d, expanded ed. (New York, [1954] 1965), passim. From a somewhat different perspective, Larson has described this problematic situation in a similar way. "Theory," he says, is "one of the most amorphous terms in science." It may be "as broad as all thought or as narrow as a single thought" and may "vary from complete conjecture to solid confirmation, from unarticulated impression to precisely defined prediction." (*Major Themes*, p. 4.)

5. In describing this two-dimensional continuum for scientific thought, I am articulating the kind of framework that would make it possible to be "realistic" about empirical truth without abandoning the commitment to relativism imposed by historically-specific cultural frameworks. This understanding is only possible if one understands that every scientific statement is, in fact, composed of different levels of generality and that *within* a presuppositional framework one may be as accurate as possible in one's orientation to the empirical world. Yehuda Elkana calls for precisely such a reconciliation of relativism and realism in his "Two-Tier Thinking: Philosophical Realism and Historical Relativism," *Social Studies in Science* 8 (1978): 309–326.

6. Toulmin, *Philosophy of Science*, p. 80, italics added.

7. Strictly speaking, of course, the framework I have described in sec. 1 can be violated in two directions, that is, the continuum can be distorted not only in the inductive and empirical manner but also in a reduction toward the metaphysical side as well. In this type of reduction of

two-directionality, rather than theory having to wait for the accumulation of empirical facts as in the positivist fallacy, it is held that the accumulation of facts must wait upon the prior formulation of a fully articulated theoretical schema. Certain aspects of Parsons' work violate two-directionality in such a manner as I will indicate in vol. 4. It is even possible to argue that the current positivist tendency in American sociology is, in some small part, a reaction against some of Parsons' exaggerated claims for theoretical thinking. Nonetheless, in the current intellectual climate of sociology, this kind of distortion, though in principle equally disruptive to the practice of science, is committed so rarely in actual sociological work that it is of minimal interest to the general problem of theoretical thinking in sociology.

I should also note a point which will become clear as the discussion in this section proceeds. In writing about the movement from specificity to generality, I am referring to how generalizations are formulated rather than to the debate over whether, e.g., formal deduction actually represents the most effective way to make use of theory once it has already been formulated. The later argument cross-cuts the positivist/antipositivist debate. For example, deductive theory can be conceived as inductively arrived at (see sec. 2 below) or, on the other hand, as a product of a two-directional formulation. As a result, supporters and opponents of the deductive strategy can be drawn from both positivist and antipositivist camps, as Leon Warshay has pointed out (*The Current State of Sociological Theory* [New York, 1975], pp. 108–115).

For a discussion of the pervasiveness of the positivist tendency in contemporary sociology, see Lewis Coser's "Presidential Address: Two Methods in Search of a Substance," delivered at the meeting of the American Sociological Association, August 25, 1975, reprinted in *American Sociological Review* 40 (1975): 691–700.

8. For a similar distinction between "positivism" in its specific historical sense and in its more generic sense, see in Anthony Giddens, ed., *Positivism and Sociology* (London, 1974), Giddens' Introduction, pp. 1–4.

9. These postulates parallel the three "presuppositions" that Jürgen Habermas has described as the focus of Hegel's critique of Kant's epistemological justification for an objectivist approach to natural science. "Hegel radicalizes the approach of the critique of knowledge," Habermas writes, by criticizing "the secure foundations of transcendental consciousness, from which the a-priori demarcation between transcendental and empirical determinations ... seemed certain" (*Knowledge and Human Interests* [Boston, 1971], pp. 13–17). Habermas discusses these propositions in greater detail in his criticism of the early positivism of Comte and Mach (pp. 71–90). In its connection of positivism to materialism and its simultaneous rejection of "objective idealism," Habermas' critique of positivism closely resembles the position outlined in this chapter.

French structuralist theory expresses the elimination of this nonempirical referent very clearly: it is the collapse of the signifier and the referent in symbolic discourse. Hayden White has applied this formula to the historial discipline, arguing that it is empiricist because it gives the false impression of literalness, as if the narrative "story" is objectively true rather than a symbolic and creative act of the imagination, i.e., a form of "signification" ("The Discourse of History," *Humanities in Society* 2, no. 1 [1979]: 1–16).

10. Catton, *From Animistic to Naturalistic Sociology* (New York, 1966), p. 52.

11. Ibid., pp. 51–52.

12. Zetterberg, *On Theory* (n. 4 above), p. 8.

13. Goode, *Explorations in Social Theory* (New York, 1973), "The Social Topography of the Field," p. 8.

14. Ibid.

15. Ibid., p. 10.

16. Ibid., p. 8. At different points throughout his discussion, it is unclear whether Goode's reference to "philosophical" problems refers to the debate of cultural versus natural science, i.e., to the ability to formulate lawful regularities in regard to social action (see sec. 3 below), or to the influence of what I will in ch. 3 call the presuppositional and ideological assumptions that inform these lawful predictions, or both. This lack of clarity on such a central issue is itself a reflection of his more general lack of explicit concern for non-empirical issues of any sort. I would maintain, however, that Goode's actual sociological work belies this formal intent: he has fruitfully employed a creative and distinctive general orientation.

17. Homans, *Social Behavior: Its Elementary Forms* (New York, 1961), p. 10.

18. Homans, "Bringing Men Back in," *American Sociological Review* 29 (1964): 811. For a general critique of Homans' work in terms of his misunderstanding of the nature of science, see Keith Dixon's discussion in *Sociological Theory: Pretense or Possibility* (London, 1973), p. 52.

An irony of the positivist position when it is articulated in empirical work is that it inevitably opens itself up to refutation by other positivist critics on the grounds of apriorism. This has been the fate of Homans' work, as it has also been the fate of Zetterberg's and, in part, Merton's. I will discuss this reaction to the latter two authors in succeeding notes. In regard to Homans, in a discussion that is generally sympathetic to his positivist formal perspective, M. S. Mulkay nonetheless criticizes the "abstractness" of his propositions and the generality of his concepts, accusing Homans of failing in practice to follow the principles he has formulated (*Functionalism, Exchange, and Theoretical Strategy* [London, 1971], pp. 161–166). "Homans' deductions are totally inadequate,"

Mulkay writes, for they "either make use of analytic propositions which are not amenable, even in principle, to empirical test or they are merely unsupported *ad hoc* interpretations" (p. 171).

And, indeed, the fallacy of Homans' own self-understanding and self-presentation is substantively demonstrated by Peter Ekeh in *Social Exchange Theory: The Two Traditions* (Cambridge, Mass., 1974). Ekeh finds that a metaphysical and ideological critique of the "collectivist" tradition of exchange theory permeates the very propositions that Homans purports to be simply descriptive of nature.

19. Zetterberg, *Theory and Verification* (n. 4 above), p. 22.

20. Ibid., pp. 63–101.

21. Ibid., pp. 101–175.

22. Ibid., p. 17. For a critique of the neopositivist understanding of science that underlies Zetterberg's formal and substantive discussions, see Dixon, *Sociological Theory*, pp. 52–59. It is interesting to note, in view of the ironic logic I mentioned in discussing the response to Homans' work above, that Zetterberg's own approach has been roundly criticized by recent more mathematically precise theorists for not providing truly direct access to empirical, observational data. See the discussion of the criticisms leveled at Zetterberg by the new quantitative causal theorists in Nicholas C. Mullins, *Theories and Theory Groups in Contemporary American Sociology* (New York, 1973), pp. 218–220, 228–229. These are the very same positivist grounds, of course, upon which Zetterberg himself had attacked earlier forms of "unscientific" social theory.

On the basis of such early statements about the formulation of theory as Homans' and Zetterberg's, the movement for "theory construction" has gathered force in the 1970s. As a self-conscious effort at the "scientization" of sociology, this movement conceptualizes scientific progress as dependent upon: (a) a calculus composed of a set of axioms deductively generating theorems, (b) a set of bridge principles linking this calculus to observable phenomena, and (c) a set of deductively generated empirical claims that can be tested against empirical reality (see, e.g., Carl Hempel, "Aspects of Scientific Explanation," in his *Aspects of Scientific Explanation and Other Essays in the Philosophy of Science* [New York, 1965]). This formal explication demonstrates that the claims of theory construction still depend upon a radical theory-data split. The very notion of science as a two-directional continuum, moreover, indicates the difficulty of any more specific level completely articulating in explicit form the tacit assumptions of the general positions that inform it (cf. Charles T. O'Connell, "Theory Construction in Sociology: What a Theory Is Not," unpublished manuscript, Department of Sociology, University of California, Los Angeles).

The difficulty of such a purely axiomatic style, and the way it fails to live up to the expectations of the positivist persuasion, was eloquently expressed by John Maynard Keynes in a draft preface for his *General Theory*. "When an economist writes in a quasi-formal style," Keynes seeks to warn his readers, "he never states all his premises and his definitions are not perfectly clear-cut. He never mentions all the qualifications necessary to his conclusions. He has no means of stating once and for all, the precise level of abstraction on which he is moving, and he does not move on the same level all the time. It is, I think, of the nature of economic exposition that it gives, not a completed statement . . . but a sample statement . . . intended to suggest to the reader the whole bundle of associated ideas, so that, if he catches the bundle, he will not be the least confused or impeded by the technical incompleteness of the mere words." The nonempirical intentions and intuitive quality of this economic "science," in other words—despite its axiomatic form—make it virtually impossible to conduct economic argument on the purely evidential basis that positivist and "theory construction" wisdom suggest. "An economic writer," Keynes continues, therefore "requires from his reader much goodwill and intelligence and a large measure of co-operation; and, on the other hand, . . . there are a thousand futile, yet verbally legitimate, objections which an objector can raise. In economics you cannot *convict* your opponent of error—you can only *convince* him of it. And, even if you are right, you cannot convince him, if there is a defect in your own powers of persuasion and exposition or if his head is already so filled with contrary notions that he cannot catch the clues to your thought which you are trying to throw to him." (Quoted in D. E. Moggridge, *John Maynard Keynes* [London, 1976], pp. 28–29, italics in original.) Between axioms, bridge principles, and empirical tests, in other words, there seems to be a great deal of subjective, intuitive space, even for one of the greatest economic scientists who ever "constructed" theory.

23. Catton, *From Animistic to Naturalistic* (n. 10 above), p. 346.

24. Stinchcombe, *Constructing Social Theories* (n. 1 above), p. 15.

25. Ibid., p. 4.

26. Ibid., p. 3.

27. Ibid., p. 25.

28. It should be noted, however, that this formal aspect of Stinchcombe's book is often contradicted by its content. Despite these arguments for the positivist reduction of theory that Stinchcombe has advanced in his first chapters, his later analysis actually clarifies, and at a highly abstract level, certain fundamental issues that are distinctively "theoretical" (ibid., pp. 57–103; see ch. 2, section 4 below). In fact, much of the book appears to have been written in an effort to sensitize mathematical sociologists to such generalized theoretical issues. Even more incongruous, however, is the section "Levels of Generality in Social Theory," with which Stinchcombe concludes the discussion of the nature of science I have described in the text. This short section actually pre-

sents an excellent explanation, based upon an assumption of the inter-relatedness of theory and fact, of why more generalized sociological argument cannot be "refuted" by purely empirical exercises (pp. 47–53). This analysis is in every way directly contrary to the premises of the positivist persuasion. (For a critique of Stinchcombe's proposals for theory construction and argument, see Dixon, *Sociological Theory* [n. 18 above], pp. 14–17.) The same incongruous tensions between formal empiricism and latent consideration for a priori assumptions inform Stinchcombe's later *Theoretical Methods in Social History* (New York, 1978). See my "Looking For Theory: 'Facts' and 'Values' as the Intellectual Legacy of the 1970's," *Theory and Society*, 10 (1981): 279–292.

29. In "Theoretical Pluralism, Methodological Dissension and the Role of the Sociologist: The West German Case" (*Social Science Information*, June–August, 1972, pp. 59–102), Klima applies to the social sciences the analogy, first developed by G. Scherhon, of scientific development as a market. If scientific development has been a progressive approximation of objective truth, there has occurred the "vertical differentiation of products" (pp. 74–75); where development presents the possibilities of circularity and does not increasingly approximate such objective reality, there has been a "horizontal differentiation." Although Klima develops a powerful argument that social scientific development is horizontal, he remains committed to the conception of a purely "vertical" development in the natural sciences.

30. See, for example, Goode, "Social Topography" (n. 13 above), p. 18.

31. Stinchcombe, *Constructing Social Theories* (n. 1 above), p. 21.

32. Goode, p. 9.

33. For a consideration of mathematical and formalist movements, see Warshay's discussion of "neopositivist sociology" (*Current State of Sociological Theory* [n. 7 above], pp. 89–92) and Mullins' discussion of "new causal theory" (*Theories and Theory Groups* [n. 22 above], pp. 215–249).

Pitirim A. Sorokin's metaphors "quantophrenia" and "numerology" aptly characterize the broader tendency I am referring to. Although Sorokin's polemic against sociology's growing preference for mathematical precision over intellectually substantive generalization was made more than twenty years ago and is highly exaggerated in its indictment, it still contains some of the most penetrating analysis of the manner in which empirical failures of particular quantitative studies can be linked to certain a priori general assumptions (*Fads and Foibles in Modern Sociology and Related Sciences* [Chicago, 1956], pp. 102–173).

C. Wright Mills also links the general tendency toward quantification with the pervasive quality of positivist philosophies of science in his chapter on the "methodological inhibition," which though less detailed and less polemical than Sorokin's is also still highly relevant (*The Sociological Imagination* [New York, 1961], pp. 50–73).

34. As Warshay has recently summarized a number of studies of the state of American sociology: "Probably the greater part of sociological activity does not explicitly use theory as a basis of research. . . . Theory (large or small) is given lip service at best or is treated with hostility and disdain as unfounded, scientifically dangerous speculation. The role of theory is seen to follow research inductively as its product or summary." (*Current State*, p. 10.)

35. Barney G. Glaser and Anselm L. Strauss, *The Discovery of Grounded Theory* (Chicago, 1967), pp. 2–3.

36. Walter L. Wallace, ed., *Sociological Theory* (New York, 1969), "Preface," pp. vii–ix.

37. Wallace, "Overview of Contemporary Sociological Theory," ibid., pp. 1–59. I quote p. 58.

38. I am referring in the following discussion to the version of this essay in Merton, *On Theoretical Sociology* (New York, 1967), pp. 39–72. The central ideas of the essay were first presented at the American Sociological Association meetings of 1947 and published in the *American Sociological Review* 13 (1949): 164–168.

39. A striking illustration of this manner of interpreting Merton's essay, which is directly relevant to the preceding discussion, is Zetterberg's use of a quotation about the middle-range approach as the epigraph to his own influential effort at formulating the logic for reducing theory to empirical practice (On Theory [n. 4 above], p. v).

40. Merton, *On Theoretical Sociology*, p. 40, italics added.

41. Ibid., p. 41.

42. Ibid., p. 51, italics in original.

43. Ibid.

44. Ibid., p. 66.

45. Ibid.

46. Ibid., p. 145, "The Bearing of Sociological Theory on Empirical Research."

47. Ibid., p. 144, italics in original.

48. Ibid., p. 39, "On Sociological Theories of the Middle Range."

49. Ibid., p. 46.

50. Ibid., pp. 1–37, "On the History and Systematics of Sociological Theory."

51. Ibid., p. 46, "On Sociological Theories of the Middle Range."

52. Ibid., p. 43.

53. Ibid., p. 40–41.

54. Ibid., p. 68.

55. In connection with this contradictory view of the nature of Marx's influence, it is relevant to note that, like Stinchcombe, Merton at-

tempts to portray the sociological founders—with, perhaps, the partial exception of Marx—as directing their energies toward "severely delimited problem[s]" on the empirical level rather than as being concerned with more "general" issues (ibid., p. 63). In effect both Stinchcombe and Merton give positivist readings of the sociological founders at the same time that both deny the relevance of such nonempirical influences as "readings."

It is also interesting that just as their positivist approach to theory construction inevitably made Homans' and Zetterberg's own formulations particularly vulnerable to the positivist criticism of a priorism, so has Merton's own partial commitment to positivism exposed his own work. Zetterberg, for example, who quotes from Merton's writing on middle-range theory in his own epigraph, ends up by criticizing Merton's substantive middle-range theories as insufficiently specified generalizations (*On Theory* [n. 4 above], pp. 74–75). See also Mulkay's critique of Merton for not connecting his theoretical formulations to the complexities of real social observations, for being overly general and imprecise (*Functionalism* [n. 18 above], pp. 106–121).

56. Merton, *On Theoretical Sociology*, p. 69, n. 52.

57. In his most recent essay on this problem of theoretical conflict, Merton's position remains an ambiguous one. On the one hand, he acknowledges a "chronic crisis" in contemporary theoretical sociology, denying only that it "constitute[s] a deep crisis in the sense of involving basically *new* controversy over fundamentals" ("Structural Analysis in Sociology," in Peter M. Blau, ed., *Approaches to the Study of Social Structure* [New York, 1975], p. 26, n. 5, italics added). Instead, Merton describes the present situation "as a continuum of theoretical issues long under debate" (ibid.). Yet later in the same essay, Merton argues that this "plurality of theoretical orientations" actually refers to the vitality of a variety of theories of the middle range, demonstrating, once again, that sociology cannot be organized around a single, comprehensive theory (p. 39 ff). "Diverse paradigms," in this latter treatment, are not arguments from different general, non-empirical positions, but simply arguments about "differing kinds of [empirical] *phenomena*" (p. 49, italics in original).

58. Wilhelm Dilthey, *Gesammelte Schriften* (Leipzig and Berlin, 1914), 1:37–38, quoted in H. A. Hodges, *Wilhelm Dilthey: An Introduction* (London, 1944), pp. 145–146; on this general topic, see Dilthey, "An Introduction to the Human Studies," in H. P. Rickman, ed., *Dilthey: Selected Writings* (Cambridge, 1976), pp. 159–167.

59. Winch, "The Idea of a Social Science," in Bryan R. Wilson, ed., *Rationality*, (London, 1970), p. 15.

60. In other words, despite the essential common denominator of the "human studies" position, there are important variations, just as there

are more extreme and more moderate expressions of the basic positivist position I outlined in sec. 2. As Hodges (*Wilhelm Dilthey*, p. 68–70), H. Stuart Hughes (*Consciousness and Society* [New York, 1958], pp. 192–200), and Habermas (*Knowledge* [n. 9 above], pp. 140–146) all emphasize, Dilthey differentiated his own position from the more romantic expressions of idealism which were even antagonistic to the techniques of the natural sciences and not simply to their application to social life. In contrast to Dilthey, such idealists as Windleband and Rickert would have excluded from the human studies all attempts at generalization, whereas Dilthey acknowledged that the human studies contained both "historical" and "systematic" disciplines. These thinkers, in fact, actually identified as "natural sciences" disciplines like economics and experimental psychology simply because they attempted to move beyond the purely idiographic emphasis on individual types. Nonetheless, there existed fundamental agreement on both sides of this dispute about the basic distinction between social and natural science, as expressed in the dichotomization of "understanding" and "explanation."

For general discussions of the idealist "human studies" position in contrast to the positivist conception of social science, see Hughes (*Consciousness*, pp. 183–191) and Parsons (*Structure* [n. 3 above], pp. 473–487). For discussions of this debate with specific reference to sociology, see Rex (*Key Problems* [n. 3 above], pp. 156–158) and Don Martindale, *The Nature and Types of Sociological Theory* (Cambridge, Mass., 1960), pp. 377–379. More recently, see Anthony Giddens, *New Rules of Sociological Method* (New York, 1976), and Richard J. Bernstein, *The Restructuring of Social and Political Theory* (Philadelphia, 1978). Both authors take an unacceptably subjectivist position, in my view, as I have noted in "Looking for Theory: 'Facts' and 'Values' as the Intellectual Legacy of the 1970's" (n. 28 above).

61. The position is taken most seriously in certain schools of contemporary anthropology, the discipline which more than any other has influenced the "human studies" position's most articulate contemporary spokesman, Peter Winch (see, e.g., his "The Idea of a Social Science" [n. 59 above], p. 15); see also A. K. Louch, *Explanation and Human Action* (Berkeley and Los Angeles, 1969).

Alfred Schutz's discussion of science makes it clear that a phenomenological perspective need not imply an antiscientific stance. The central point of Schutz's position is a formulation—the possibility of which will be explored in more detail in the following section—that natural as well as social science must be seen as resting on an intersubjective understanding.

It is a misunderstanding of the essential character of science to think it deals with reality if we consider as the pattern of reality the world of everyday life. The world of both the natural and the social scientist is neither more or less than the world of thought in general can be. ("The Problem of Rationality in the Social World," in Dorothy Emmet and Alasdaire Macintyre, eds., *Sociological Theory and Philosophical Analysis* [London, [1943] 1970], p. 113.)

When Schutz goes on to refer to the "historical boundaries" of science and to the "postulates of adequacy," he is pointing to the manner in which certain kinds of subjective understandings can and do become the basis of scientific objectivity in a nonpositivist sense of that term.

Paul Ricoeur's discussion of "The Model of a Text: Meaningful Action Considered as a Text," represents a later argument, within the phenomenological and hermeneutic tradition, against Dilthey's separation of understanding and explanation (*Social Research* 38 [1971]: 529–562).

62. Max Weber, "Objectivity in Social Science and Social Policy," in Edward A. Shils and Henry A. Finch eds., *The Methodology of the Social Sciences: Max Weber* (New York, 1949), pp. 50–112, and "Critical Studies in the Logic of the Cultural Sciences," ibid., pp. 164–188.

In *Key Problems in Sociological Theory* (n. 3 above), Rex confronts the arguments of Dilthey and Winch from an explicitly Weberian position (pp. 166–174). For general discussions of Weber's refutation of the "human studies" position, see Parsons (*Structure*, pp. 577–601) and Hughes (*Consciousness*, pp. 301–314). As for whether Weber's own exposition of the objectivity of the social sciences is itself tenable, see Raymond Aron's refutation of Weber's philosophy of science in "Max Weber and Michael Polanyi," in Marjorie Grene, ed., *The Logic of Personal Knowledge: Essays Presented to Michael Polanyi* (Glencoe, Ill., 1961), pp. 99–116, to which I will refer below (n. 86); also see the analysis of the impact of certain of Weber's intellectual presuppositions on his empirical observations in vol. 3, passim.

63. Ernest Nagel, *The Structure of Science: Problems in the Logic of Scientific Explanation* (New York, 1961), pp. 450–485.

64. Ibid., pp. 80–90, 107–117.

65. Ibid., pp. 489–490.

66. Ibid., p. 530.

67. Sorokin, *Fads* (n. 33 above), pp. 31–50.

68. In contrast to Sorokin, for example, Neil J. Smelser's detailed analysis, "Classification, Description, and Measurement" (ch. 6 of his *Comparative Methods in the Social Sciences* [Englewood Cliffs, N.J., 1976]), demonstrates how a commitment to the tasks of elaborating a "scientific" methodology of experiment, verification, and explanation can be combined with a full comprehension of the independent importance of generalized elements in social scientific formulations. By showing that virtually none of the methodological literature on comparative social development actually meets the positivist standards of meth-

odological precision, Smelser's discussion indicates, in effect, the degree of indeterminacy that conflict over generalized conceptualization must introduce into any empirically oriented analysis.

69. Precisely because it vulgarizes Nagel's "naturalistic" approach, Catton's book affords a good illustration of how the rejection of the "human studies" position is taken to lead to the automatic acceptance of the positivist argument. In *From Animistic to Naturalistic Sociology* (n. 10 above, passim) Catton offers extensive documentation that the imputation of cultural meaning to action does not prevent the applicability of statistical manipulation and causal analysis, and following Nagel he calls this methodological position the "naturalistic" approach to social science. But it is the conclusion that Catton draws from this demonstration that is significant: he believes that by indicating the compatibility of cultural subject matter and "scientific" technique he has demonstrated the validity of the radical positivist perspective.

70. In terms of the debate between "human studies" and "natural science," I am proposing, in other words, that natural science itself should be seen as a hermeneutical exercise. In this way, it can be seen that the pursuit of generalization and explanation is often—subject to the limitations described below (sec. 6)—available for extension to the social world. In fact, many of the contemporary exercises in, and arguments for, a "hermeneutical" social science would agree with this position if they were confronted with it. Their antagonism to the positivist persuasion, however, creates an atmosphere of polarization which makes such agreement publicly infrequent, undermining the desire for clarification of possible commonality between the two positions. (Good examples of this often tacit agreement can be found in Paul Rabinow and William M. Sullivan, eds., *Interpretive Social Science: A Reader* [Berkeley and Los Angeles, 1979]). The acceptance of a dichotomy between natural science and the "human studies" in something like the terms I have described represents, e.g., one of the major problems in Habermas' otherwise penetrating critique of positivism. Despite his disagreements with Dilthey, Habermas deliberately follows him in seeing substantive presuppositions as relevant only to social science. The only apriori commitment that Habermas attributes to natural science is the "technical" interest in adapting to social conditions by controlling behavior through prediction and explanation. But the argument set forth below makes it clear that science has, in Habermas' terms, "practical" interests as well: it too is guided by meanings that are rooted in tradition. (For this definition of "practical interest," see *Knowledge and Human Interests* [n. 9 above], p. 310.)

Herminio Martins, in a review of developments in the philosophy of science, has put the dangers of this dichotomization between natural and social science—and the possibility for a third, synthetic and postpositivist position—very clearly in his excellent essay, "Time and Theory in Sociology," in John Rex, ed., *Approaches to Sociology* (London, 1974), pp. 246–294.

> A major overarching assumption prevailed that the choice lay between either a general positivistic or naturalistic philosophy of the sciences (including natural and social sciences) *or* a nonpositivistic non-naturalistic philosophy of the social and cultural studies. A third alternative, that positivism and especially logical empiricism was wrong about natural science and that one could formulate a plausible nonpositivistic philosophy of the natural sciences just as much as a nonpositivistic philosophy of the social sciences—that one could formulate a meta-science in which the conception of a *verstehende Naturwissenschaft* could run parallel to that of a *verstehende Soziologie*—was rarely seriously entertained.... The dilemma facing sociologists was perceived, rather, as either to accept a unified theory of science (at the time almost inevitably a logical empiricist one) in which case the social sciences and the social studies as a whole appeared as fantastically prescientific, if not worse, or to embrace a dualistic theory of scientific knowledge with a comparably depressing bifurcation between natural science (characterised in positivist terms) and sociological knowledge (which appeared to lose its autonomy anyway in the light of some idealist interpretations, as a branch of either philosophy or history). (P. 286, italics in original.)

71. For a good general introduction to and documentation of these different phases, see Anthony Giddens, "Positivism and Its Critics," in T. B. Bottomore and R. N. Nisbet, eds., *A History of Sociological Analysis* (New York, 1978), pp. 237–286; Ian Barbour, *Myths, Models, and Paradigms* (London, 1974); and Stephen Toulmin, "From Form to Function: Philosophy and History of Science in the 1950's and Now," *Daedalus* 106 (Summer 1977): 143–162. This historical discussion by Toulmin is particularly interesting for its autobiographical elements, since he is a historian and philosopher of science who has personally experienced, in terms of the reception of his own work, the transition from abstracted positivism and empiricism to postpositivist thinking, for his work presented some of the earliest criticisms of these approaches. Referring to his books of 1953 and 1961, Toulmin comments: "The direct influence of those books seems to me to have been comparatively slight." He adds: "When I wrote [them] I certainly felt . . . much 'out in the cold.' . . . The new style of philosophizing about science came into favor [only] during the late 1960's" (pp. 161–162).

72. The "received view" is Hilary Putnam's term for the analysis of scientific theories as "axiomatic calculi which are given a partial observational interpretation by means of correspondence rules" (quoted in Frederick Suppe, "The Search for Philosophic Understanding of Scientific Theories," in Suppe, ed., *The Structure of Scientific Theories* [Ur-

bana, Ill., 1974], p. 3); Putnam proposed the phrase in "What Theories Are Not," in Nagel, Suppes, and Tarski, eds., *Logic, Methodology, and the Philosophy of Science: Proceedings of the 1960 International Congress* (Stanford, Calif., 1962), pp. 240–251. This notion developed out of the original logical positivism proposed by the Vienna Circle in the 1920s. Many of the difficulties with the original formulation of logical positivism were noticed by members of the Vienna Circle themselves, and in papers like Rudolph Carnap's "Testability and Meaning," *Philosophy of Science* 3 (1936): 240–268, and 4 (1937): 1–40, they both weakened the positivist program and ushered in its liberalized successor, logical empiricism (for a general discussion of this point, see Harold I. Brown, *Perception, Theory, and Commitment: The New Philosophy of Science* [Chicago, 1979], p. 23). As Suppe points out (p. 6), many philosophers who rejected logical positivism as a general epistomology were prepared to accept it in the guise of logical empiricism for the specialized case of scientific knowledge. Probably much of empiricism's staying power was a result of its evolution in the hands of the original positivists.

73. Karl Popper, *The Logic of Scientific Discovery* (New York, [1934] 1959), p. 41. This ambiguity in Popper's work is implicitly illustrated by Imre Lakatos' use of "Popper$_0$," "Popper$_1$," and "Popper$_2$," in referring to three distinctive nonpositivist positions that have been attributed to Popper by historians and philosophers of science, although Lakatos himself contends that only the last two Popperian positions were actually articulated by Popper himself ("Criticism and the Methodology of Scientific Research Programmes," *Proceedings of the Aristotelian Society* 69 [1969]: 149–186).

74. In the more technical terminology I have introduced here, the "positivist persuasion" elaborated above may be viewed as including both positivism and the reductionist aspects of empiricism. With this qualification, I will refer to "positivism" and "empiricism" strictly considered as interchangeable with the positivist persuasion.

In the light of the description I have made of the changing perspectives among leading historians and philosophers of science, it is revealing to note that after the consensus on the radical positivist perspective had long since crumbled, the leaders of the positivist persuasion in sociology continued to invoke the "discoveries" of "philosophers of science" as justification for their own position. Invariably, these references, if actually specified, were to the radical positivist position that had already been sharply challenged by empiricism and was in the process of being even more radically confronted by the third, antiempiricist critique.

For example, despite the fact that he was writing in 1966, Catton argues as follows:

The emphasis on evidence [in modern sociology] was strongly reinforced when philosophers in the 20th century formulated the verifiability theory of meaning—declaring a sentence meaningless if its truth cannot be ascertained by observation, direct or indirect. [Therefore] insistence of scientists upon objectivity, or verifiability, often entails ignoring factors which might seem important to the layman but for which no adequate observational techniques yet exist. (*From Animistic to Naturalistic Sociology* [n. 10 above], p. 49.)

Homans actually wrote in 1964 that his emphasis on propositional, inductive theorizing had until that date been ignored "because the philosophers of science had not given as clear an answer to the question about theory as they have now" ("Bringing Men Back in" [n. 18 above], p. 811). The "answer" he refers to, he continues, can be found in the work of a philosopher like Braithwaite, who was writing in terms of a general position which had, by then, been subject to criticism for several decades. Similarly, Goode explicitly refers for legitimation to what he regards as the self-evidently "positivist" canons of the scientific method (*Explorations in Social Theory* [n. 13 above], p. 9), and Stinchcombe roots his argument in the "common basis of the sciences" which he describes in radical positivist language as the "logical forms of scientific inferences, or 'induction' " (*Constructing Social Theories* [n. 1 above], p. 15). Finally, Zetterberg, who vacillates between a radical positivist emphasis on verification, as indicated by the very title of his book, *On Theory and Verification in Sociology* (n. 4 above), and a more moderate empiricism, indicates his confusion by claiming that Thomas Kuhn's perspective, which sharply departs from both positivism and empiricism, is actually complementary to his own (p. 176).

Nagel and Merton represent the most important exceptions to such philosophical naïveté, which rather than simply taking one side of the epistemological controversy actually denies its very existence. Nagel deliberately placed himself in the empiricist framework. Although Merton also clearly eschewed the radical positivist framework, his vacillation makes his philosophical commitment ultimately unclear.

In addition to the contradictions I have pointed to above—which can be interpreted as a conflict between empiricist and postempiricist orientations—Merton has recently made a qualified endorsement of the work of Gerald Holton, a strongly postempiricist philosopher and historian of science whose work I will discuss below (sec. 4.2). See Merton's "Thematic Analysis in Science: Notes on Kuhn's Concept," *Science*, April 25, 1972, pp. 335–338.

75. Although Polanyi at first attracted little interest from his fellow philosophers of science, the relatively few sociologists who have encountered his work have not failed to appreciate its profundity. Raymond Aron's penetrating essay "Max Weber and Michael Polanyi" (n. 62 above) analyzes the "error of the Weberian formulation" of objectivity (p. 105) in the light of Polanyi's interpretation of science (see n. 86 below). Polanyi's reformulation of the traditional conception of science also ap-

pears to have been significant for Edward Shils' conceptualization of his "center and periphery" notion, which he first formulated in the essay of that name in Grene, ed., *The Logic of Personal Knowledge* (n. 62 above), pp. 117–130.

Two other dissenters from the positivist persuasion, with more influence in their own discipline, emerged during the 1950s: Stephen Toulmin and Norwood Russell Hanson. Like the positivists of the Vienna Circle, Toulmin and Hanson were greatly impressed with Wittgenstein, but with the *Philosophical Investigations* (1953), not the *Tractatus Logico-Philosophicus* (1922). While the *Tractatus* dealt with propositions, Wittgenstein's later work turned to an examination of "language games." The implication of this was, in Toulmin's words, that "rather than allowing the axiomatic method of analysis [i.e., formal logic] any monopoly, what was most needed was a functional taxonomy of explanatory procedures and techniques" ("From Form to Function" [n. 71 above], p. 145). Scientific theorizing, Toulmin held, took place in its own language game, and that language game could be studied like any other. In my terms, this means a rejection of the first positivist postulate, the radical distinction between the empirical and the nonempirical, a position which Hanson promoted in a particularly forceful way (see below, n. 99). Toulmin also emphasized the "hierarchy" and "stratified language" of science (*Philosophy of Science* [n. 1 above]), a position that presents an early example of the hierarchy I have conceptualized in my "Continuum of Scientific Thought" (figs. 1, 2). See my references to his work in nn. 1 and 6 above.

76. Polanyi's most important book on this subject is *Personal Knowledge* (New York, 1958). Some of his major essays are collected in Marjorie Grene, ed., *Knowing and Being* (London, 1969). His first major explication of this position appeared in *Science, Faith, and Society* (London, 1946).

77. Polanyi, *Personal Knowledge*, p. 312.

78. Ibid., p. 38.

79. Ibid., p. 36.

80. Ibid., pp. 34–35, italics in original.

81. Ibid., p. 37.

82. Ibid., p. 311.

83. Ibid., p. 300.

84. Ibid., p. 308.

85. Ibid., p. 315.

86. Ibid., p. 300. The relationship between this articulation of universality and objectivity and Polanyi's earlier discussion of the formative impact on observation of the scientist's internal conception of the order which he expects to find can be seen in the following passage.

> Orderly patterns are not subjective. My recognition of a scientific pattern *may* be subjective, but only in the sense that it is mistaken. The

shapes of the constellations are subjective patterns, for they are due to accidental collocations; and the alleged confirmations of horoscopes recorded by astrologers are likewise subjective. But . . . man has the power to establish real patterns in nature, the reality of which is manifested by the fact that their future implications extend indefinitely beyond the experience which they were originally known to control. The appraisal of such order is made with universal intent and conveys indeed a claim to an unlimited range of as yet unspecifiable true intimations. (*Personal Knowledge*, p. 37, italics in original.)

It is in terms of this reconstruction by Polanyi of the subjectivity-objectivity dilemma that Aron criticizes Weber's positivist definition of objectivity. In response to Weber's assertion that objectivity is based on the complete separation of facts and values once the admittedly value-directed choice of scientific subject matter has been completed, Aron writes:

If the intention of the historian is not separated from that of the historical person, or the intention of the sociologist from that of the citizen, is not the *scientific* intention, that of universality, at once undermined? . . . It was to resolve this difficulty that Max Weber was forced to effect a rigorous distinction between subjective questions and objective replies and so assumed that the knower, having expressed his historical subjectivity in the question, proceeded to efface himself before the object. It is true that the historical person becomes an historian . . . only on condition that he transcends, through the effort of knowledge, the temptation to justify, to condemn, and to distort. The error of the Weberian formulation is to transform into an objective duality a duality in fact internal to the consciousness of the knower. . . . But if the historical account is never depersonalized, neither is it ever reduced to a simple elaboration of prejudices and passions, at least so long as it preserves a scientific character in the eyes of competent men. ("Max Weber and Michael Polanyi" [n. 62 above], p. 105.)

It might also be noted that Aron supports the position that Polanyi's conception of science is not an idealist one:

[For Polanyi] the conceptual systems of the social sciences are neither the result of arbitrary choices . . . nor reflections of a structure inscribed in reality itself. Both formulae falsify what we may call the dialogue or dialectic which constitutes the authentic experience of social science . . . (p. 108.)

(For a similar discussion, also drawing on Polanyi's work, which indicates how scientific standards of objectivity can be rooted in an antipositivist perspective on the interrelation of knower and known, see Robert N. Bellah's article, "Between Religion and Social Science," in his *Beyond Belief* [New York, 1970], pp. 237–259.)

For an analysis of how a thoroughly anti-objectivist position can also be anti-idealist—can recognize, that is, the external limitations of objective nature without at the same time objectifying that perception of nature—see Habermas' discussion of the dialectical philosophy of science implicit in Marx's early writings in ch. 2 of *Knowledge and Human Interests* (n. 9 above). Habermas contrasts Marx's position to Hegel's in the following way:

> Nature does not conform to the categories under which the subject apprehends it in the unresisting way in which a subject can conform to the understanding of another subject on the basis of reciprocal recognition under categories that are binding on both of them. The unity of the social subject and nature . . . cannot eradicate the autonomy of nature and the remainder of complete otherness that is lodged in its facticity. . . . [Nature's] independence manifests itself in our ability to learn to master natural processes only to the extent that we subject ourselves to them. This elementary experience is expressed in the language of natural "laws" that we must "obey." The externality of nature manifests itself in the contingency of its ultimate constraints. (P. 33.)

87. Alexandre Koyré, *Metaphysics and Measurement* (Cambridge, Mass., 1968), "Galileo and the Scientific Revolution of the Seventeenth Century" and "Galileo and Plato," pp. 1–15, 16–43.

88. Ibid., p. 7.

89. Ibid., p. 6.

90. Ibid., p. 3. Fifteen years after Koyré wrote these words, Herbert Butterfield discussed the same phenomenon in *The Origins of Modern Science* (New York, [1957] 1965), and arrived at a very similar conclusion about the role of generalized nonempirical frameworks in creating the observations that led to the Galilean revolution in modern physics:

> It is not relevant for us to argue that if the Aristotelians had merely watched the more carefully they would have changed their theory of inertia for the modern one—changed over to the view that bodies tend to continue either at rest or in motion along a straight line until something intervenes to stop them or deflect their course. It was supremely difficult to escape from the Aristotelian doctrine by merely observing things more closely, especially if you had already started off on the wrong foot and were hampered beforehand with the whole system of interlocking Aristotelian ideas. In fact, the modern law of inertia is not the thing you would discover by more photographic methods of observation—it required a different kind of thinking-cap, a transposition in the mind of the scientist himself; for we do not actually see ordinary objects continuing their rectilinear motion in that kind of empty space which Aristotle said could not occur, and sailing away to that infinity which also he said could not possibly exist. . . . [The problem of motion] could not be solved by close observation within the framework of the older system of ideas. (Pp. 16–17.)

For another early historical case study of the decisive influence of suprascientific cultural influences on the perception of objective fact see Ludwik Fleck's 1935 study of the scientific and clinical treatment of syphilis, translated as *Genesis and Development of a Scientific Fact* (Chicago, 1979). "A fact," Fleck writes, "always occurs in the context of the history of thought and is always the result of a definite thought style [i.e., cultural framework]" (p. 95). "Truth . . . is always, or almost always, completely determined within a thought style. . . . Truth is . . . (1) in historical perspective, an event in the history of thought, (2) in its contemporary context, stylized thought constraint" (p. 100, italics eliminated).

91. This issue is discussed most thoroughly in a later essay on "The Growth of Science in Society" in *Knowing and Being* (n. 76 above), pp. 77–78. The three criteria of scientific merit Polanyi establishes are: (1) plausibility; (2) scientific value: accuracy, systematic importance, and intrinsic interest; and (3) originality. E.g., he writes: "A scientific fact is one that has been accepted as such by scientific opinion, both on the grounds of the evidence in favor of it and because it is sufficiently plausible in face of the scientific conception of the nature of things" (p. 65).

92. Ibid., pp. 4, 135.

93. Ibid., p. 167; cf. p. 254.

94. Koyré, *Metaphysics and Measurement* (n. 87 above), pp. 18–19.

95. Ibid., p. 19. At about the same time, this point was also articulated by the philosopher and historian R. G. Collingwood, with specific reference to the most general level of the scientific continuum. In the following statement, he discusses the status of the "Absolute Presuppositions" which he describes as that dimension of a scientific statement "which stands, relatively to all questions to which it is related, as a presupposition . . ." (*Metaphysics* [London, 1940], p. 31):

> Absolute presuppositions are not verifiable. This does not mean that we should like to verify them but are not able to; it means that the idea of verification is an idea which does not apply to them, because . . . to speak of verifying a presupposition involves supposing that it is a relative presupposition. If anybody says "Then they can't be of much use in science," the answer is that their use in science is their logical efficacy, and that the logical efficacy of a supposition does not depend on its being verifiable. . . . (P. 32.)

Later, Collingwood compares this position to what he calls "Positivist Metaphysics":

> Positivists have always tried more or less consistently to say . . . that scientific thought has no [such] presuppositions. For if the function of thought is to classify observed facts, there must be facts available for classification before thought can begin to operate. And once facts are available there is no need to presuppose anything. (P. 146.)

96. Koyré, p. 90. If this were truly representative of Koyré's under-

standing of the role of experiment in science, which I believe it is not, it would represent the return to a one-directional perspective on science, only this time from an idealist perspective. On this reversal as the second type of possible violation of the two-directional schema set forth here, see the discussion in sec. 3 above.

97. In light of the degree to which Kuhn's work has become the single point of focus for both supporters and critics of the postpositivist position, it is important to appreciate its nonidiosyncratic character, its very direct continuity with earlier antipositivist, nonidealist formulations which were, for the most part, widely footnoted by Kuhn himself but which have rarely been mentioned by others. Following Polanyi, Kuhn utilizes the literature from Gestalt psychology to establish both his basic epistemological position and the importance of social "communication" in upholding a particular scientific perspective (Thomas Kuhn, *The Structure of Scientific Revolutions*, 2d ed. [Chicago, 1970], pp. 111–115; Polanyi, *Knowing and Being* [n. 76 above], p. 80). Following Polanyi and Koyré, and, of course, Wittgenstein, Kuhn relies heavily on the analogies of language and persuasion for comprehending the a priori aspect of science (*Scientific Revolutions*, pp. 202–204; idem, "Reflections on My Critics," in Imre Lakatos and Alan Musgrave, eds. *Criticism and the Growth of Knowledge* [London, 1970], pp. 266–277; Polanyi, *Personal Knowledge* [n. 76 above], pp. 69–131; Koyré, *Metaphysics and Measurement* [n. 87 above], pp. 18–19). Following Koyré, Kuhn emphasizes the general philosophical and metaphysical assumptions that inform the "views of nature" that underlie paradigms (*Scientific Revolutions*, pp. 2, 4–5, 121). Following Koyré and Butterfield, Kuhn relies for one of his major illustrations of the relationship between paradigm revolution and extrascientific change on discussions of the pendulum experiment in the conflict between Aristotelian and Galilean physics (ibid., pp. 123–126). And following Butterfield and Polanyi, Kuhn utilizes the term *anomaly* to describe situations of theoretical conflict over the same empirical observation (ibid., pp. 52–65; Butterfield, *Origins of Modern Science*, [n. 90 above], p. 17; Polanyi, *Personal Knowledge*, p. 20). Stephen Toulmin has noted the general parallels between Kuhn's book and Collingwood's discussion in *Metaphysics* (Toulmin, *Human Understanding* [Princeton, N.J., 1972], pp. 98–100). Merton is, I think, correct in describing Kuhn's book as "drawing explicitly upon and also significantly recombining and developing earlier ideas" ("Structural Analysis in Sociology," in Blau, ed., *Approaches* [n. 57 above] p. 43).

98. Masterman actually identifies twenty-one different kinds of references for the paradigm concept, but many of these are overlapping ("The Nature of a Paradigm," in Lakatos and Musgrave, *Criticism and the Growth of Knowledge*, pp. 59–90). In describing the different references Masterman identifies, I am employing my own terms, not hers.

99. An extreme example of this phenomenon is illustrated by Hanson's argument that even the simplest observations are theory-laden: "Let us consider Johannes Kepler: imagine him on a hill watching the dawn. With him is Tycho Brahe. Kepler regarded the sun as fixed: it was the earth that moved. But Tycho followed Ptolemy and Aristotle in this much at least: the earth was fixed and all other celestial bodies moved around it. *Do Kepler and Tycho see the same thing in the east at dawn?*" Norwood Russell Hanson, *Patterns of Discovery: An Inquiry into the Conceptual Foundations of Science* (Cambridge, 1958), p. 5, italics in original. In the present case, we might argue that while both Tycho and Kepler had major presuppositional disagreements, and perhaps that they even saw different things in the east at dawn, they probably still shared common commitments somewhere along the theoretical continuum: to the methodological importance of observation, to the relevance of geometric models to astronomy, to the conviction that astronomy ought to be an autonomous area of investigation.

100. In *Human Understanding*, Toulmin has spoken directly to this latter point:

> The parties to such a fundamental debate—both those who cling to the older theory, and those who put forward a newer one—would still share some common ground: not any common body of theoretical notions, perhaps, but rather certain shared disciplinary conceptions, reflecting their collective intellectual ambitions and rational methods, selection-procedures and criteria of adequacy. (P. 79.)

In another essay, Toulmin has applied the same kind of reasoning, arguing that scientists need not share metaphysical assumptions in order to submit to the same empirical authority ("Does the Distinction between Normal and Revolutionary Science Hold Water?" in Lakatos and Musgrave [n. 97 above], pp. 39–48).

The significance of common methodological commitments amid sharp conflicts at other levels, and Toulmin's observation in this regard about the importance of the disciplinary matrix, is borne out in a revealing way by a recent polemic in Marxist theorizing. In his slashing attack on the work and thought of the French structuralist Marxist Louis Althusser, the British Marxist historian E. P. Thompson disputes Althusser's claim that all empirical historical work can be reduced to ideological theories between which there can remain only political conflict. "His comments," Thompson writes about Althusser, "display throughout no acquaintance with, nor understanding of, historical procedures: that is, procedures which make of 'history' a *discipline* and not a babble of alternating ideological assertions: procedures which provide for their own relevant discourse [about] proof" (*The Poverty of Theory and Other Essays* [London, 1978], pp. 205–206, italics in original). This democratically minded Marxist historian, in other words, finds the existence of a disciplinary framework the last anchor of "scientific rationality." That in other respects he wavers about the actual role of scientific theory does not detract from the importance of this insight.

101. I believe that this way of understanding the problems in Kuhn's formulation provides two points of leverage for clarifying the debate over his work. First, it becomes possible to see a certain degree of commonality that runs through his disparate critics and commentators. For example, the charge that Kuhn has been inflexible in fusing the different elements of scientific paradigms has been made in so many words not only by his empiricist critics, like Karl Popper ("Normal Science and Its Dangers," in Lakatos and Musgrave [note 97 above], pp. 51–58) but also by Gerald Holton (*Thematic Origins of Scientific Thought: Kepler to Einstein* [Cambridge, Mass., 1973], passim) and Masterman (pp. 59–90), who support in different ways Kuhn's general postempiricist position. Toulmin, for example, has emphasized the need for a more differentiated conception of scientific statement in a manner that is similar to that described here. He argues that the notion of "concept systematicity" gives too little autonomy to the different levels of the scientific continuum and should be replaced by a notion of "concept populations."

> Rather than treating the content of a natural science [i.e., the elements of the scientific continuum] as a tight and coherent logical system, we shall therefore have to consider it as a conceptual aggregate, or "population," within which there are—at most—localized pockets of logical systematicity. (*Human Understanding*, p. 128.)

On this basis, Toulmin has also argued against Kuhn's theory of scientific revolution, primarily on the grounds that long-term continuity in methodological and disciplinary frameworks ensures that science is guided more by "rational argument" and accumulation than Kuhn would admit. He uses the same base point to discuss the problems of Kuhn's relativism (pp. 98–130).

The approach I have suggested also makes it possible to reconcile the positions of some of Kuhn's sharpest critics with important aspects of his own work. This is true, for example, in regard to the criticisms by Imre Lakatos, one of the most interesting and forceful of Kuhn's critics. Despite the fact that he can be described as a neo-Popperian and has deliberately couched his work as an elaboration of one aspect of Popper's own reasoning, Lakatos actually made a decisive break with empiricism—presumably under the influence of the early postpositivists and also of Kuhn himself. In fact, the term I have chosen to describe the principal weakness of Kuhn's formulation of paradigm—"conflation"—is the term that Lakatos uses to criticize Popper's empiricist contention that the experimental disproof of a scientific theory will produce its rejection or refutation (Lakatos, "Criticism and the Methodology" [n. 73 above], pp. 155, 162, 177, 178; Lakatos, "Falsification and the Methodology of Scientific Research Programmes," in Lakatos and Musgrave, p. 109). For an analysis of the complementary relation of Lakatos' specific formulation of the "scientific research programme" and Kuhn's formulation of paradigms, see n. 110 below.

A similar middle ground can be found, on this basis, between Toulmin's and Kuhn's positions. For while the above criticisms by Toulmin are well directed, there is the distinct tendency in his own writing to focus greatest attention on the shared methodological and disciplinary frameworks that allow scientific progress. In this way, though he effectively criticizes empiricism, he pushes the philosophy of science away from a primary concern with developing distinctive criteria for evaluating the most generalized, nonempirical aspects of scientific argument. Toulmin apparently underestimates the real incommunicability that still occurs at levels more general than the methodological and disciplinary matrix, even if this is not so radical a breakdown as Kuhn has portrayed. Further, Kuhn's relativism is not as radical as Toulmin contends. As Kuhn later emphasizes in a formulation that, despite Toulmin's characterization, remains consistent with the earlier phase of his thinking, empirical accumulation—which can be taken as a sign of the "ultimate rationality" of science that Toulmin upholds against scientific relativism—is not incompatible with vast breakdowns in communication and continual disagreement over basic assumptions.

102. The artificial unity produced by such conflation is indicated also by the temporal, as well as intellectual, distortions Robert W. Friedrichs is forced to introduce. (1) While he describes the functionalist paradigm as solidifying its domination in the 1940s and 1950s, Friedrichs himself introduces evidence of fundamental "paradigm conflict" emerging in precisely the same period (A Sociology of Sociology [New York, 1970], pp. 25–26). (2) Friedrichs artificially places the "search for paradigmatic alternatives"—such as evolutionism, action theory, Freudianism, behaviorism, mechanism, and phenomenology—in the 1960s (pp. 33–45), whereas such analytic approaches actually had significant followings throughout the previous period of supposed functionalist domination. (3) Friedrichs claims that explicit concern for philosophy-of-science issues in sociology—a sign, according to Kuhn, of the emergence of paradigm conflict—started only in the early 1960s (p. 36), whereas there had actually been extensive debate over such issues, as exemplified by Nagel's writing, throughout the 1950s. (For a critique of Friedrichs' application of "paradigm" analysis that raises many of the issues mentioned here, see Donald N. Levine's review of Friedrichs' book, American Anthropologist 74 [1972]: 6–8.)

Another example of the artificial conflation of sociological levels of analysis derived from adopting Kuhn's original concept of paradigm is George Ritzer's discussion, "Sociology: A Multi-Paradigm Science," (*American Sociologist* 10, no. 3 [1975]: 156–167; also Ritzer's *Sociology: A Multi-Paradigm Science* (Boston, 1975). Although the three paradigms Ritzer proposes—"Social Facts," "Social Definition," and "Social Behavior"—represent points of agreement in themselves, they do not provide the key to theoretical divergence at all levels of analysis, as Ritzer contends. There are, in fact, a number of fundamental disputes between the followers of each of these supposedly unified perspectives and, in addition, equally important areas of agreement between members of the different paradigmatic schools Ritzer has chosen to identify as coherent units.

The same artificial conflation and intellectual distortion occurs in all the other attempts to strictly apply Kuhn's paradigm concept to sociology, for example in Timothy Lehmann's and T. R. Young's discussion of the "conflict methodology" which is purported to accompany the newly emerging "conflict paradigm" ("From Conflict Theory to Conflict Methodology: An Emerging Paradigm for Sociology," *Sociological Inquiry* 44, no. 1 [1974]: 15–28), and in Henrika Kuklick's discussion, "A Scientific Revolution: Sociological Theory in the United States, 1940–1945" (ibid., 43, no. 1 [1973]: 3–22), which despite its illumination creates a thoroughly false sense of paradigmatic unity in sociology. Andrew Effrat's application of Kuhn's paradigm concept, in "Power to the Paradigms: An Editorial Introduction" (ibid., 42, no. 3–4 [1972]: 3–34), represents an important although partial exception to these conflationary applications (see n. 151 below). More than the other approaches, Effrat clearly differentiates the scientific continuum into a number of different levels and also describes a number of different paradigms in sociology today. He fails, however, to assert the autonomy *within* any given paradigm unit of these different analytic levels, describing as necessarily interrelated certain kinds of philosophical assumptions, ideological commitments, propositions about conflict and equilibrium, methodological techniques and exemplary empirical studies (e.g., pp. 14–15, 17).

103. Kuhn, "Postscript," *Scientific Revolutions* (n. 97 above), p. 182.

104. Ibid., pp. 174–210; and Kuhn, "Reflections on My Critics" (n. 97 above), pp. 231–278; Kuhn, "Second Thoughts on Paradigms," in Suppe, ed., *The Structure of Scientific Theories* (n. 72 above), pp. 459–482.

105. Ritzer ("Sociology: A Multi-Paradigm Science" [n. 102 above]) is, therefore, reversing the actual situation when he suggests that, in comparison with the exemplar focus, Kuhn's original formulation of paradigm produced a greater emphasis on power and the organizational sources behind scientific development as opposed to the traditional emphasis on cognitive factors. For a more elaborate evaluation of Kuhn's later work, see my "Kuhn's Unsuccessful Revisionism: A Rejoinder to Selby," *Canadian Journal of Sociology* 7, no. 2 (1982).

106. Mullins (n. 22 above), passim. In the "Postscript" to the second edition of *Scientific Revolutions* (pp. 174–210), in which he proposes his new reformulation with its explicit emphasis on exemplars and groups, Kuhn cites Mullins' doctoral dissertation on biology, which uses much the same method as his later study on sociology, as an example of the kind of group-oriented analysis he has in mind to operationalize his exemplar concept (p. 176).

107. Mullins, p. 12.

108. Ibid., pp. 13, 39, 79. The most extreme example of how such an approach obscures basic intellectual issues in theoretical work is Mullins' dismissal (p. 68) of Walter L. Wallace's essay (n. 36 above) for focusing only on the structural-functional school. In fact, most of the theorists Mullins discusses as members of "new" paradigmatic groups can quite clearly be located in one of the number of nonfunctionalist analytic categories that Wallace has identified.

Actually, despite Mullins' claim to be applying Kuhn's analysis, he fails to utilize scientific exemplars to establish the *criteria* of group commitments. Consequently, not only does Mullins' organizational emphasis make him relatively indifferent to intellectual issues per se, but he has acquired little of the compensatory accuracy that attends to the use of the exemplar over the earlier paradigm concept. This confounds Mullins' errors, because the conflation of levels created by the paradigm concept makes it even more difficult to distinguish truly distinctive theoretical agreement and conflict.

In an article in which Mullins adheres more accurately to Kuhn's exemplar focus, the manner in which the "group" focus distorts the intellectual issues at stake is still very clear, and much easier to differentiate (Belver C. Griffith and Nicholas C. Mullins, "Coherent Social Groups in Scientific Change," *Science*, September 15, 1972). For example, in discussing the restriction on the perception of conflicting information that characterizes the kind of tightly-knit sectarian groups which create revolutionary paradigm shifts, Griffith and Mullins make no reference whatever to the impact of shared intellectual perspectives but refer rather to a "conscious effort to direct the group's work toward a specified series of problems . . . on the part of the leader or cadre of students" (p. 961). In reviewing Mullins' book, Marcello Truzzi makes a similar judgment of its central problems, although he considers them unrelated to problems in Kuhn's own formulation:

> [The] groups discussed [by Mullins] certainly demonstrate degrees of in-group solidarity and consciousness of kind. But these differences and similarities do not necessarily represent significant areas of agreement and disagreement in true theoretical-analytic terms. Once the reader compares Mullins' statements of the "paradigm content" for the different groups, these show little inclusion-exclusion criteria in terms of important intellectual dimensions. . . . This book is about associations of

scientific workers more than it is about *theory groups* in the usual sense. (*Contemporary Sociology* 4 [May 1975]: 223, italics in original.)

109. In *The Scientific Community* (New York, 1965), which relies on Kuhn's earlier formulations, Hagstrom demonstrates that it is possible to emphasize the group aspect of scientific activity without reducing the cognitive component to an epiphenomenon. He emphasizes this, first, by defining the paradigm community as a normative one, in contrast to the organizational, political, and economic aspects emphasized by such Kuhnians as Friedrichs, Mullins, and Ritzer. Second, Hagstrom asserts that these normative constraints are effective only insofar as they are integrated with the distinctive values of science in general and the individual disciplinary emphases in particular. (See especially pp. 24, 34, 48, 168–173.)

In subsequent work, Hagstrom has been one of the few sociological "Kuhnians" to recognize the full significance of Kuhn's shift to the "exemplar" usage. Hagstrom now defines a paradigm as a hierarchical grouping of scientific elements at different levels of generality, and he asserts that if theories are to belong to the same paradigm there must be agreement at every level of the continuum. The result is that Hagstrom can acknowledge the historical indeterminacy of the elements within any given scientific formulation. "The extent to which these elements constitute a unified whole or a loose assemblage," Hagstrom writes, "is left ambiguous and constitutes a serious problem in evaluating Kuhn's [earlier] theory" ("The Sociology of Scientific Revolutions and Disputes," unpublished manuscript, Sociology Department, University of Wisconsin, Madison, p. 3); see also Hagstrom's "Notes on Paradigms and Related Concepts" (ibid., pp. 17–23). He concludes: "It is logically possible that the really interesting phenomena concerning scientific change involve very diffuse sets—conceptual schemes in which methods, concepts, etc., are easily detached from the theories of their originators and [adhere] to open networks rather than groups" (pp. 12b–13).

For a comprehensive critical discussion of the numerous attempts by sociologists to utilize the "paradigm" concept to clarify theoretical debate over the last decade, see "The Paradigm Concept and Sociology: A Critical Review," by Douglas Lee Eckberg and Lester Hill, Jr. (*American Sociological Review* 44 [1979]: 925–936). The authors conclude that none of the twelve major sociological attempts they examine have adhered to Kuhn's basic distinction between exemplars and his earlier multifold paradigm conception. Instead, these attempts have usually taken a single level of the scientific continuum and argued that consensus at that level is the definitive point of theoretical division in sociological analysis. In emphasizing the early/late Kuhn distinction, however, the authors fail to recognize the problematic elements in Kuhn's conceptualization, problems which have, in the later as well as earlier periods, made it difficult to "operationalize" in an accurate way.

For a more discursive and theoretical analysis of the misperceptions by sociologists, and social scientists more generally, of Kuhn's paradigm concept, which takes a position similar to that presented here, see Herminio Martins, "The Kuhnian 'Revolution' and Its Implications for Sociology," in T. J. Nossiter, A. H. Hanson, and Stein Rokkan, eds., *Imagination and Precision in the Social Sciences: Essays in Honor of Peter Nettl* (New York, 1972), pp. 13–58.

110. As with the first phase, I believe that by understanding how the problems of this second phase of Kuhn's formulation derive from a basically accurate insight which, nevertheless, opens the door to a drastic intellectual reduction, it becomes possible to reconcile certain aspects of Kuhn's own work with a common line of criticism offered by writers who in their own minds differ greatly with Kuhn and among themselves as well.

For example, Lakatos is clearly wrong when he charges Kuhn with a desire to subordinate "truth" to an alternative scientific criterion such as degree of "psychological commitment" or "the greatest numbers" (Lakatos, "Criticism and the Methodology" [n. 73 above], p. 151, n. 19), and Kuhn quite legitimately responds to this as follows:

> To say that, in matters of theory-choice, the force of [methodological] logic and [empirical] observation cannot in principle be compelling is neither to discard logic and observation nor to suggest that there are not good reasons for favouring one theory over another. (Kuhn, "Reflections on My Critics," p. 234.)

But in another sense—in terms, that is, of the kind of impact this Kuhnian orientation could have on the analysis of science—Lakatos is quite correct. Kuhn's interest, as he himself readily admits ("Reflections on My Critics," pp. 264–265), does tend to shift the focus of attention entirely to the noncognitive criteria of scientific acceptance.

Similarly, it is in an effort to avoid the reductionist possibility of Kuhn's work that other critics have emphasized the importance of making certain significant distinctions. For example, Harriet Zuckerman distinguishes the "cognitive" from the "social" aspects of scientific conflict ("Cognitive and Social Conflict in Science," *Minerva* 12 [January 1974]: 131–135); Levine ("Review," n. 102 above) criticizes Friedrichs (who follows Kuhn) for not differentiating between the utilization of a given piece of sociological work as a "theoretical model" or an "empirical model"; and Joseph Ben-David, in discussing the "community" emphasis of the second edition of Kuhn's book, emphasizes that Kuhn's approach should be understood as explaining only the course of scientific activity and not its substantive contents (*The Scientist's Role in Society* [Englewood Cliffs, N.J., 1971], pp. 3–5, 13–14).

111. Holton, *Thematic Origins* (n. 101 above), pp. 13–14.

112. Gerald Holton, "On the Role of Themata in Scientific Thought," *Science*, April 25, 1972, pp. 328–329.

113. *Thematic Origins*, p. 22.

114. Ibid., p. 24.

115. Ibid.

116. Ibid., p. 22.

117. See, for example, Holton's analysis of the philosophical, cultural, and psychological influences that underlie Bohr's revolutionary articulation of the complementarity theme (ibid., pp. 115–116).

118. That among those theorists I have described as postpositivist there often exists disagreement should, indeed, be emphasized. Some writers exhibit strains toward idealism, others toward empiricism. Nonetheless, in terms of the specific criteria I have set out, I believe their work can be classified under this common framework.

119. Paul K. Feyerabend, "Consolations for the Specialist," in Lakatos and Musgrave (n. 97 above), pp. 209–210.

120. Lakatos, "Criticism and the Methodology" (n. 73 above), p. 161.

121. Ibid.

122. Ibid., p. 156. Lakatos' position on this issue has been amplified by a number of subsequent writers who consider themselves to be highly influenced by his work and, like him, take a decidedly cautious, often critical, approach to various aspects of Kuhn's work and the work of the more "radical" postpositivist thinkers. For example, Barbour writes:

> The decision to look on a given statement as primarily theoretical or primarily observational is relative, pragmatic, and context-dependent. . . . Those descriptions which one considers stable and more directly accessible will be taken as data, but this judgment will itself reflect theoretical assumptions." (*Myths* [n. 71 above], p. 97.)

And in the introduction to his critical evaluation of empiricism in sociology (see above, nn. 18, 22, 28), Keith Dixon also puts this issue very well, relating it directly to the significance of theoretical assumptions:

> All data, whether in the natural or social sciences . . . must necessarily be viewed through the lenses of theory or accumulated together with a series of background assumptions which render the data less than neutral. . . . In theoretical activity one is forced to treat some data as "harder" than others and it is this judgment . . . that enables theorists to erect a series of empirical tripwires. . . . The possibility of treating data as hard almost always depends upon the prior existence of a *well-founded and established theoretical framework*. (*Sociological Theory* [n. 18 above], p. 10, italics in original.)

The network model of science outlined by Mary Hesse takes a similar position, emphasizing the impossibility of distinguishing between fact and linguistic, i.e., prototheoretical, expressions, so that theory and observational data must be considered different analytical parts of a single subjective system of classification. "The absence of distinction between fact and linguistic expression here is not accidental," Hesse writes. "As soon as we begin to try to capture a practical fact in language, we are committed to some theoretical interpretation. Even to say of the solid body that 'its points are more or less worn down and blunt' is to commit ourselves to the categories of an ideal geometry." (*The Structure of Scientific Inference*, Berkeley and Los Angeles, 1974, p. 25.) Thus, "while it need not be denied that there is sometimes a useful distinction to be made between comparatively theoretical and comparatively observational descriptions," Hesse insists, at the same time, that "this does not mean that the distinction is more than pragmatically convenient" (p. 40). The distinction between facts and theories presents, rather, the contrast between more or less "entrenched" analytical statements (pp. 17–24). Yet Hesse insists, much as the present argument does, that this antipositivist position on data does not eliminate the significant role of observation. If science is a two-directional process, inputs from the metaphysical and empirical realms both must affect the construction of data. "Not all primary recognitions of empirical similarity can be overridden in the interest of preserving a given [theoretical] law," Hesse writes, "for it is upon the existence of some such recognitions that the whole possibility of language with empirical reference rests" (p. 16).

123. Polanyi, *Knowing and Being* (n. 76 above), p. 92.

124. Lakatos, "Criticism and the Methodology of Scientific Research Programs," pp. 176–177.

125. Holton, "Role of Themata" (n. 112 above), pp. 185–195.

126. Ibid., pp. 261–380. For other articulate critiques of the notion that any ultimately "crucial experiment" is possible in science, see Ken Menzies, *Talcott Parsons and the Social Image of Man* (London, 1976), "Programmatic Assertions and Programmes," pp. 11–17, and David C. Bell, "Theories, Metatheories and Paradigms: the Doctrine of the Crucial Test," paper prepared for the Annual Meeting of the American Sociological Association, New York, August 30–September 3, 1976. The remarkably insightful statement by John Maynard Keynes on the enormous logical gaps that must be filled in by scientific tuition—see n. 22 above—provides another strong explanation of the difficulties that any single new piece of evidence has in producing scientific change. For a phenomenological approach that argues for the "normalizing tendencies" of scientific investigation as one form of common sense knowledge, see Harold Garfinkel's discussion of scientific investigation as a "documentary method," i.e., a perception that tends to document the validity of prior understandings, in his important essay "Common Sense Knowledge" in *Studies in Ethnomethodology* (Englewood Cliffs, N.J., 1967), ch. 3.

127. This second postulate does not mean, of course, that science is not an "empirical" method in terms of its specialization vis-à-vis other kinds of social thought (see my related point in sec. 1 above). Indeed, the historical differentiation in Western society of self-consciously empirical thinking produced systematic reorientation at every level of social thought and must be regarded as one of the most decisive breaks with traditional culture. This postulate does mean, however, that even a branch of thought which is so specialized cannot be strictly empirical in the one-directional sense outlined above. In regard to sociology, Martindale's discussion illustrates how these two perspectives on science can be combined. His introductory chapters make a concise case for the origins of sociology in the differentiation of the pursuit of "objective, empirically testable knowledge" from folk wisdom, religion, and philosophy, a differentiation that resulted in the "extension of the scientific method first pioneered in art and confirmed in applications to the physical world to the social world of man himself" (*Nature and Types* [n. 60 above], p. 27, generally pp. 3–47). That this description of sociology's origins does not imply the actual elimination of nonempirical ideological and cognitive assumptions from sociological practice is clear from the fact that the succeeding 500 pages of Martindale's book are devoted to the categorization of "schools" of sociology according to their different philosophical and ideological bases. Martindale's positivist definition of science, however, results in equivocation, and he sometimes presents empirical evidence as the sole factor in deciding theoretical change (e.g., p. 128). Nonetheless, at its best, his discussion describes theoretical advance as motivated by an admixture of philosophical debate, ideological exigencies, and empirical-methodological advances.

128. For the definition of horizontal and vertical differentiation in scientific development by Rolf Klima, see the discussion in n. 29 above.

129. Popper, *Logic of Discovery* (n. 73 above), p. 42.

130. It is interesting that this kind of theoretical recourse was actually very well formulated by Popper himself.

> It is always possible to find some way of avoiding falsification, for example by introducing *ad hoc* an auxiliary hypothesis, or by changing *ad hoc* a definition. It is even possible without logical inconsistency to adopt the position of simply refusing to acknowledge any falsifying experience whatsoever. (Ibid.)

But although logically conceivable, Popper argues that this is not the actual recourse of the "empirical method," whose purpose "is not to save the lives of untenable systems" (ibid.). The postpositivist position implies the opposite: what is logically admissible is, usually, what theoretically occurs.

This faith in the disinterested rationality of the scientist is itself, of course, a certain type of nonempirical assumption. As Habermas wrote in reference to Popper, "a critique of knowledge that claims to be free of presuppositions . . . must always already know more than it can know according to its own stated premises" (*Knowledge and Human Interests*, [n. 9 above], p. 12).

131. Polanyi, *Personal Knowledge* (n. 76 above), p. 292.

132. Lakatos, "Criticism and the Methodology" (n. 73 above), pp. 168–176.

133. Ibid., pp. 168–169.

134. Ibid.

135. Ibid., p. 171. As these quotations indicate, Lakatos and Kuhn are not so far apart in their conception of scientific development as Lakatos evidently believed. But although he would not disagree with Kuhn that most contradictory experimental evidence is ignored or explained in ad hoc ways, he chooses to emphasize that when major theoretical shifts finally do occur they are usually "progressive," in that they will explain more empirical variation than the theoretical systems which they succeeded. I do not believe that Kuhn actually disagrees with either of these statements, but his emphasis is the opposite of Lakatos'. In the first edition of his book, Kuhn seeks to underline the significance of the nonempirical aspects of theoretical development, and in this context he points out that scientific development may not always be progressive, that new paradigms are sometimes accepted which may not actually explain as much empirical variation overall but rather simply explain more effectively a theoretically-crucial empirical anomaly. But Kuhn does acknowledge in that first edition, and emphasizes in his later "Reflections on My Critics" that there usually is an overall growth in the explanatory power of scientific systems (n. 97 above, p. 264).

The real difference between the two writers, in this respect, is less significant than Lakatos believed it to be. It rests on the fact that Lakatos appears to view the ultimate abandonment of a general theoretical system as a deliberate decision based on the awareness of a failure of theoretical explanatory power ("Falsification and the Methodology of Scientific Research Programmes" in Lakatos and Musgrave [n. 97 above], pp. 174–175). Kuhn, in contrast, holds that although the abandonment is related to unresolved empirical anomaly, it is more of a nondeliberate gestalt decision that ultimately rests upon more general and less explicit assumptions. (See Kuhn's criticism of Lakatos' emphasis on the deliberate and conscious quality of decision making in paradigm shifts, "Reflections on My Critics" [n. 97 above], pp. 238–241.)

The idea that overall factual accumulation is not inconsistent with the dogmatic and horizontal development of any particular theoretical system is articulated by Martindale in the conclusion to his book on the massive and continuing controversies that have marked the history of theoretical sociology.

A common stock of terms, concepts, and empirical generalizations is increasingly shared by all schools; indeed, the ability to explain the established "facts" of the field becomes a kind of first step in determining the acceptability of a theory. . . . Each new formation of theory remains inconclusive until it is able to explain successfully those facts explained by its rivals. (*Nature and Types* [n. 60 above], p. 541.)

136. Stinchcombe, "Levels of Generality" (n. 1 above), p. 53. Stinchcombe's formulation is also important because it makes particularly clear that the postpositivist position is not an argument against the possibility of refuting any particular theoretical formulation per se, but rather an argument against the possible falsification of an entire theoretical orientation. In specifying the different levels of possible refutation, Stinchcombe's discussion resembles Holton's in contributing to a more cautious, nonconflationary elaboration of the kind of postpositivist position initiated by Kuhn.

I have earlier noted how incongruous this formulation is in relation to the positivist philosophy of science which dominates the initial section of Stinchcombe's book (see n. 28 above).

137. Butterfield, *Origins of Modern Science* (n. 90 above), p. 17. Koyré expresses this same point:

If and when he [the Aristotelian physicist] encounters a "fact" that does not fit into his theory, he denies its existence. And if he cannot deny it, he explains it. And it is in the explanation of this fact apparently incompatible with his theory that Aristotle gives us the measure of his genius. (*Metaphysics and Measurement* [n. 87 above], p. 27.)

138. Lakatos, "Criticism and the Methodology," (n. 73 above), p. 155.

139. Thus, Lakatos continues: ". . . even if Keplerian ellipses had refuted the Cartesian theory of vortices, only Newton's theory made us reject it; even if Mercury's perihelion refuted Newtonian gravitation, only Einstein's theory made us reject it" (ibid.).

140. This problem indicates how, just as the four postulates of the positivist persuasion were logically interdependent, so are these four postpositivist postulates. (1) If scientific data were not theoretically informed, (2) there would ultimately be no grounds for accepting evidence other than the experimental, (3) nor for envisioning anything but vertical, progressive scientific development, (4) nor for accepting the inherent need for generalized argument in any major shift in scientific commitment.

The interrelationship of these postulates is illustrated in the writings of the philosopher of science Abraham Kaplan. Even more strongly than Nagel, Kaplan criticizes radical positivism and argues for the independent importance of sociological theory. For example, he writes:

We say that a theory is true if it "fits the facts," that is, if the predictions made on the basis of the theory are in fact fulfilled. Yet it cannot be forgotten that how we conceptualize the facts in turn depends on the theories which play a part in this cognition. (*The Conduct of Inquiry* [New York, 1964], p. 313.)

Yet Kaplan cannot, in the last analysis, break away from the concrete perception of empirical data. As he continues his argument:

> The circle here is not, so far as I can see, a vicious one, necessarily; it becomes vicious only if the facts are wholly constituted by the theory they are adduced to support, if they lack *an observational core.*" (ibid., italics added).

For this reason, despite his obvious intention, Kaplan must ultimately undermine the autonomy of the non-empirical element of science.

> Every appeal to "the facts" rests on a bedrock of common sense. . . . Every problematic situation occurs within a . . . matrix of the unproblematic. . . . It is perfectly proper to criticize a theory by showing how much violence it does to what is already accepted as fact . . .
> Science is governed fundamentally by the reality principle, its thought checked and controlled by the characteristics of the things it thinks about. There is in science a kind of natural piety, a submission of the will to a world not our making; we have learned that when nature is in command our will prevails only when we have first obeyed. (Pp. 312–313.)

By being unable to fully accept the first postpositivist principle, Kaplan has been forced to concede all the rest.

The same kind of problem besets the argument advanced by John Rex in *Key Problems in Sociological Theory* (n. 3 above). Like Kaplan's work, Rex's discussion presents one of the most powerful nonpositivist perspectives on the need for sui generis theoretical argument in the social sciences. Yet, also like Kaplan, Rex's support for independent theoretical argument founders because of his reluctance to accept the analytic as opposed to concrete distinction between theory and fact. Specifically, Rex provides strong criticisms of the logical inconsistencies and scientific inadequacies in Popper's empiricist argument that theory should be directly falsifiable (pp. 17–20). But Rex is himself ultimately forced back into the Popperian framework on these grounds: "We can say definitely," he asserts, " . . . that in the event of widespread and consistent falsifications of the basic statements deduced from them scientists reject general hypotheses" (p. 19). But if the role of theory in constituting different perceptions of fact is ignored, such apparent falsification only supports an empiricist perspective. The contradictory situation within which Rex finds himself is indicated by the ad hoc hypotheses he must now attach to the falsification thesis, qualifications which rob it of its predictive power. Falsification, Rex writes, "cannot be applied too rigidly" because "ultimately this question is a moral one" and should be left to the "discretion" of the individual scientist (p. 19).

141. Holton, *Thematic Origins* (n. 101 above), p. 99, italics added.

142. Barbour, *Myths* (n. 71 above), p. 114.

143. Holton, *Thematic Origins*, p. 26.

144. Ibid., p. 190.

145. Aron, "Max Weber and Polanyi" (n. 62 above), p. 106.

146. Holton, for example, writes that while "the three-dimensional (xyz) space . . . is required for a more complete analysis . . . of scientific statements," it is not his intention to argue for the introduction of

> thematic discussions or even a self-conscious awareness of themata into the practice of science itself. It is indeed one of the great advantages of scientific activity that in the xy plane many questions—for example, concerning the "reality" of scientific knowledge—cannot be asked. Only when such questions were ruled out of place in a laboratory did science begin to grow rapidly. ("On the Role of Themata" [n. 112 above], pp. 330–331.)

Kuhn expresses his support for this perspective by his claim that continuous philosophical conflict marks a science as "preparadigmatic." See n. 151 below.

147. Collingwood articulates this position by emphasizing in a particular manner the distinction he has drawn between the "absolute presuppositions" that occupy the most metaphysically-related position in science and the "propositions" that are the most directly empirical:

> Absolute presuppositions are not propositions. . . . Absolute presuppositions are never . . . propounded. . . . To be propounded is not their business; their business is to be presupposed. The scientist's business is not to propound them but only to presuppose them. (*Metaphysics* [n. 95 above], pp. 32–33.)

148. Kuhn (n. 97 above), p. 91.

149. In other words, even though there is more disagreement in normal periods of natural science than Kuhn proposes, there remains significantly less disagreement in the relative terms generated by a contrast with social science.

For Dilthey's discussion of the greater proximity of social science to political and cultural concerns, see his "Life and the Human Studies," particularly Part 5, "The Emergence of the Human Studies from the Life of Individuals and Communities," in *Dilthey: Selected Writings* (n. 58 above), pp. 181–182; cf. Hodges, *Wilhelm Dilthey* (n. 58 above), pp. 75–79. For a specific analysis of the political-ideological aspect of this proximity, see Klima's discussion, "Theoretical Pluralism" (n. 29 above), passim. These two factors affecting the degrees of consensus possible in the natural and social scientific communities—the ideological and the methodological barriers—are consistent with the factors cited by Hagstrom in his discussion of the causes for shifting degrees of consensus in natural science. Hagstrom argues that the possibilities for consensus depend, among other things, on the "intellectual scope of disagreement" that occurs in a given discipline and on the degree of quantification that is consistent with that discipline's scientific goals (*Scientific Community* [n. 109 above], pp. 256–258). Specifically addressing the comparative lack of ideological dispute in the natural sciences, he writes that while groups within the scientific community have ideologies, their "specific *theories* are only remotely linked to such ideologies." As a result, natural "scientific theories are only rarely, and then pathologically, ideologies to justify the power of groups. . . . Thus changes in the content of science do not usually imply changes in social structures" (p. 285, italics added). In the social sciences, of course, exactly the opposite is the case.

150. As Eckberg and Hill put the matter in their critical review of recent attempts to utilize Kuhn's paradigm concept:

> Those who state so emphatically that sociology "has" a paradigm (or paradigms) must support their assertions by showing that research in sociology is guided by concrete examples of scholarship, upon which the new research is modeled in a continuous process. What we often actually find is research modeled upon no other research at all, upon a short, soon extinguished line of research, or upon a theorist's speculations. There is little of the puzzle-solving of which Kuhn speaks. ("Paradigm Concept" [n. 109 above], p. 26.)

151. The argument that continual generalized conflict represents only the "preparadigmatic," preparatory stage of social science was first advanced by Kuhn and has been supported by those social scientists who have strictly adopted his framework—e.g., Friedrichs (see also Larsons, *Major Themes* [n. 2 above], p. 32). The effect of this argument has been, paradoxically, to reinforce the positivist persuasion that a truly mature social science can be concerned only with strictly empirical concerns. (Even Holton, who views his own emphasis on themata as an endorsement of the more metaphysically-oriented writing in contemporary social science, still associates such general argument with the relative youth of the social sciences [*Thematic Origins*, p. 13]).

Those analysts who have wished to take a more positive approach to theoretical conflict in the social sciences and to remain, nevertheless, within the Kuhnian framework have been led to modify Kuhn's association of scientific maturity with theoretical agreement, at least for the case of sociology. These two different approaches to Kuhn on this issue are clearly, though implicitly, manifest in two essays on paradigm conflict in sociology written by Andrew Effrat. Whereas in his first essay, in 1968, Effrat suggested the notion that efforts to elaborate Parsonian theory are contributions to the resolution of the preparadigmatic period of sociology ("Editor's Introduction," *Sociological Inquiry* 38, no. 2 [1968]:

103), in his 1972 essay he suggests that the "complete liberation" of sociology from paradigm conflict "may be impossible—perhaps even undesirable" ("Power to the Paradigms" [n. 102 above], p. 32). See also Ritzer's discussion, "Sociology: A Multi-Paradigm Science" (n. 102 above), passim.

152. Habermas similarly connects the perception of objectivity in the natural sciences to consensus rather than to its ontological status in his discussion of Charles Pierce's early critique of positivism:

> We term information scientific if and only if an uncompelled and permanent consensus can be obtained with regard to its validity. . . . The genuine achievement of modern science does not consist primarily in producing true, that is, correct and cogent statements about what we call reality. Rather, it distinguishes itself from traditional categories of knowledge by a method of arriving at an uncompelled and permanent consensus of this sort about our views. (*Knowledge and Human Interests* [n. 9 above], p. 91.)

CHAPTER TWO

1. Each of the following books begins with a refutation of positivist or empiricist theories of scientific development as a justification for the exercise in general theoretical argument that is the focus of the remainder of each work: Talcott Parsons, *The Structure of Social Action*, New York, [1937] 1968; John Rex, *Key Problems of Sociological Theory* (London, 1961); Percy Cohen, *Modern Social Theory* (London, 1968); M. S. Mulkay, *Functionalism, Exchange, and Theoretical Strategy* (London, 1971); Alvin W. Gouldner, *The Coming Crisis of Western Sociology* (New York, 1970); Anthony Giddens, *Capitalism and Modern Social Theory* (Cambridge, 1971); Peter P. Ekeh, *Social Exchange Theory: The Two Traditions* (Cambridge, Mass., 1974). Although these do not, of course, exhaust the major theoretical efforts of recent times, they are more than simply a representative sample.

2. In a series of reviews that discuss a wide range of contemporary social thought, from Marxism and psychoanalysis to functionalism, critical theory, and empiricism, I have tried to examine the relationship between problematic conceptions of science and substantive theoretical difficulties. The reviews are of T. B. Bottomore, *Sociology as Social Criticism* (*American Journal of Sociology* 81 [1976]:1220–1223); S. N. Eisenstadt and M. Curelaru, *The Form of Sociology: Paradigms and Crises* (*Contemporary Sociology* 6 [1977]:658–661); Leo Rangell, *The Mind of Watergate* (*New Republic*, March 29, 1980); John Goudsblom, *Sociology in the Balance* (*American Journal of Sociology* 85 [1980]:1259–1262); Arthur L. Stinchcombe, *Theoretical Methods in Social History*, and Richard J. Bernstein, *The Restructuring of Social and Political Theory* (*Theory and*

Society 10 [1981]:272–292); François Bourricaud, *L'Individualisme In-*
stitutionnel (*Contemporary Sociology* 10 [1981]:500–505).

3. Despite the fact that, as I have argued above (ch. 1, sec. 4.2), his
analysis of what these metaphysically oriented aspects are must be
viewed as seriously in error, Robert W. Friedrichs provides an excellent
formal analysis of the range of nonempirical commitments involved in
specific scientific processes like problem selection, hypothesis construction, and validation (*A Sociology of Sociology* [New York, 1970], pp. 135–
165).

4. A good example on the most abstract, philosophical level of analysis of the kind of confusion that develops if the generality criterion is not
modified by this stricture about triviality can be found in R. G. Collingwood's insightful argument in *Metaphysics* (London, 1940, ch. 4, 5). Collingwood emphasized that every scientific statement "presupposes"
more general "questions." There exists, according to this analysis, a
whole range of such presuppositional questions which differ in generality and specificity. At the most general level of thought are what Collingwood called "absolute presuppositions" that address the most
metaphysically-related issues. In terms of this presentation of the problem, my purpose here is to find those "absolute" presuppositions which
cannot be subsumed under what Collingwood calls "relative" presuppositions. But the distinctions in terminology should also be noted. In
Collingwood's terms, each of the levels of the scientific continuum beyond the observational are "presuppositions." In my terms, only the
most general level of such nonobservational elements, which he calls the
absolute presuppositions, are categorized as presuppositions.

There is, however, a problem that is posed by the manner in which
Collingwood presents his arguments—for how can one determine what
are really absolute and not simply relative presuppositions? There can,
in principle, always be more general questions which logically precede
those that I have chosen. Yet many of these, though more general, would
undoubtedly be inconsequential in terms of the gist of a particular argument. To avoid this problem, one should modify Collingwood's argument
in the following way. Absolute presuppositions vary according to the nature of the particular kind of scientific or intellectual activity at hand.
Criteria for establishing them can be established only according to specific and differentiated kinds of intellectual purposes. Given such a modi-
fication, one can also avoid the residue of relativism that detracts from
Collingwood's argument about science; for, as I will try to demonstrate in
ch. 4, one can "objectively" evaluate the validity of absolute presuppositions in terms of whether or not they accomplish their distinctive scientific task.

For an excellent secondary discussion which draws out the implications of Collingwood's rather unfocused discussion in a manner that is

complementary to the present analysis, see Stephen Toulmin's *Human Understanding* (Princeton, N.J., 1972, pp. 65–83). In particularly emphasizing the problem of relativism in Collingwood's approach, however, Toulmin overstates his case. It is not true, as Toulmin charges, that for Collingwood absolute presuppositions simply cannot be evaluated. Collingwood's point, rather, is that they cannot be evaluated "scientifically"; they can, he believes, be evaluated "metaphysically." The confusion here lies in the conception of science. As I argued in the preceding chapter, it is possible to understand a certain type of generalized argument as "objective" if science is not identified as an activity that considers only empirical phenomena. Toulmin does support such a postpositivist understanding. Perhaps the reason that he nevertheless arrives at this radical criticism of Collingwood is that he himself is concerned primarily with the problem of finding criteria to evaluate the basis of scientific change, while this issue is not Collingwood's central concern. As a result, though Collingwood does evaluate different metaphysical assumptions in themselves, his argument offers no criteria for evaluating the progress or regress of scientific change. To the extent, however, that Toulmin criticizes Collingwood's anti-objective conception of metaphysical evaluation, his criticism is on the mark.

5. For a description of these questions as defining the most general, nonempirical level of scientific debate, see Koyré's analysis of the influence of Greek culture on Aristotelian physics in ch. 1, sec. 4.1, above.

6. For the argument that intellectual integrity depends upon maintaining complexity and, more particularly, the autonomy of generalized analytical concerns, see my "Looking for Theory: 'Facts' and 'Values' as the Intellectual Legacy of the 1970's," *Theory and Society* 10 (1981):279–292.

7. This definition of ideology is consistent with that provided by Clifford Geertz in "Ideology as a Cultural System," in his *The Interpretation of Cultures* (New York, 1973), pp. 193–233.

8. Karl Mannheim, "Conservative Thought," in Kurt H. Wolff, ed., *From Karl Mannheim* (New York, 1971), p. 142.

9. Ibid.

10. Ibid.

11. The logical conclusion of this position, in fact, leads to the redefinition of the term "positivism" itself. Instead of the postpositivist persuasion being identified with the recognition of nonempirical elements in science, it is now characterized by the existence only of those nonempirical elements that can be associated with a particular type of social action, namely, those that are opposed to the political status quo. This is the main point of Herbert Marcuse's approach to positivism in *Reason and Revolution* (Boston, [1941] 1960).

12. Mannheim, "The Problem of a Sociology of Knowledge," in *From Karl Mannheim*, p. 65, italics in original.

13. Ibid.

14. Ibid., italics in original.

15. Mannheim, "Conservative Thought," ibid., p. 148, italics added.

16. Stark, *The Fundamental Forms of Social Thought* (London, 1962).

17. See Reinhard Bendix, "Social Science and the Image of Man," and his and Bennett Berger's "Images of Society and Problems of Concept Formation in Sociology," in Bendix, *Embattled Reason* (New York, 1970), pp. 3–17, 116–138.

18. I will discuss this work in more detail below; see note 72.

19. Mills, "Situated Actions and Vocabularies of Motive," *American Sociological Review* 5 (1940):904–913.

20. See Mills, "The Professional Ideology of Social Pathologists," *American Journal of Sociology* 49 (1943):165–180, and idem, *The Sociological Imagination* (New York, 1961), pp. 78–118.

21. Coser, *The Functions of Social Conflict* (New York, 1956), pp. 15–20, 26–29.

22. Horton, "Order and Conflict Theories of Social Problems as Competing Ideologies," *American Journal of Sociology* 71 (1966):701–713.

23. The criticisms made in ch. 1 against Kuhn's conceptualization of the paradigm notion, particularly the more recent focus on exemplars and groups as the basis of scientific commitment, can be reformulated in terms of the perspective developed here. The conflation inherent in the paradigm concept promotes the reduction of intellectual argument to the sociology of knowledge. In addition to Friedrichs' work, this reduction is well illustrated by Mullins' discussions. It is significant that those few analysts of social science who have attempted a more differentiated use of the paradigm concept, like Andrew Effrat, have simultaneously argued, at least formally, against any exact correspondence between the ideological component of sociological thought and other theoretical elements (see Andrew Effrat, "Power to the Paradigms," *Sociological Inquiry* 43, no. 3–4 [1972]:3–34.) Among the early formulations of the postpositivist perspectives, Alexandre Koyré's work contains an argument against the equation of a nonpositivist conception of science with ideological determinism. Koyré contends that Galileo's presuppositional framework must be understood in terms of more general cultural and intellectual issues rather than in terms of more specific changes in social and economic patterns. (*Metaphysics and Measurement* [Cambridge, Mass., 1968], passim.)

24. Friedrichs, *A Sociology of Sociology* (n. 3 above) pp. 135 ff.

25. Gouldner, *Coming Crisis* (n. 1 above), pp. 12–13 ff.

26. Ibid., pp. 88–163.

27. For a recent utilization of this kind of distinction to describe a major theoretical orientation in contemporary sociology, see T. B. Bottomore's discussion in "Competing Paradigms in Macrosociology," *Annual Review of Sociology*, Alex Inkeles, James Coleman, Neil Smelser, eds. (1975):195–197. An example of the use of the designation "critical" to cover a broad range of otherwise disparate sociological theories is David L. Sallach's "Critical Theory and Critical Sociology: A Second Synthesis," *Sociological Inquiry* 43, no. 2 (1973):131–140. Among many others, Rolf Klima's article "Theoretical Pluralism, Methodological Dissension and the Role of the Sociologist: The West German Case" (*Social Science Information*, June–August 1972, pp. 59–102) is a representative illustration of the utilization of one of the thrusts of Habermas' work to portray sociological theory as facing the simple choice between empiricism and "critical" theory, with no other alternatives possible. Actually, Habermas himself describes three independent choices as determinant of what he calls "cognitive interest": technical-empirical, hermeneutic-value oriented, and critical-ideological. However, in one aspect of his writing, which I will discuss in the following section, Habermas argues that these three phases are tightly connected in a manner determined by the thinker's philosophy-of-science commitments and his social situation.

In terms of this contemporary and less orthodox application of Mannheim's reductionist understanding, I should also mention here an attempt to apply this reduction to natural science itself, which Mannheim himself actually allowed a transcendental, nonsocial status. Of course, in a broader and less directly Mannheimian sense a "social" approach to natural scientific knowledge is precisely the position that all postpositivist philosophy and history of science recommends; but recently a more literal sociology-of-knowledge approach to natural science has been promoted by the Social Studies Unit at Edinburgh University. A social approach to natural science becomes objectionable only when its explanation follows Mannheim's latently instrumentalist sociology of knowledge too closely. In doing so, it reduces scientific knowledge to the objective interests of scientists rather than understanding how science forms a distinctive cultural tradition mediated by a number of independent factors, both cultural and material. Within the Edinburgh group, just this bifurcation can be observed. Barry Barnes, in *Scientific Knowledge and Sociological Theory* (London, 1974), offers a nuanced and culturally sensitive approach to the determinism of natural science. David Bloor, in contrast, proposes what he terms the "strong programme in the sociology of knowledge" in his *Knowledge and Social Imagery* (London, 1976), a program overtly materialistic and reductionist in its approach to explanation. Though Bloor identifies his approach as Durkheimian, I will try to demonstrate in volume 2 that such a materialistic sociologism cannot be viewed as an accurate application of Durkheim's mature work.

28. Elie Halévy, *The Growth of Philosophic Radicalism*, pts. 1–3 ([1901–1904] Clifton, N.J., 1972), pp. 136–140 and passim.

29. See, for example, ibid., pp. 181–224, 318–341.

30. See, for example, Nisbet's "Ideology and Sociology" in his *The Sociological Tradition* (New York, 1966), pp. 16–18. It is Nisbet's own ideological intentions which are illuminated by the fact that despite the separation he achieves between ideology and other kinds of general presuppositions he still chooses to characterize his distinctively theoretical concepts as "conservative" categories.

31. Lukes, *Emile Durkheim* (New York, 1972), pp. 245–54, 320–360, 538–546; Bellah, ed., *Emile Durkheim on Morality and Society* (Chicago, 1973), pp. xv–xviii, xxxvi–xxxvii; Marks, "Durkheim's Theory of Anomie," *American Journal of Sociology* 80 (1974):329–363; J-C Filloux, *Durkheim et le socialisme* (Geneva and Paris, 1975).

It is, nonetheless, a testimony to Mannheim's greatness as a social theorist—in terms of the criterion I advanced in ch. 1—that in his essay on "Conservative Thought" he actually anticipated exactly these challenges to his attempt at ideological reduction. To rebut them he added onto his central arguments a series of qualifications, or ad hoc hypotheses which, if fully incorporated, would have destroyed the consistency and efficacy of his basic line of argument. For example, to avoid the kinds of problems Halévy raises, Mannheim claimed, on the one hand, that natural-rights theory was actually a form of rationalist utilitarianism, a position that Halévy refutes, and, on the other hand, that the thought of some of the principals of radical thought, like Rousseau and Montesquieu, was actually intermixed with the irrationalist romanticism that characterizes conservative thought, a fact which though true is completely inconsistent with Mannheim's basic explanation. In relation to the types of problems raised by the recent discussions of Durkheim, Mannheim further qualifies his theory by asserting that while the proletariat could be viewed as the most rationalistic of all social groups, it also absorbed the Romantic irrationalism of the conservative critique of capitalism, hence the organicist quality of much of socialist thought. Here, in other words, after already qualifying his theory's application to the bourgeois case, he stipulates that it not be applied at all to the proletariat's. Finally, in regard to the sorts of propositions raised by Nisbet, we can find in Mannheim the qualification that once a style of thought has first been formulated, its contents can, in the course of subsequent historical development, become relatively dissociated from their original ideological implications. If taken seriously, this qualification would vitiate entirely the applicability of Mannheim's categories to late-nineteenth- and twentieth-century thought.

32. Dick Atkinson, *Orthodox Consensus and Radical Alternative* (New York, 1972); Bob Jessop, *Social Order, Reform, and Revolution* (London, 1972); Ekeh, *Social Exchange Theory* (n. 1 above); Jonathan H. Turner, *The Structure of Sociological Theory* (Homewood, Ill., 1974); Harold Bershady, *Ideology and Social Knowledge* (New York, 1973); Guy Rocher, *Talcott Parsons and American Sociology* (New York, 1975).

33. Bottomore, "Karl Marx: Sociologist or Marxist," in his *Sociology as Social Criticism* (New York, 1974), pp. 80–84. For an elaboration of this problem in Bottomore's thought, see my review in *American Journal of Sociology* 81 (1976):1220–1223.

34. Ernest Nagel, *The Structure of Science* (New York, 1961), 488–494.

35. In order to support his positivist distinction between fact and theory (described in ch. 1), Goode engages in an extensive demonstration of the possibility for sociology to produce propositions that are not coextensive with political statements (William J. Goode, *Explorations in Sociological Theory* [New York, 1973], pp. 14–16, 33–63). And Catton, in a historical sketch of the origins of sociology, writes that

> Before a genuine social science could emerge, [it] had to become possible to suspend ethical judgment so that social phenomena could be studied cognitively rather than evaluatively, [and sociology] had to outgrow the tendency to appraise its theories in terms of their moral impact rather than their empirical validity (William R. Catton, Jr., *From Animistic to Naturalistic Sociology* [New York, 1966], p. 49.)

Catton relies here on Don Martindale's description of the importance of the differentiation between moral, philosophical, and empirical thought in the origins of modern science in *The Nature and Types of Sociological Theory* (Cambridge, Mass., 1960). Yet as I argue in ch. 1, it is clear from Martindale's book considered in its entirety that, despite his ambiguity, such a notion of differentiation does not prevent him from allowing great causal significance to all kinds of nonempirical presuppositions.

36. Jürgen Habermas, *Knowledge and Human Interests* (Boston, 1971), p. 311, italics in original.

37. M. J. Mulkay, *Functionalism, Exchange and Theoretical Strategy* (London, 1971), passim.

38. Friedrichs (n. 3 above), pp. 135–258.

39. Habermas, *Toward a Rational Society* (Boston, 1970), particularly "Technical Progress and the Social Life World" and "Technology and Science as Ideology," pp. 31–49, 81–122. This Habermasian tendency is carried to its logical extreme in the work of Richard J. Bernstein, who argues, in *The Restructuring of Social and Political Theory* (Philadelphia, 1978), that all "empirical" theory is fundamentally conservative. For a critique of the conflationary element in Bernstein's work, and a discus-

sion of how such reduction parallels the logic of empiricism itself, see my "Looking for Theory: 'Facts' and 'Values' as the Intellectual Legacy of the 1970's," (n. 6 above).

40. The logic of Parsons' description of the effects of the positivist position is the following. "Being rational," Parsons writes, "consists in these [positivist] terms precisely in becoming a scientist relative to one's own action." From this he is led to the conclusion that

> "Short of the ultimate boundaries of science, irrationality, then, is only [held to be] possible so long as actors are not in possession of the logically possible complement of knowledge affecting human affairs."

In other words, positivism cannot perceive, cannot countenance, a social theory that allows for irrational action.

> It follows further: if the explanation of irrationality on a positivistic basis must lie in factors not in fact known, but intrinsically capable of being known scientifically to the actor, these factors must be found . . . capable of non-subjective formulation, that is in the material conditions of action. (*The Structure of Social Action* [n. 1 above], pp. 66–67.)

By tracing Habermas' conflation back to Parsons, I do not wish to imply that Parsons' *Structure* was his only inspiration. The identification of positivism with a rationalistic perspective on action is deeply rooted in the history of social thought, as I will indicate in chapter 3.

41. Horton, "Order and Conflict Theories of Social Problems as Competing Ideologies" (n. 22 above), p. 702.

42. See Neil J. Smelser, *Essays in Sociological Explanation* (Englewood Cliffs, N.J., 1968), pp. 262–268, the section "The Organization of Variables into Equilibrium Systems to Analyze Social Change," in the article entitled "Toward a General Theory of Social Change."

43. Coser, *The Functions of Social Conflict* (n. 21 above), passim.

44. Ralf Dahrendorf, *Class and Class Conflict in Industrial Society* (Stanford, Calif., 1959), ch. 5; on Dahrendorf's relation to Coser, see particularly his remarks on p. 209.

45. Rex, *Key Problems* (n. 1 above), particularly ch. 5. Rex pointedly criticizes Coser's functionalism and value emphasis, and Dahrendorf's failure to link conflict with the economy, pp. 115–120.

46. Martindale, *The Nature and Types of Sociological Theory* (n. 35 above), pp. 127–175.

47. Friedrichs, *A Sociology of Sociology* (n. 3 above), pp. 26–27.

48. Timothy Lehmann and T. R. Young, "From Conflict Theory to Conflict Methodology: An Emerging Paradigm for Sociology," *Sociological Inquiry* 44, no. 1 (1974): 15–88. For a discussion of the problems in this essay, see ch. 1, n. 102.

49. Dahrendorf (n. 44 above), chs. 5, 6.

50. Lockwood, "Some Remarks on 'The Social System,'" *British Journal of Sociology* 7, no. 2 (1956):134–146. For a detailed and penetrating critique of this essay from a perspective that accepts the need for theoretical emphasis on conflict and change but challenges Lockwood's particular emphasis on coercion and factual elements, see Cohen's discussion in *Modern Social Theory* (n. 1 above), pp. 107–118, 190–191. (Note, however, that in a later and widely cited essay, "Social Integration and System Integration," in George K. Zollschen and Walter Hirsch, eds., *Explorations in Social Change* [Boston, 1964], pp. 244–257, Lockwood implicitly reverses his position, offering a devastating critique of the argument by "conflict theorists" that disequilibrium is necessarily tied to the predominance of instrumental over normative action and order.)

51. Horton (n. 22 above), p. 704.

52. Collins, *Conflict Sociology* (New York, 1975), p. 57.

53. Coser, *The Functions of Social Conflict* (n. 21 above). Only this contestation over a theoretical level of analysis that is not explicitly acknowledged by conflict theory itself can explain the critical review by Coser of Collins' *Conflict Sociology*. In terms of the present schema, although Coser applauds Collins' emphasis on conflict at the level of empirical proposition, he takes Collins to task for his exclusive concern with coercion at a more general level of argument:

> I am prepared to go a long way with Collins along this road, but I must part with his company when his emphasis on the conflictful elements in human interaction threatens ... to become a pan-conflict imperialism.... This book ... neglects those areas where scarcity is not a factor. In the religious order, or in the universe of nationalism, success of some does not depend on the failure of others.... Had Collins paid more attention to these noncompetitive spheres, he would have gained access to an understanding of integrative forces in the social order that are now a closed book for him. (*American Journal of Sociology* 81 [1976]:1509–1510.)

Although Coser characteristically presents this critique as one of an overemphasis on conflict as opposed to equilibrium, he is clearly referring to a cross-cutting problem on a more general level.

54. Rex, *Key Problems in Sociological Theory* (n. 1 above), pp. 124–126. Atkinson, in his major theoretical work, (*Orthodox Consensus and Radical Alternative* [n. 32 above], pp. 88–89), recognizes only this aspect of Rex's argument, emphasizing its continuity with Rex's later work on racial conflict. In terms of this interpretation, it is quite correct, as I noted above, to emphasize as Atkinson does the continuity between Rex's position and that of Parsons. For example, at an earlier point in his discussion Atkinson characterizes Parsons in a manner that points, quite obviously, to his later discussion of Rex:

It seems important to emphasize that there is nothing in his [Parsons'] theory, as we have so far seen it develop [i.e., through 1954], which precludes the possibility of offering an explanatory model of conflict. It is quite reasonable to imagine two or more opposed groups, each integrated in exactly the way we have discussed, in place of the assumption of a single unified system. (P. 25.)

55. Rex, *Key Problems*, pp. 92–115, 136–144. It should perhaps be added that Rex still considers himself at this point to be speaking within the action framework. I will elaborate on this break in his theoretical analysis further in my discussion of rationality in ch. 3.

56. Shils polemicizes against the attempt to monopolize the study of empirical conflict by the "conflict theory" approach in the introduction to his *Center and Periphery: Essays in Macrosociology* (Chicago, 1975, pp. xii–xiii), in which he focuses on the origins of social conflict in the cultural tension between sacred and profane ideals. John Finley Scott, in *Internalization of Norms* (Englewood Cliffs, N.J., 1971, pp. 42–44), and Blake and Davis, in "Norms, Values, and Sanctions" in R. E. L. Faris, ed., *Handbook of Modern Sociology* [Skokie, Ill., 1964], pp. 456–484), argue that conflict theorists incorrectly oppose the existence of norms per se and suggest, instead, a recognition of normatively-inspired conflict. In "Some Further Comments on Chronic Controversies," Robin M. Williams, Jr., responds to Horton's article by emphasizing the possible role of value orientations in originating conflict (*American Sociological Review* 71 [1966]:717–721). (See also in this regard Williams' *American Society* [New York, 1963], chs. 10, 11.) For Smelser's emphasis on the conflict-creating possibilities of value commitments, see his *Social Change in the Industrial Revolution* (Chicago, 1959, pp. 66–79), *Theory of Collective Behavior* (New York, 1962, chs. 9 and 10), *Essays in Sociological Explanation* (n. 42 above, chs. 6, 8), and "Growth, Structural Change, and Conflict in California Public Higher Education, 1950–1970," in Smelser and Gabriel Almond, eds. *Public Higher Education in California* (Berkeley and Los Angeles, 1975).

57. Dahrendorf, *Class and Class Conflict in Industrial Society* (n. 44 above), pp. 206–279.

58. Walter L. Wallace's "Overview of Sociological Theory" (in Wallace, ed., *Sociological Theory* [New York, 1969], pp. 1–59) relegates the issue of stability versus change to a level below his basic cross-cutting taxonomy. His dichotomy follows, in a rough way, the truly presuppositional choices I will present below, though there seem to me to be some difficulties with it as well. For my critique of Wallace's general dichotomy, see ch. 3, nn. 30, 153. Although Turner takes conflict theory as an independent generalized category, he still sharply differentiates between the different kinds of conflict theories, in part at least according to their

more general presuppositional differences (*The Structure of Sociological Theory* [n. 32 above], pt. 2). Atkinson makes this distinction very clear by asserting that there actually exists a "convergence" in contemporary sociology about the issues of conflict and equilibrium; and in doing so, he frees himself to discuss the divergence between theoretical writing at more general levels of analysis (*Orthodox Consensus and Radical Alternative* [n. 32 above], pp. 128–140). For discussion of Atkinson's treatment of this more generalized level, see ch. 3, secs. 1, 3.2.

59. *Conflict Sociology*, p. 43.

60. Ibid., pp. 20–21. Collins is actually ambivalent about the precise path by which systems theory is anti-conflict. Here he argues that the path is mediated via systems theory's ideological conservativism.

61. Adams, "Coercion and Consensus Theories: Some Unresolved Issues," *American Sociological Review* 71 (1966):714–717.

62. It is relevant, I think, to quote Giddens' entire statement about this issue:

> It is a familiar theme that, whereas Marx saw society as an unstable system of groups (classes) in conflict, Durkheim conceived of it as a unified whole—as a entity "greater than the sum of its parts"; and that consequently he provided no analysis of the sources of social conflict. The misleading factor in this is the use of the blanket term "society." In order to adjudge upon the validity of the contrast, the only proper comparison is between Marx's and Durkheim's respective analyses of specific *forms* of society, and especially of that type of society which Marx called "bourgeois society" or "capitalism." For if conflict, or class conflict, plays an essential part in Marx's analysis of extant societies, he did, after all, envisage the emergence of a type of society in which such conflict would disappear.... The differences lie, not in the fact that one recognized the fact of class conflict in nineteenth century Europe, while the other ignored it, but in their respective diagnoses of the origins of—and hence the "remedies" for—that conflict. ("Four Myths in the History of Social Thought," *Economy and Society* 1 [1972]:371–372, italics in original.)

In his Introduction to *Karl Marx on Society and Social Change* (Chicago, 1973), Neil J. Smelser also emphasizes that Marx's conception of the social system contains distinctive equilibriating aspects.

63. Friedrichs, *A Sociology of Sociology* (n. 3 above), pp. 294–296.

64. For these points, see, e.g., Blumer, *Symbolic Interactionism: Perspective and Method* (Englewood Cliffs, N.J., 1969), "The Methodological Position of Symbolic Interactionism," pp. 57–60; Martindale, *The Nature and Types of Sociological Theory* (n. 35 above), ch. 17, "The Nature and Origins of Sociological Functionalism," and ch. 18, "Macro-Functionalism in Contemporary Sociology"; Mulkay, *Functionalism, Exchange and Theoretical Strategy* (n. 1 above).

65. Rex, *Key Problems*, "The Need for Models in Sociological Explanation," and "The Model of the Organism," pp. 60–63.

66. Gluckman, *Rituals of Rebellion in South-East Africa* (Manchester, 1954).

67. Coser, *The Functions of Social Conflict* (n. 21 above), Turner, *The Structure of Sociological Theory* (n. 32 above), "Conflict Functionalism," pp. 106–120. See also Piotr Sztompka's refutation of this criticism, "The Charge of Static Bias," in his *System and Function* (New York, 1974), pp. 153–161.

68. Cohen, *Modern Social Theory* (n. 1 above), "Functionalism or the 'Holistic' Approach," pp. 56–58.

To emphasize this aspect of Malinowski's work is not to say, however, that he viewed action exclusively as a rational phenomenon. Peter P. Ekeh has emphasized the "anti-contractual" aspect of Malinowski's work that has been underemphasized in recent sociological writings, particularly those of Homans and Blau. See Ekeh, *Social Exchange Theory* (n. 1 above), pp. 24–30.

69. Alvin W. Gouldner, "The Norm of Reciprocity," *American Sociological Review* 25 (1960):161–179; Piotr Sztompka, "The Logic of Functional Analysis in Sociology and Social Anthropology," *Quality and Quantity* 5, no. 2 (1971):369–388; idem, "Marxism and Functionalism: Foundations of Affinity" (unpublished essay, 1972), and *System and Function* (n. 67 above). In *System and Function*, for example, Sztompka describes the "rational mechanism" of the "purposive-system model" as one approach to the "problem of motivation which makes individuals act in a way functional to the preferred states of the system" (pp. 146–148).

70. Eisenstadt, *The Political System of Empires* (New York, 1963), chs. 4, 9, 12; Smelser *Social Change in the Industrial Revolution* (n. 56 above), passim, and "Growth, Structural Change, and Conflict in California Public Higher Education, 1950–1970" (n. 56 above). As with the discussion of utilitarian functionalism, in referring to this aspect of Eisenstadt's and Smelser's writing I am not implying that they do not consider other types of action but rather that the nonrational, normative reference is combined in their work with an emphasis on conflict. In volume 4 I will argue, in fact, that their theories represent a combination of different approaches to action.

71. Jessop, *Social Order, Reform, and Revolution* (n. 32 above), p. 26, italics added.

Although this second type of conflationary argument usually runs in the sequence I have described—functionalism→normative emphasis→equilibrium commitment→anti-conflict assumptions—it is also possible to view this argument as basing itself on the direct identification of a systems model with an equilibrium emphasis, and the latter, in turn, with the anti-conflict bias. But as Cynthia Eagle Russett forcefully demonstrates in *The Concept of Equilibrium in American Social Thought* (New Haven, Conn., 1966, pp. 160–161, 90–91, 118–119), neither of these identifications is correct. First, and most importantly from the present perspective, a systems model can be adopted without any reference to equilibrium notions, as Russett shows in her discussion of David Easton's theories as well as in her analyses of the "autonomy" of both commitments as they came to be emphasized in the work of Pareto and L. J. Henderson.

Moreover, even if equilibrium systems are assumed, the concept of equilibrium involves choices along at least three different dimensions. Stable versus unstable equilibrium refers to whether or not social development is predictable; stationary versus moving equilibrium refers to whether individual variables change over time; static versus dynamic equilibrium refers to whether there can occur fundamental historical transformations in the nature of the systems concerned. Russett characterizes most contemporary behavioral scientists as adopting the stable–moving–dynamic approach. In other words, her discussion clearly indicates that the equilibrium commitment of systems theory cannot be reduced to a decision about whether or not conflict exists; the matter is rather how this conflict or lack of it should be conceptualized. As Russett concludes her discussion:

> It is simply not accurate, historically or logically, to align equilibrium unequivocally with integration and harmony [since there] is not an a priori reason why a conflict model of equilibrium theory could not be constructed. And so it has been—Gumplowicz, Bentley, and Pareto, to name no others, conceived the social equilibrium as a hotbed of strife among conflicting interests. Pareto even glorified class conflict as the instrument of progressive evolution. Equilibrium cannot safely be identified with concord. (Ibid., pp. 167–168.)

This distinction between the adoption of a systems model and a particular type of systems approach, that of an equilibrium system, and the further distinction within the latter between different approaches to equilibrium systems represents excellent examples of the point made briefly in ch. 1: the levels of the scientific continuum I have identified represent only the grossest level of distinction. Within each category there can be a number of further distinctions made along the same line of generality and specificity.

72. In addition to Martindale's discussion of contemporary functionalism cited above, see his *The Nature and Types of Sociological Theory* (n. 35 above), pp. 51–123, "Positivist Organicism."

Even if one were to accept the reductionist framework of sociology of knowledge, Martindale's argument blurs the more subtle distinctions which Mannheim's utilization of the "organicist" notion sought to achieve. As mentioned above, despite the logically contradictory nature of this insight, Mannheim realized that nonrational organicism could not truthfully be classified simply as a conservative notion, for it also formed a vital part of much socialist theory and ideology. In his attempt to establish the inherent relation between functionalism and conservatism—which serves as the theoretical foundation for his entire work—Martindale largely ignores this refinement.

Since I have mentioned Martindale's *The Nature and Types of Sociological Theory* as containing each of the three major kinds of reductionist arguments discussed in this chapter, a word might be said here about the book taken as a whole. Not surprisingly in view of its extraordinary scope—Martindale discusses almost every major work in social theory over the last two hundred years—the work criticizes theory from a number of different positions that present a range of different conflationary possibilities. Although the plasticity of Martindale's categories make them difficult to define in an exact manner, their main outlines are clear. He presents five "schools" that cover all social theory: Organicism, Conflict Theory, Formalism, Social Behaviorism, and modern Functionalism. The progression of social science is viewed as a response, most of all, to the weaknesses of the first school, Organicism, defined by Martindale as embodying tightly interrelated positions at every level of science—a model of system determinism, empirical propositions about equilibrium and stasis, an ideology of conservatism, and idealist presuppositions.

Critical of each of these commitments, Martindale describes subsequent development as disengaging from this school in distinctive ways. (Basically, this disengagement involves only Conflict Theory and Social Behaviorism, because Formalism is defined in an ad hoc way in relation to Martindale's central categories, and modern Functionalism is taken to be merely a latter-day elaboration of Organicism.) Conflict Theory is described as breaking away from Organicism's equilibrium approach, idealist emphasis, and conservativism, as the figures of Marx and Machiavelli indicate. Yet this classification breaks down. For example, Hegel's emphasis on conflict leads Martindale to describe him as a major figure here, yet his equally great idealism and ideological conservativism would clearly qualify him, according to the standards Martindale has set, for the organicist position. Similarly, while Adam Smith's and Malthus' rationalism and conflict emphases place them, in Martindale's terms, in the conflict school, they certainly were more conservative than the socialist and democratic theorists Tönnies and Durkheim. Yet Martindale has defined conservatism as produced principally by holism and an idealist emphasis—emphases that both Tönnies and Durkheim embraced. Martindale's classifications cannot tolerate the actual variety of social theory because they attempt to make different levels of theory overly dependent on decisions about conflict.

The same kind of problem arises for the other major classification, Social Behaviorism, which is described by Martindale as emphasizing a nominalist approach over and against both organicist and conflict theory, as well as transcending Organicism's static and conservative biases. Here again, this category is too broadly defined actually to describe the variations and patterns of social theory. Max Weber, for example, is described by Martindale as one of the principal figures in this school and is placed, therefore, alongside the theorists of symbolic interactionism. Yet Weber certainly emphasizes conflict as much as any member of Martindale's Conflict school, and he conceptualizes nonindividualistic *groups* more than Smith, and as much as Bentham, Marx, or Malthus. Or to consider the symbolic interactionist Mead, does Mead's Social Behaviorism make him any more nominalist or partial to conflict than Smith? In other words, significant commonality between Behaviorists and so-called Conflict theorists is camouflaged by Martindale's classifications. The same goes for some of the distinctions between Behaviorism and organicist Functionalist theory. Is Weber more ideologically radical than Tönnies? Does his individualism make him more subjectivist, as Martindale claims, than Parsons? We see, once again, how the attempt to emphasize one theoretical level as decisive over all others—in this case the presuppositional problem about the role of the individual in creating social order—makes a framework too inflexible to encompass theoretical variation.

It is because of this general tendency for conflationary argument that Martindale's book, despite its fantastic erudition, has appeared to many critics as overly vague and general in its critical aspect.

73. Mills, *The Sociological Imagination* (n. 20 above), pp. 40–44; Zeitlin, *Ideology and the Development of Sociological Theory* (Englewood Cliffs, N.J., 1968), pp. 234–280; Gouldner, *The Coming Crisis of Western Sociology* (n. 1 above), pp. 138–156, 246–338; Bottomore, "Conservative Man" and "Out of This World: The Sociological Theory of Talcott Parsons," in his *Sociology as Social Criticism* (n. 33 above), pp. 19–43. The fact that I have previously cited most of these same writings in my criticisms of other forms of reductionism simply indicates the extent to which these authors conflate the different levels of theoretical analysis.

74. See Robert K. Merton, *On Theoretical Sociology* (New York, 1967), "Manifest and Latent Functions," pp. 73–138, particularly the section "Functional Analysis as Ideology," pp. 91–100; and Cohen, *Modern Social Theory* (n. 1 above), "Functionalism or the 'Holistic' Approach," pp. 34–68, particularly the section "Criticisms: Ideological," pp. 58–64. Cohen's discussion specifically addresses the critiques of "functionalist" stratification and power theories.

75. Merton, pp. 73–138; Kingsley Davis, "The Myth of Functional Analysis as a Special Method in Sociology and Anthropology," *American Sociological Review* 24 (1959):757–773; Goode, *Explorations in Sociological Theory* (n. 35 above), "Functionalism: The Empty Castle," pp. 64–94; Cohen, pp. 34–68; Sztompka, *System and Function* (n. 67 above), particularly "System-Functional Models: Substantial Continuities in Sociological Theory," pp. 35–132.

A specific qualification must be made here with reference to Davis' discussion. While Davis cogently illuminates the broad kinds of commitments that functionalism implies, he also puts forward the proposal that these commitments are convergent with those that any sociological analysis entails. Such a position is reductionistic, either eliminating the autonomy of the model level of analysis or claiming that there can be only one such model. In fact, Davis can make this argument only by claiming that the approaches which have been called antifunctionalist—psychologism, interactionism, idealism, empiricism—are actually antisociological and should not be considered as competing forms of sociological analysis. In so doing, Davis seriously conflates presuppositional, propositional, ideological, and model levels of analysis.

This criticism leads to a more general point that should also be emphasized. The correctness of this broad approach to "systems" does not imply the validity of these theorists' overall approaches to "functional" analysis. In Merton's case, for example, this broad notion of system is one of the few nonempirical elements of science he will allow in his ambiguous effort to define "middle range" theory (see ch. 1, sec. 2). Somewhat paradoxically, the openness of the conception is, therefore, used by Merton to support an empiricist approach to the effect that observed data will now be able to "specify" the system concept's "generality." From the present perspective, in contrast, the system concept's openness is important precisely because it allows recognition of the determinate qualities of other kinds of equally nonempirical components of the scientific continuum. In actuality, of course, Merton does "fill in" his system concept with a range of other nonempirical commitments, both more and less general; if this were not true, the fruitfulness of his specific theories would be inexplicable.

76. Rex, *Key Problems* (n. 1 above), p. 68. This is one of six different definitions of "functionalism" offered by Rex, and it so well expresses why the concept of "functional effect" need imply no reification of individual action that it is worthwhile to quote from the definition at length:

> [In this version of functionalism] an individual's action is explained as being due to the need to ensure that some other individual's ends are attained. The action is seen as purposive in terms of a model which starts from the ends of the other individual [but] when a very high degree of complexity is attained it is sometimes imagined that a particular

action has the sole purpose of maintaining the structure of society. But the "structure of society" is itself something which can be explained. Different societies have different "structures" because they fulfill different purposes. Thus what passes as necessary for maintaining a particular set of social relations in turn is only necessary given that certain purposes must be attained. If this is true our model of sociological explanations is again cast in terms of [individual] purpose and we should not have any qualms about using the term function instead of the term effect.

77. Buckley, *Sociology and Modern Systems Theory* (Englewood Cliffs, N.J., 1967), pp. 94–113.

78. Turner, *The Structure of Sociological Theory* (n. 32 above), pp. 15–28.

79. Stark, *The Fundamental Forms of Social Thought* (n. 16 above), pp. 44–46.

80. Levine, review of Robert W. Friedrichs, *A Sociology of Sociology*, in *American Anthropologist* 74 (1972):7.

81. This is the criticism, for example, made against Davis' article by Martindale, who by virtue of his own conflation wishes to make the functional commitment much more particularized than it actually is (*The Nature and Types of Sociological Theory* [n. 35 above], pp. 246–247). Of course, to the degree that Davis' article, as mentioned above (n. 75), does overstep the task of broadly defining functionalism to identify such a commitment with all sociological thought, the criticisms of his attempt are indeed justified. See Cohen, *Modern Social Theory* (n. 1 above), p. 64.

82. Wallace, *Sociological Theory* (n. 58 above). For my criticisms of the substantive content of Wallace's classification system, see above, ch. 1, sec. 2, and below, ch. 3, nn. 30, 153.

83. Sztompka, *System and Function* (n. 67 above), pp. 168–170. For references to Sztompka's articles, see n. 69 above.

84. *System and Function*, p. 177. Also interesting in terms of the more general argument presented here is Sztompka's decision to carry out this differentiation between particular types of Marxist and functionalist theories according to their degree of commitment to a rationalist frame of reference. It is particularly revealing in this respect to compare Sztompka's theoretical writing with Mulkay's. Both writers consider exchange theory as the most important recent development in sociological theory. But because Mulkay has a conflationary perspective on the functional commitment, cross-cutting it with perspectives on conflict and value coercion, he describes exchange theory as a theoretical decision on the same level as, and antithetical to, the "functionalist" approach. Sztompka, on the other hand, because he has a more properly differentiated understanding of the nature of the functionalist commitment, can argue simultaneously for both systems and exchange theory. It should be

noted, perhaps, that Sztompka's designation of "particular" and "general" in reference to assumptions about "model" and "rationality" is the opposite of that presented here.

85. Hobsbawm, "Karl Marx's Contribution to Historiography," in Robin Blackburn, ed., *Ideology in Social Science* (New York, 1973), pp. 273–275.

86. See particularly Althusser, "The Errors of Classical Economics," in Althusser and Etienne Balibar, *Reading Capital* (London, 1970), pp. 96–100, 104–105, 107–108, and "Marx's Critique," ibid., pp. 180–181; also, idem, *For Marx* (London, 1966), pp. 87–128, "Contradiction and Overdetermination." For a secondary discussion of this overlap, see Erik Olin Wright and Luca Perrone, "The Structuralist-Marxist and Parsonian Theories of Politics: A Comparative Analysis" (unpublished essay, University of California, Berkeley, March 1973), particularly pp. 6–7, "Formal Convergences."

The common Marxian/Parsonian commitment at the model level is perhaps best articulated by Maurice Godelier, who applies the Althusserian approach to his comparative study of economic systems, *Rationality and Irrationality in Economics* (New York, 1971). In his introductory essay, "Functionalism, Structuralism, and Marxism," Godelier describes what he calls the "points of agreement":

> There is first the methodological principle that social relations must be analyzed as forming "systems." Then, there is the principle that the inner logic of these systems must be analyzed before their origin is analyzed. We see at once that, as regards these two principles, Marxism is not opposed either to structuralism or to functionalism. (P. xxi.)

Clarifying further, Godelier writes that

> [What Marxism rejects is not] the principle that science must take as its subject of analysis the relations between men, or the principle that relations must be analyzed in their unity within a whole, or the principle that priority must be given to studying the logic of these relations and this whole before studying their origin and evolution. (P. xviii.)

The emphasis, in other words, is on interpreting the system concept in a broad, open-ended manner (see also, ibid., "The Idea of a 'System,'" pp. 257–259).

87. Jürgen Habermas, *Legitimation Crisis* (Boston, 1975).

88. Smelser, *Karl Marx on Society and Social Change* (n. 62 above), "Introduction," p. 9.

89. Ibid., pp. 17–18, italics in original.

90. Loomis, "In Praise of Conflict and Its Resolution," *American Sociological Review* 32 (1967):876.

91. Lipset, "Social Structure and Social Change," p. 173, in Peter

Blau, ed., *Approaches to the Study of Social Structure* (New York, 1975), pp. 172–208.

92. Arthur L. Stinchcombe, *Constructing Social Theories* (New York, 1968), pp. 93–98.

93. Atkinson (n. 32 above), p. 51.

94. See Atkinson's discussions of Parsons and Marx (ibid., pp. 9–65), and his discussion of the convergence of the classical schools into what he sees as a "modern consensus," which is really only a consensus on the model level (ibid., pp. 105–143).

95. This can be seen, for example, in terms of the "functionalist" argument. Thus, in arguing against what he views as the recent over-emphasis on theoretical crisis and for a qualified version of the convergence argument, Eisenstadt refers specifically to the systems perspective shared by Marxists and structural-functionalist alike ("Some Reflections on the 'Crisis' in Sociology," *Sociologische* 4 [July–August, 1973]:259–260). In terms of the crisis proposal, one of the major points of reference for Gouldner's arguments in *The Coming Crisis in Western Sociology* (n. 1 above) chs. 9, 12, is the pervasive agreement around what he calls a "functionalist" commitment, erroneously described by him as a form of social utilitarianism. Donald G. MacRae has also used what is simply a common orientation to the systems model to evoke a crisis created by the convergence between what are actually radically divergent sociological theories. See his "The Crisis of Sociology," in J. H. Plumb, ed., *Crisis in the Humanities* (London, 1964), pp. 124–138, and his "Introduction" to Cohen's *Modern Social Theory* (n. 1 above), pp. vii–viii. In regard to the latter, for example, although MacRae correctly perceives the nature of Cohen's contributions, he puts forward the inexplicable proposal that Cohen's argument, which actually outlines a certain distinctive and polemical theoretical position, actually indicates that a "genuine" theoretical "integration" has been "largely achieved" in the sociological discipline.

CHAPTER THREE

1. In this sense, I strongly disagree with the position taken by S. N. Eisenstadt and M. Curelaru in *The Form of Sociology: Paradigms and Crises* (New York, 1976) ch. 10, which contends that the latent "cross-cuttings" of the theoretical debate of the 1960s and 1970s should be read as a theoretical "convergence" toward a more complex and truly generalized social theory. The latent commonality among participants in this debate is mainly confined to the unselfconscious form of residual categories: most of the discussion has occurred in the context of attempts to build the kind of philosophically closed "schools" that Eisenstadt and Curelaru do, in fact, recognize as a possibility (pp. 300–308). Yet with the

exception of this "whiggish" reading, and of a latent faith in the pure objectivity of social science, the position I am outlining here parallels the insightful analysis in Eisenstadt's and Curelaru's work.

2. Parsons, *The Structure of Social Action* (New York, [1937] 1968), particularly ch. 2, "The Theory of Action," and ch. 3, "Some Phases of the Historical Development of Individualistic Positivism in the Theory of Action."

3. See, for example, *The Politics of Aristotle*, ed. and trans. by Ernest Barker (New York, 1962), bk. 7, pt. 3.4, "The Social Structure," pp. 297–299. For Augustine, see the discussion of *The City of God* (XIV) in Robert N. Bellah's essay, "Religion and Polity in America," *Andover-Newton Quarterly* 15, no. 2 (1974): 107–123. This essay provides a concise overview of the kinds of theoretical and political tensions generated by traditional epistemological issues in the history of theological and classical thought.

4. In the stampede to relieve sociology of its Parsonian heritage, a number of authors have challenged the "intellectual history" of *The Structure of Social Action*, in which Parsons sought to buttress his analytical claims for the superiority of a noninstrumental perspective on action with a linear, evolutionary reading of the actual historical victory of normative over instrumental theorizing. (For the best of these critical efforts, see Robert Alun Jones, "On Understanding a Sociological Classic," *American Journal of Sociology* 83 [September, 1977]: 279–319; Charles Camic, "The Utilitarians Revisited," *American Journal of Sociology* 85 [1979]: 516–550; Donald N. Levine, *Simmel and Parsons: Two Approaches to the Study of Society* [New York, 1981], pp. v–lxix.) It is certainly true that Parsons did seek this historical sustenance: his accumulationist understanding of science led him to postulate empirical convergence on the kind of theorizing he felt to be most analytically promising. Yet the real upshot of Parsons' first book is surely that theoretical problems have an independent status, and that they must be addressed without historical consolation. Just as the validity of the "action" problem, then, cannot be identified with the particular form of Parsons' later theorizing, neither can the validity of any particular presuppositional position be tied to any particular reading of intellectual history. Implicitly, Parsons used intellectual history simply as a vehicle for talking about purely analytical-epistemological problems, and although his intellectual history is limited and often superficial his articulation of the theoretical issues is usually profound. The analytic-epistemological issues were fundamental points of cleavage before and after Parsons wrote, and they will remain tensions as long as social thought is produced. Camic and Levine tend, by contrast, to reduce the relevance of these general problems of order and action to specific historical contexts, inadvertently (and ironically) following the predilection they identified

in Parsons to conflate history and theory. They describe, for example, the challenge posed by the "utilitarian" and "individualistic" positions as limited to a few anomalous decades in the late nineteenth and early twentieth centuries and primarily, within this time period, to the American and Anglo-Saxon traditions. It is my basic contention, to the contrary, that the relation between subject and object and the understanding of how this relationship is socially aggregated continue to provide a fundamental structuring problem—though by no means the only one—for all of social thought. In this context it is not irrelevant to note that both Camic and Levine actually rely in their historical reconstructions on the analytic vocabulary provided by Parsons himself. Their "historical" arguments rest, in other words, on certain assumptions about theoretical logic that could be disputed on purely analytical grounds, and for which there is certainly no contemporary theoretical consensus.

5. *The Structure of Social Action*, p. 732.

6. Translated and quoted by Nathan Rotenstreich, *Basic Problems of Marx's Philosophy* (Indianapolis, 1965), p. 23, italics in original. Rotenstreich's book is one of the most extensive analyses of Marx's epistemological framework available in English. For his elaboration of the meaning of this first thesis, see his discussion on pp. 27–39. See also the excellent discussion of Marx's epistemological position, and its relation to certain broader aspects of his thinking, in Shlomo Avineri, *The Social and Political Thought of Karl Marx* (Cambridge, 1968), pp. 69–75. Avineri's book, which will be critically discussed in the chapters on Marx in vol. 2, is particularly valuable for comparing Marx's epistemological position in relation to Engels' more conventional philosophical materialism and to the epistemological reductionism of some of Marx's followers. My understanding of the relationship between Parsons' and Weber's conception of "action" and Marx's conception of "praxis" could not be more different from that of Goran Therborn, the Althusserian Marxist who offers what seems to me a reductionistic and ideological reading of the two terms (see "Social Practice, Social Action, Social Magic," *Acta Sociologica* 16, no. 3 [1973]:157–174). For Therborn, the epistemological dimension is not really relevant: Marx's "praxis" should be understood only as class struggle and political action, while Parsons' and Weber's "action" reflects liberal ideology and the lack of commitment to revolution. When he does refer to epistemology, Therborn offers a tendentious reading, contrasting Marx's multidimensional "praxis" with the purported idealism of Parsons' and Weber's notion of "action."

7. Bottomore, "Competing Paradigms in Macro-Sociology," in *Annual Review of Sociology*, Alex Inkeles, James Coleman, and Neil Smelser, eds., 1 (1975): 196.

8. Max Weber, *The Theory of Social and Economic Organization*, ed. Talcott Parsons (New York, 1964), pp. 88–90. In the edition of Weber's

work entitled *Economy and Society* (Berkeley and Los Angeles, 1978), this discussion is in pt. 1, ch. 1, sec. 1. In subsequent references to Weber, I cite both individual volumes and the *Economy and Society* edition.

9. Emile Durkheim, *The Elementary Forms of Religious Life* (New York, 1965), pp. 662–696, "Conclusion."

10. For a similar attempt to use certain philosophically defined problems as models for approaching specifically sociological issues, rather than use them literally or not at all, see the discussions of "sociological realism and sociological nominalism" in Werner Stark, *The Fundamental Forms of Social Thought* (London, 1962), p. 3, and the similar analysis of "social realism" and "social nominalism" in J. David Lewis and Richard L. Smith, *American Sociology and Pragmatism: Mead, Chicago Sociology, and Symbolic Interactionism* (Chicago, 1980), passim.

11. See Don Martindale, *The Nature and Types of Sociological Theory* (Cambridge, Mass., 1960), ch. 15, "The Social-Action Branch of Social Behaviorism," pp. 376–412. For a similar discussion of "action theorists" as Weberian analysts who emphasize the individual as opposed to the collective, more Durkheimian approach to symbolic representations, see the analysis of theoretical divisions within political anthropology in Abner Cohen, *Two Dimensional Man* (Berkeley and Los Angeles, 1974), pp. 40–43.

12. Martin Hollis, *Models of Man: Philosophical Thoughts on Social Action* (London, 1977); Anthony Giddens, *New Rules of Sociological Method* (New York, 1976), and *Central Problems in Social Theory* (Berkeley and Los Angeles, 1979); Alan Dawe, "Theories of Social Action," in Tom Bottomore and Robert N. Nisbet, eds., *A History of Sociological Analysis* (New York, 1978). Giddens' work, it should be noted, is informed by more collectivistic strands as well (see n. 135 below).

13. See, for example, the first chapter in Parsons, *The Social System* (New York, 1951), pp. 3–23, "The Action Frame of Reference and the General Theory of Action Systems: Culture, Personality and the Place of Social Systems."

14. Walter L. Wallace, *Sociological Theory* (New York, 1969), pp. 1–59, "Overview of Contemporary Sociological Theory," esp. p. 36.

15. Pope, "Classic on Classic: Parsons' Interpretation of Durkheim," *American Sociological Review* 38 (1973):408–409.

16. John Rex, *Key Problems in Sociological Theory* (London, 1961), p. 78.

17. Alfred Schutz, "The Problem of Rationality in the Social World," in Dorothy Emmet and Alasdaire Macintyre, eds., *Sociological Theory and Philosophical Analysis* (London, [1943] 1970), p. 110. I should emphasize that neither in Schutz's nor Rex's references, nor in the reference presented here, does the concept of "motivation" imply "human nature." A theorist's perspective on human nature provides a broad com-

pass from which his perspective on social motivation in a particular theoretical system can be drawn. Not to make this distinction is to open the door to some insuperable theoretical problems, as will be seen in my discussion of some of the secondary literature on Marx in vol. 2.

Among the large number of writings on the action problem, Percy Cohen's is particularly interesting from the perspective developed here. Cohen initially defines the action approach, in a manner similar to Martindale and Wallace, as a particular school of sociological theory parallel, for example, to functionalism. In his following substantive discussion, however, Cohen, first, describes action in the broadest epistemological terms, employing much of the same vocabulary utilized here; second, he argues that a focus on both "action" and "system-function" must be part of any fully supplied social theory (*Modern Social Theory* [London, 1968], pp. 69–94). In other words, in the course of his discussion, Cohen has effectively accorded to action a generic status—distinguishing it as analytically separated from the level of "model."

18. Keith Dixon has put the matter in a way that parallels the present discussion: "All explanations of human behavior involve reference either directly or parasitically to the concept of what is deemed 'rational' for men to engage in" (*Sociological Theory: Pretense or Possibility* [London, 1973], p. 66).

19. David Hume, *Inquiry Concerning the Principles of Morals*, app. 1, quoted in Elie Halévy, *The Growth of Philosophic Radicalism* (Clifton, N.J., [1901–1904] 1972), p. 13, italics altered.

20. Jeremy Bentham, *An Introduction to the Principles of Morals and Legislation* (1789), quoted in Halévy, p. 26. (Bentham is actually here paraphrasing Helvétius, himself a disciple of Hume.) This point is also particularly clear in Bentham's discussion later in this same work of what he calls the four basic sanctions of social life: political, moral, religious, and physical. The first three, Bentham contends, are all reducible to the last, for only can the fear of physical material pain and the hope for physical material pleasure address the true, instrumental motivation of human beings.

I should emphasize here that I am talking about Bentham's "perception of action" as it is embodied in a self-contained and relatively formal explanatory scheme, not about his perception of action in general in the human species. Indeed, many of the thinkers most responsible for formulating the explanatory scheme that became political economy—the prototypically "instrumental" theory—were moral philosophers who recognized, in other segments of their work, that men may be committed to nonrational norms and who, on these grounds, sought to utilize their instrumental explanatory schemas for higher moral interests. Thus, when Charles Camic objects that Adam Smith simply "was abstracting 'economic motivations and processes' from a more comprehensive anal-

ysis of social action provided in his earlier *Theory of Moral Sentiments*,"
he has missed the essential *theoretical* point ("The Utilitarians Revisited"
[n. 4 above], p. 531). It is precisely the explicit and abstracted explanatory system that is, in fact, our concern—and the presuppositions that
underlie it. This distinction, and the internal conflict it often signals, is
clearly articulated by one of the preeminent later utilitarians, J. S. Mill.
After emphasizing that to view mankind as occupied solely in acquiring
and consuming wealth is a useful if limiting abstraction, he adds the
caveat—"not that any political economist was ever so absurd as to sup-
pose that mankind are really thus constituted, but because this is the
mode in which science must necessarily proceed" (*A System of Logic*
[1843], bk. 6, ch. 9, sec. 4). There is, indeed, often the widest possible gap
between a theorist's personal knowledge, interest, and insight, and his
understanding of the proper "mode in which science must necessarily
proceed," as we shall see throughout the course of this volume and the
volumes that follow.

Although Mill is seeking to justify the independence of the science of
political economy, it can be argued—and will so be argued below—that
even this discipline cannot assume a purely instrumental framework on
action. Here the argument is more concerned, however, with the assumption that action is *generally* instrumental—instrumental, that is,
throughout the entire social area covered by social-scientific theorizing.
In this, of course, Mill was not an instrumentalist theorist, but Bentham
and many others certainly were, and are. Mill himself makes exactly this
observation (ibid., bk. 6, ch. 8, sec. 3), when he argues against the scientific validity of the narrowly self-interested and calculating action postulated by the Benthamite Utilitarians—even though he recognizes that
they employed this presupposition of instrumental rationality for heuristic purposes and not necessarily as an assumption about human nature
in an abstract and general sense.

21. This characterization of instrumental rationality as "technical"
follows Weber's classification of the types of social action and Habermas'
reformulation of classical German discussions of reason. Regarding
Weber's definition, technical rationality can be seen to correspond
roughly to one of the two definitions that Weber applies to his concept of
Zweckrationalität (*Theory of Social and Economic Organization* [n. 8
above], pp. 115–118; *Economy and Society* [n. 8], pt. 1, ch. 1, sec. 2). I
discuss these different possible meanings of the *Zweck* concept in sec. 2.3
below as well as in the interpretation of Weber in vol. 3. For Habermas'
discussion of the technical rationality concept, see his chapter "Reason
and Interest: Retrospect on Kant and Fichte," in *Knowledge and Human
Interests* (Boston, 1971), pp. 191–213, particularly pp. 196–198. This analysis is vital for relating the differences in the rationality concept discussed here to the debates over the concept of reason that developed in

the classical philosophical discussions about the source of human morality and the nature of motivation. For other references by Habermas to the technical version of rationality, see the conclusion to his discussion of Pierce, ibid., p. 137, and *Toward a Rational Society* (Boston, 1970), pp. 91–93.

22. See particularly Parsons' section on "The Positivist Theory of Action," pp. 60–69. I will discuss his blurring of these different questions later in this chapter (sec. 3.4.3.).

23. Habermas, *Knowledge and Human Interests*, pp. 260, 197, respectively.

24. In historical terms, the manner in which the rationalist commitment can underlie substantively different types of social theories has been demonstrated by H. Stuart Hughes in *Consciousness and Society* (New York, 1958, pp. 33–66), particularly in his critical discussion of the essential interchangeability in nineteenth-century thought of mechanism, materialism, and naturalism. The same historical point has been argued in certain parts of Parsons' *The Structure of Social Action*, which particularly emphasizes the parallel structure of hedonism, Darwinism, and economic utilitarianism (pp. 51–60, 110–121).

25. George C. Homans, *Social Behavior: Its Elementary Forms* (New York, 1961), pp. 12–14.

26. Peter M. Blau, *Exchange and Power in Social Life* (New York, 1964), p. 20. Throughout his work, Blau insists that the *assumption* of rationality is necessary for the effective study of social life whether or not action really is so rationally motivated. He adds that to the degree action may not actually be rational, the rationality assumption can be preserved by constructing a number of parameters that should be taken as givens of sociological analysis. It is the contention of the present work that, on the contrary, the effective study of social life requires the positive definition of precisely the kinds of residual categories that must be so constructed if a rationalist position is to be maintained. In this positive redefinition, the parameters are eliminated, and the true nature of human motivation, which cannot be simply technically rational, is revealed.

For a penetrating critique of the rationalist, instrumental perspectives that underlie the work of Homans and Blau, see Peter P. Ekeh's *Social Exchange Theory: The Two Traditions* (Cambridge, Mass., 1974), particularly pp. 3–34, 111–126, 168–187. Ekeh also discusses the relation of this sociological exchange theory to the earlier anthropological tradition that emphasizes instrumental rationality, exemplified in the work of Spencer and Frazer, and in parts of Malinowski's. In the course of his analysis, Ekeh makes it clear that exchange is a general concept which can actually be applied in ways other than the instrumentally rational one. He discusses what I will later call the "nonrational" and "internal order" versions of the exchange tradition in the work of Lévi-Strauss and Mauss.

27. Hughes, *Consciousness*, pp. 33–66, "The Revolt Against Positivism"; Parsons, *Structure*, pp. 69–72, "Empiricism."

In order not to confuse the point I made about the "positivist reduction" in ch. 1, or to give the appearance of including in this identification of rationalism and positivism all of the protagonists of the "positivist persuasion" discussed there, I should emphasize here that because of the different levels of theoretical commitment involved, it is quite possible for a theorist to be a positivist in terms of his philosophy of science without manifesting also a rationalist commitment in his perspective on action. It is true that such dual commitments would be contradictory to one another, but given the relative autonomy of different elements on the scientific continuum, combined with the lack of contemporary self-consciousness about generalized theoretical issues, it should not be surprising that both of these commitments are in fact often simultaneously made.

Although Parsons certainly does not identify science with rationalism, one of the relatively minor but nevertheless bedeviling problems of *The Structure of Social Action*, as I mentioned in ch. 2, sec. 2, is Parsons' tendency to equate a rationalist approach to action with a positivist approach to science.

28. Habermas, "Science and Technology as Ideology," *Toward a Rational Society*, pp. 81–121.

29. J. H. M. Beattie, in Brian Wilson, ed., *Rationality* (London, 1970), p. 247, italics in original.

30. In this sense, the fundamental issue in the philosophy of science is the nature of scientific "rationality." To the degree such rationality is viewed in a narrowly instrumental way, the historical and cultural context of the scientific actor is not taken into account and a positivistic, atheoretical understanding of science results. If a more multidimensional perspective on action is adopted, however, it becomes clear that the rationality of the scientist is very much the result of a certain kind of normative commitment and, further, that this norm of scientific objectivity can never be extricated from the broader evaluative framework—of culture, history, and "theory"—within which it is naturally imbedded. The scientist is rational, in other words, but not in a "rationalistic," or instrumentalist, way.

Robert K. Merton has formulated a normative approach to the scientist's rationality in a classical way in his famous paper, "The Normative Structure of Science" (pp. 267–278 in Merton, *The Sociology of Science* [Chicago, (1942) 1973]), which argues that scientists must internalize such values as universalism and organized scepticism; yet he has maintained, at the same time, a rather ahistorical understanding of the rationality of science as a whole (see my discussion of Merton's approach in ch. 1, sec. 2). Insofar as he argues that scientific growth is enhanced only by specific and empirically oriented theorizing and that empirical data can be sharply separated from more general theorizing, Merton treats the rationality of science in an empiricist fashion. He believes that although the form of scientific regulation is culturally rooted, its contents can be impartially evaluated in terms of their objective rationality. Merton's later work on the social structuring of the reward system of science (pp. 286–412) implicitly relativizes such objective rationality, but the full implications of social structure can be appreciated only if cultural influence on the *content* of science is explained—something which Merton does not do. (An understanding of rationality which more closely resembles the approach taken here is forcefully presented by Larry Laudan in *Progress and Its Problems* [Berkeley and Los Angeles, 1977]). I will try to articulate my own position on scientific rationality more fully in ch. 4.

It is relevant to note here that Wallace's classificatory schema—which in certain respects resembles the distinctions proposed here—considers a theory's position on scientific methodology to be the most general indication of its epistemological position on the idealism-materialism continuum. ("Overview of Contemporary Sociological Theory," [n. 14 above]). As in the present approach, Wallace finds two basic dimensions as cross-cutting the "property space" from which he attempts to derive the crucial variations within social theory. Further, he identifies as one of these dimensions the subjectivism/objectivism duality. But he then defines the latter as relating to the observational criteria that govern a theory's approach to empirical data rather than as relating to the criteria that govern the activities of the individuals whose action the theory seeks to explain. Thus, according to this standard, he puts Durkheim in the materialist, objectivist camp because of his emphasis on the externality of social facts, and Weber in the idealist, subjectivist category because of his emphasis on *Verstehen*. He also classifies as objectivist not only Homans' utilitarian theory but also the symbolic interactionists—the latter because, despite their non-rational, normative emphasis, they respect the "obdurate" nature of empirical reality. Although such classifications are not incorrect, given the criteria Wallace sets out, they do fail to distinguish the most crucial, epistemological framework that governs general theoretical logic. To establish this, the frameworks of the actors themselves must be the focus of attention. Wallace has, in other words, attempted to raise methodological assumptions to a presuppositional status.

A classificatory schema more complementary to the present position is the approach to epistemological issues formulated by Andrew Effrat in "Power to the Paradigms" (*Sociological Inquiry* 42, no. 3–4 [1972]: 3–34). Effrat establishes as one of his two basic cross-cutting dimensions the nature of the "substantive factors" that compose any social theory, a question that is a rough parallel to my "problem of action." He distinguishes four main types of factors: material, affective, interactional, and idealist or symbolist. The only drawback of this schema, from the perspective presented here, is that it overlays fundamental epistemological conflict with certain more empirically oriented concerns. For example, in establishing a distinction between affective and symbolic foci, Effrat has divided two approaches that are both epistemologically idealist and has brought into his most general category specifications about the nature of this action that can only be spelled out by model and concepts.

31. *The Republic of Plato*, pt. 2, ch. 9, secs. 2, 4, and pt. 5, chs. 31–32, trans. F. M. Cornford (London, 1945), pp. 80–85, 88–92, 321–336. For Augustine, see the discussion by Bellah (n. 3 above).

32. Mead, "Social Psychology and Behaviorism," in Anselm Strauss, ed., *George Herbert Mead on Social Psychology* (Chicago, 1964), p. 117.

33. Ibid., pp. 121–122.

34. In ontological terms there is an asymmetry, then, between rational and nonrational action. Whether or not an element functions as a condition is not determined by its corporeal nature, for an ideal element may function objectively if the sanctions that sustain it make it stand in relation to the actor as an unmoveable force. In this case, the actor adopts toward it an instrumental motive, treating it as a condition rather than an end in itself. By contrast, an element can be the reference point for nonrational action only if it has a nonmaterial status, since it must occupy a position that is internal rather than external to the actor. Ultimately, of course, it is a matter of theoretical decision—a decision itself influenced by assumptions about the relative rationality of action—whether or not an element is understood as having a material or ideal status.

35. Douglas, *Purity and Danger* (London, 1966), p. 33; Robertson Smith, *Lectures on the Religion of the Semites* (London, [1889] 1927); Marcel Mauss, *The Gift* (New York, [1925] 1954); Victor Turner, *The Ritual Process* (Chicago, 1969). For secondary discussions of Smith and Mauss, which emphasize that aspect of their writing which I designate here as the nonrational approach to action, see, respectively, Douglas, *Purity and Danger*, pp. 20–31, and Ekeh, *Social Exchange Theory*, pp. 30–33. In Ekeh's discussion, as I will point out later in this chapter, the emphasis on non-rationality remains only implicit because it overlaps with his analysis of Mauss' treatment of the order issue. For a similar, more recent anthropological approach to the same problem, see Abner Cohen's *Two Dimensional Man* (n. 11 above), in which "symbolism" is identified as the principal antithesis to "power," and is described as denoting "normative, non-rational, non-utilitarian behaviour" (p. ix).

36. Hatch, *Theories of Man and Culture* (New York, 1973).

37. Sahlins, *Culture and Practical Reason* (Chicago, 1976), particularly chs. 1–3.

38. See Hughes' discussions of Gide, Mann, Hesse, Proust, and Pirandello in *Consciousness and Society* (n. 24 above), pp. 367–368, 378–391.

39. See, e.g., Charles Renouvier, *Science de la Morale* (Paris, 1869); cf. the discussions of Renouvier's writing on ethics and morality in Steven Lukes, *Emile Durkheim: His Life and Work* (New York, 1972), pp. 54–57.

40. See Robert Nisbet, *Community and Power* (New York, 1962), and particularly *The Sociological Tradition* (New York, 1966). The emphasis on these aspects of nonrationality and their relation to voluntarism is clear in Nisbet's description of the meaning of "community" in nineteenth-century conservative thought: "Community is a fusion of feeling and thought, of tradition and commitment, of membership and volition" (ibid., p. 48). Yet as Steven Seidman has shown in his excellent doctoral dissertation, "Enlightenment and Reaction: Aspects of the Enlightenment Origins of Marxism and Sociology" (University of Virginia, 1979), despite popular perceptions, the "classical" Enlightenment tradition itself embodied significant "nonrational" emphases.

41. For Parsons' most specific definition of how "normative" functions for him as the antithesis to "rational," see *The Structure of Social Action*, pp. 74–77, "On the Concept of 'Normative.'"

42. Habermas, *Knowledge and Human Interests* (n. 21 above), pp. 137, 157, 196–197, 214, 260; idem, *Toward a Rational Society* (n. 21), pp. 91–94. Sahlins' contrast of cultural versus practical reason (n. 37) also has a strongly generalized reference.

43. Schutz, "The Problem of Rationality in the Social World" (n. 17 above), p. 97.

44. I. C. Jarvie and Joseph Agassi, "The Problem of the Rationality of Magic," in Brian R. Wilson, ed., *Rationality* (London, 1970), p. 173. For the centrality of Lucien Lévy-Bruhl's formulations as the starting point for one strand of the anthropological polemic over rationality, see Wilson's and Beattie's discussions, ibid., pp. xiii–xiv, 240–241; see also E. E. Evans-Pritchard, *Theories of Primitive Religion* (London, 1965), pp. 78–99.

45. Dixon, *Sociological Theory* (n. 18 above), p. 76.

46. Sigmund Freud, "Formulations Regarding the Two Principles in Mental Functioning," in John Rickman, ed., *A General Selection From the Works of Sigmund Freud* (New York, 1957), pp. 38–45.

47. Heinz Hartmann, *Essays on Ego Psychology* (New York, 1964), p. 50, "On Rational and Irrational Action."

48. Weber, *Theory of Social and Economic Organization* (n. 8 above), pp. 115–116; *Economy and Society* (n. 8), pt. 1, ch. 1, sec. 2.

49. James Coleman, "Foundations for a Theory of Collective Decisions," *American Journal of Sociology* 71 (1966): 615.

50. Schutz (n. 17 above), p. 115.

51. See "Parsons' Theory of Social Action: A Critical Review by Alfred Schutz," in Richard Grathoff, ed., *The Theory of Social Action: The Correspondence of Alfred Schutz and Talcott Parsons* (Bloomington, Ind., 1978), pp. 8–70, esp. pp. 34–36.

52. Dick Atkinson, *Orthodox Consensus and Radical Alternative* (New York, 1972), p. 175.

53. Schutz, "Parsons' Theory of Social Action" (n. 51), particularly pp. 34–36.

54. Beattie, "On Understanding Ritual" (n. 29 above), p. 247.

55. For example:

> Internalization means that regulations that have been accepted on the basis of continued interaction with objects in the external world are replaced by inner regulations. This internal acceptance . . . forms the basis for consistent orientations to action at all institutional levels. Moreover, the better part of this "common culture" is not available for conscious examination; it exists for individuals on the unconscious level. . . . Some bases of action must remain unconscious in order to prevent the war of all against all that would be engendered by the expression of unrestrained instinctual behavior or, under the conditions of progressive rationalization of psychic structure, by the totally egoistic expression of self-interest. . . . As a result of his internalization . . . individuals remain committed to the rules even when the patterns run counter to reason and self-interest. (Weinstein and Platt, *The Wish to Be Free: Society, Psyche, and Value Change* [Berkeley and Los Angeles, 1969], pp. 5–6.)

Weinstein and Platt later move beyond this limited understanding of nonrationality in their *Psychoanalytic Sociology* (Baltimore, 1973); see also Weinstein's "Critical Views of Ego Psychology: A Critical View," *Psychoanalytic Review* 65 (1978): 203–215, particularly pp. 209 ff.

56. Hartmann (n. 47 above), pp. 58, 64.

On the general problem of psychoanalytic symbolic analysis, see, e.g., Philip Rieff, *Freud: The Mind of the Moralist* (New York, 1959), pp. 113–162, 281–328, and Charles Rycroft, "Freud and the Imagination," *New York Review of Books* 22, no. 5 (1975): 26–30. For a criticism of how this abstract theoretical problem produces empirical difficulties in an otherwise penetrating example of psychoanalytic social thought, see my review of Leo Rangell, *The Mind of Watergate*, in *The New Republic*, March 29, 1980.

57. Max Weber, *Theory of Social and Economic Organization* (n. 8 above), pp. 115–116; *Economy and Society* (n. 8), pt. 1, ch. 1, sec. 2.

58. Rex, *Key Problems* (n. 16 above), pp. 80–85, 93.

59. Ibid., p. 102. This characterization of Rex's work, which is itself internally divided, refers to only one of its strands. I have discussed the part of his work that attempts to interweave rational and nonrational in the discussion of conflict theory in ch. 2, sec. 3 above.

60. See, for example, Coleman's "Foundations for a Theory of Collec-

tive Action" (n. 49 above), and also his "Social Structure and a Theory of Action," in Peter M. Blau, ed., *Approaches to the Study of Social Structure* (New York, 1975), pp. 76–93.

61. Ludwig von Mises, *Human Action* (New Haven, 1949), p. 18.

62. For example, Alfred Schutz, "Common-Sense and Scientific Interpretations of Human Action," in *Collected Papers*, ed. Maurice Natanson, (The Hague, 1962) 1: 3–47.

63. For a conceptualization that considers each of the different kinds of activity that I will discuss below simply as different specific forms of a more general "rationalism," see the writings of Michael Oakeshott. Although Oakeshott identifies this rationalism as "technical" knowledge in contrast to "practical" or "traditional" knowledge, he uses the term "technical" in a much broader sense than the purely instrumentalist one that I use here. It includes, for him, any action governed by conscious and explicit reference to normative standards which are identified with "reason." See, e.g., "Rationalism in Politics," in his *Rationalism in Politics and Other Essays* (New York, 1962), pp. 1–36. Edward Shils takes much the same position, with similar ideological intentions (see particularly his emphasis on the dichotomy between intellectual rationalism and tradition in *The Intellectuals and the Powers and Other Essays* [Chicago, 1972]).

64. Wilson, *Rationality* (n. 44 above), p. vii.

65. Bendix, "Embattled Reason," in *Embattled Reason* (New York, 1970), pp. 13–14.

66. Jarvie and Agassi (n. 44 above), p. 173.

67. Vilfredo Pareto, *The Mind and Society* (New York, 1935), passim. Percy Cohen's analysis of rationality in his essay "Rational Conduct and Social Life" (in S. I. Benn and G. W. Mortimore, eds., *Rationality and the Social Sciences* [London, 1976], pp. 132–154), which includes a long treatment of Pareto, is one of the most insightful discussions of different approaches to the question I have encountered. Even Cohen, however, occasionally fails to maintain a consistent definition of rationality, sometimes taking "purposiveness" in general and at other times certain particular normative standards as his criterion.

68. Jere Cohen, "Moral Freedom through Understanding in Durkheim," *American Sociological Review* 40 (1975): 104–106.

69. Max Weber, *Theory of Social and Economic Organization* (n. 8 above), pp. 185–186, "The Formal and Substantive Rationality of Economic Action"; *Economy and Society* (n. 8), pt. 1, ch. 2, sec. 9. For Weber's other discussions, see, on religion, the Introduction to *The Protestant Ethic and the Spirit of Capitalism* (New York, 1958), pp. 13–31; on law, "Formal and Substantive Rationalization in the Law (Sacred Laws)," in Max Rheinstein, ed., *Max Weber on Law in Economy and Society* (New York, 1954), pp. 224–255; *Economy and Society*, pt. 2, ch. 7, sec. 5; for a

general discussion, see "Critical Studies in the Logic of the Cultural Sciences," in Edward A. Shils and Henry A. Finch, *The Methodology of the Social Sciences: Max Weber* (New York, 1949), pp. 124–125.

70. Karl Mannheim, *Man and Society in an Age of Reconstruction* (New York, 1940), p. 58. There are different and often contradictory approaches to substantive rationality in Weber's work. The analysis of economic rationality cited above, for example, allows substantive rationality to be achieved in relation to such nonvaledictory ends as social distinction and prestige. The discussion in the cultural sciences essay, by contrast, asserts that the ends must be limited to those which increase individual freedom. It is not usually appreciated how divergent Mannheim's definition of substantive rationality is from some of those offered by Weber. Mannheim's actually corresponds to Weber's own definition of one type of *Zweckrationalität*, following the logic of the *Zweck/Wert* distinction by asserting that any commitment to an "ultimate," "previously defined" end—a commitment that would result from, e.g., the influence of tradition or religion—is inconsistent with the achievement of substantive rationality (ibid., p. 54). By contrast, in Weber's discussions of economic rationality, *Wertrationalität* is actually considered to be a necessary though not sufficient condition of substantive rationality. For a general analysis of different types of rationality in Weber, see Ann Swidler, "The Concept of Rationality in the Work of Max Weber," *Sociological Inquiry* 43 (1973): 35–42; also Stephen Kalberg, "Max Weber's Types of Rationality: Cornerstones for the Analysis of Rationalization Processes in History," *American Journal of Sociology* 85 (1980): 1145–1179, and Donald N. Levine, "Rationality and Freedom: Weber and Beyond," paper presented at the Max Weber Symposium, University of Wisconsin, Milwaukee, May 5, 1977, forthcoming in *Sociological Inquiry* 51, no. 1 (1981).

71. Herbert Marcuse, *Reason and Revolution* (Boston, [1941] 1960), p. 45. For a description of the concept of reason in the work of various members of this Frankfurt school, see Martin Jay, *The Dialectical Imagination* (New York, 1973), pp. 60–79.

72. See Habermas' critique of Marcuse in *Toward a Rational Society* (n. 21 above), pp. 85–90.

73. Jeffrey C. Alexander, "Formal and Substantive Voluntarism in the Work of Talcott Parsons: A Theoretical and Ideological Reinterpretation," *American Sociological Review* 43 (April 1978): 177–198, and "The Mass News Media in Systematic Historical and Comparative Perspective," in Elihu Katz and Tamàs Szecskö, eds., *Mass Media and Social Change* (London, 1981), pp. 17–51.

74. Not all the problems in the theoretical debate over the order concept have developed for reasons related to the structure of theoretical logic itself. There is, e.g., the purely historical fact that from the 1940s

through the early 1970s theoretical debate in Western sociology usually has taken its bearings, either positively or negatively, from reference to the order concept in Parsons' work, a reference which, as will be seen below, is itself permeated by ambiguity and self-contradiction. But beneath such contingent problems that arise from the particular formations of contemporary debate, there exist more fundamental reasons for the theoretical confusion.

75. Edward Shils, *Center and Periphery: Essays in Macrosociology* (Chicago, 1975), pp. 3–16, 256–275, "Charisma, Order, and Status," and "Center and Periphery," and idem, *The Intellectuals and Other Essays* (Chicago, 1972), pp. 3–22, "The Intellectuals and the Powers."

76. S. N. Eisenstadt, "Charisma and Institution Building: Max Weber and Modern Sociology," S. N. Eisenstadt, ed., *Max Weber on Charisma and Institution Building* (Chicago, 1968), pp. ix–lvi, particularly xxiv ff.

77. Ralf Dahrendorf, *Class and Class Conflict in Industrial Society* (Stanford, Calif., 1959), ch. 5; David Lockwood, "Some Comments on 'The Social System,' " *British Journal of Sociology* 7, no. 2 (1956): 134–145.

78. Anthony Giddens, "Four Myths in the History of Social Thought," *Economy and Society* 1 (1972): 358–361, 365.

79. Another plausible though less frequently mentioned sequence is proposed by Bob Jessop in his *Social Order, Reform, and Revolution* (London, 1972). Separating the empirical issue of the extent of social conflict from ideological and presuppositional concerns, Jessop argues that Marxism, which he describes as a radical, materialist theory, also recognizes the significance of the "order" question. It does so through its emphasis on the possibility during certain historical periods of "peaceful coexistence" between different social classes. The same point is made by Neil J. Smelser in his introduction to *Karl Marx on Society and Social Change* (Chicago, 1973), pp. vii–xxxviii.

80. Polanyi, *Personal Knowledge* (New York, 1958), p. 38. See my discussion in ch. 1, sec. 4.1.

81. Mary Douglas, *Purity and Danger* (note 35 above), p. 48.

The literary analyses of Kenneth Burke employ the same kind of treatment of order. In his essay "On the First Three Chapters of Genesis," for example, Burke contends that theological speculation inherently involves reference to the idea of "order," which he defines as the first term in the basic cluster "order-disorder-obedience-disobedience" which every religious rhetoric, no matter what its specific ideational differences, must address. (*Daedalus*, Summer 1958, pp. 37–64; on the same theme see also Burke's *The Rhetoric of Religion* [Boston, 1966], pp. 174 ff.).

82. David Little, *Religion, Order, and Law* (New York, 1969), p. 6.

83. Ibid., pp. 33–166.

84. E.g., Weber's *Theory of Social and Economic Organization* (n. 8

above), pp. 148–151; *Economy and Society* (n. 8 above), pt. 1, ch. 1, sec. 13. See my discussion of the relation between this treatment of legitimate "orders" and Weber's historical analysis in vol. 3, ch. 4.

85. Cohen, *Modern Social Theory* (London, 1968), pp. 18–33, particularly pp. 20–21. For examples of how this generic definition allows Cohen to avoid the ideological, model, and empirical reductionism I have identified elsewhere, see my discussion of his work earlier in this chapter.

86. Turner, *The Structure of Sociological Theory* (Homewood, Ill., 1974), p. vii.

87. Peter P. Ekeh, *Social Exchange Theory* (n. 26 above), pp. 3–19. In *American Sociology and Pragmatism* (n. 10 above), Lewis and Smith provide another illuminating analysis of the significance of this theoretical decision about individual versus collective order. By doing so under the rubric of nominalism versus realism, however, certain problems are introduced. The latter debate refers primarily to the status of concepts or forms, and therefore remains largely within the realm of normative theory. Lewis' and Smith's "realism," then, cannot be cross-cut by the problem of action; thus, while its relevance for modes of nonrational theory is enormous, its status as a truly generalized dichotomy is limited, for it does not evaluate the case of a rationalist theory that is collectivist in its approach to order (see sections 3.3 and 3.4 below).

88. Homans, *Social Behavior* (n. 25 above), pp. 2–3. See Homans, "Bringing Men Back in," *American Sociological Review* 29 (1964): 809–818, for another, more polemical statement of the author's individualist position.

89. James M. Coleman, "Collective Decisions," in Herman Turk and Richard L. Simpson, eds., *Institutions and Social Change: The Sociologies of Talcott Parsons and George C. Homans* (Indianapolis, 1971), p. 273.

Coleman's work is a good example of the fact that what makes theory individualistic is not its complete neglect of social order per se but rather the manner in which it approaches the problem. Coleman is well aware of the inadequacies of Homans' theory. "The theory [of exchange] breaks down," he writes, because there is nothing postulated "to prevent those who disagree from simply withdrawing from the collectivity or refusing to accept the action or rebelling against it" ("Foundations for a Theory of Collective Decisions" [n. 49 above], p. 617). He proposes to remedy this by addressing social order directly, by explaining "joint or collective action [not] at the level of the individual actor [but] at the level of the pair or collectivity" (pp. 615–616). But he then proceeds to explain this collective phenomenon only in terms of the self-conscious actions of individuals, as an extensive series of individual barters.

90. Goffman, *The Presentation of the Self in Everyday Life* (New York, 1959), passim. More specifically, see Goffman's discussion in *Asylums* (New York, 1961), pp. 35–36.

91. Blumer, *Symbolic Interactionism: Perspective and Method* (Engle-

wood Cliffs, N.J., 1969), p. 8. It is interesting to note, in this regard, that within the contemporary tradition of symbolic interactionism there is a tension between Blumer's individualistic interpretation of George Herbert Mead and the more collectivistic strand in Mead's own social psychology of social life (see the penetrating analysis by Lewis and Smith in *American Sociology and Pragmatism* [nn. 10, 87 above]). "Self theory," for example, associated with Manfred Kuhn and later with Ralph Turner, Sheldon Stryker, and others, takes a more collectivist view of interaction. This conflict has been termed the division between the "Chicago" and "Iowa" schools of symbolic interactionism (Bernard N. Meltzer, John W. Petras and Larry T. Reynolds, *Symbolic Interactionism* [London, 1975], pp. 55–67). As this note should clearly indicate, our division between individualistic and collectivistic approaches to order has nothing whatever to do with the "micro/macro" distinction; "micro" refers only to decisions at the more specific, empirical end of the scientific continuum about level of analysis, not to the theoretical assumptions which are brought to bear on such analysis.

92. Jean Paul Sartre, *Search for a Method* (New York, 1968), passim.

93. Atkinson, *Orthodox Consensus and Radical Alternative* (n. 52 above), p. 265.

94. Ibid., p. 264.

95. See, e.g., Ernest Jones, "The Psychology of Constitutional Monarchy" and "Psychopathology and International Tension," in *Essays in Applied Psychoanalysis* (London, 1951), vol I, chs. 16, 21.

96. In *The Growth of Philosophic Radicalism* (n. 19 above), Halévy describes the historical development of utilitarianism in the following way. The intellectual center originated in the Puritan atmosphere of seventeenth-century England, moved in the eighteenth century to France and Italy, where it informed the thinking of the Enlightenment philosophes, and shifted back to England in the nineteenth century through the writings of Bentham. For an analytic discussion of the interrelationship between the historical development of Western Protestantism and utilitarianism, see Parsons' *The Structure of Social Action* (n. 2 above), pp. 51–57.

97. Halévy, *Philosophic Radicalism*, pp. 13–15.

In this particular analysis, and, indeed, throughout the three volumes of his *Philosophic Radicalism*, Halévy conceptualizes order both as a generic notion of order-as-social-arrangement and as a particularistic conception that conflates it with empirical conditions of social tranquility. This probably occurs because Halévy's analysis was directed specifically toward the political, quasi-Fabian problem of how social reforms can be created which while remedying social strains could also ameliorate social conflict. Halévy described two alternative reform strategies. Social activists could rely simply on the administratively passive theory of the natural identity of interests, or could attempt actively to create change by restructuring an artificial identity of interests. Halévy felt that nineteenth-century proponents of social change in England eventually realized that neither social tranquility nor a natural identity of interests actually existed. Unrepresentative economic interest groups acted in their own self interest and were the sources of social disharmony and conflict. Thus, the Benthamite utilitarians were philosophic radicals because they advocated that the state should step into this situation and create a more democratic society in which an "artificial" identity of interests would exist within the social fabric.

In *The Structure of Social Action*, Parsons follows Halévy in criticizing the "residual" quality of Lockean utilitarianism (pp. 95–102), and goes beyond Halévy by systematically describing the issue in distinctively epistemological terms. One problem with Parsons' treatment is that he equivocates on the order issue in the same manner as Halévy. A more serious problem is that Parsons regards Locke's problematic situation as originating from both the order and the action questions, whereas from the present perspective it is primarily only the former issue, the level of order, which is the source of strain in Locke's work. As I will elaborate later in this chapter and ch. 4, and in great detail in vol. 4, Parsons makes this mistake for two reasons: his analysis in *The Structure of Social Action* exhibits a strain of normative reduction; it also conflates the problems of order and action.

98. To consider a specific example, Halévy argues that, within the social Darwinist tradition, Malthus' population principle should be viewed as an ad hoc explanatory device that transcends the limits of individualistic analysis strictly considered (*Philosophic Radicalism*, pp. 225–248; see also Parsons' later reformulation of this insight about Malthus in *The Structure of Social Action*, pp. 102–107).

99. Homans, *Social Behavior* (n. 25 above), pp. 232–264. For a pointed critique of Homans' theory on precisely this issue, see Ekeh, *Social Exchange Theory* (n. 26 above), pp. 138–149. For Ekeh's broader analysis of the failure of Homans's work to achieve the collectivist level of analysis, see pp. 84–165 of the same work.

100. Thus, Homans admits that people "differ in their ideas of what constitutes investment, reward, and cost, and how these things are to be ranked," and he acknowledges that such ideas "differ from society to society, from group to group, and from time to time in any society or group" (*Social Behavior*, p. 246).

101. Coleman, "Foundations for a Theory of Collective Decisions" (n. 49 above), passim.

102. Goffman, *Asylums* (n. 90 above), pp. 1–125.

103. This is not to say that Sartre's confrontation with orthodox Marxism is waged solely within the context of the individualist/collectiv-

ist order debate. It also addresses itself to the problem of action, on both
an individual and collective level. In terms of this problem of action
within the Marxian tradition, Sartre's efforts are more successful, but
still present unresolved ambiguities. See vol. 2, ch. 10.

104. Sigmund Freud, *Group Psychology and the Analysis of the Ego*
(New York, 1959), pp. 15–21.

105. Schutz, "Common-Sense and Scientific Interpretations of Action" (n. 62 above), passim.

106. Schutz, *The Phenomenology of the Social World* (Evanston, Ill.,
1967), p. 171. The same tension, with a similarly ambiguous attempt at
an individualistic resolution, can be found in the treatment of "life
worlds" in Edmund Husserl's later works, from which, in fact, Schutz
drew heavily for his own theory of intersubjectivity.

107. Peter L. Berger and Thomas Luckmann, *The Social Construction
of Reality* (New York, 1967), particularly pt. 3.

108. Earlier, I connected this ambiguity in Schutz's understanding of
order with his reluctance to differentiate action into rational and nonrational forms. This led, I argued, to the phenomenological perspective
that all supra-individual controls had the same "objectivist" status and to
the belief that—since all external controls were equally inimical to freedom—the voluntary element in action had to be completely dissociated
from external control per se. If sociology, then, was to have a voluntaristic theory, Schutz concluded, it must focus exclusively on motives, a
focus that reflects, I earlier argued, a fundamental shift toward idealism.
Ethnomethodology, and Garfinkel's work in particular, continues to reflect this tension. As a student of Parsons as well as Schutz, Garfinkel is
interested in the sources of collective order, yet his exclusive focus on the
concrete individual acts of the concrete individual actor makes it difficult
for him to reveal anything other than the subject's immediate contribution to that order. This ambiguity is acutely revealed in an early article,
"A Conception of, and Experiments with, 'Trust' as a Condition of Stable
Concerted Actions," where Garfinkel tries to combine the individualistic
strain in Schutz and the collectivism of Parsons in an uneasy way. The
"way a system of activities is organized," Garfinkel writes, "means the
same thing as the way its organizational characteristics are being produced and maintained."

> Structural phenomena such as income and occupational distributions,
> familial arrangements, class strata, and the statistical properties of lan-
> guage are emergent products of a vast amount of communicative, per-
> ceptual, judgmental, and other "accommodative" work whereby per-
> sons, in concert, and encountering "from within the society" the
> environments that the society confronts them with, establish, maintain,
> restore, and alter the social structures that are the assembled products
> of temporally extended courses of action. . . . Simultaneously these so-

cial structures are the conditions of persons' concerted management of these environments. (Pp. 187–188 in O. J. Harvey, ed., *Motivation and Social Interaction*, [New York, 1963].)

As Garfinkel came to define himself as an "ethnomethodologist" and moved away from Parsons, he focused less on the "conditions" and more on the individual's strategies for creating "emergence."

109. Between Bentham and Hobbes, on the one side, and contemporary social thought on the other, there stands the mediation of Marx's and Weber's formulations of the rationalist collectivist perspective. Since Marx's and Weber's work are major considerations in my vols. 2 and 3, I do not consider them further in the present discussion, which is intended to establish the nature of the general logic of this position, its historical antecedents, and its contemporary adherents.

110. Thomas Hobbes, *Leviathan*, ch. 13.

Compare this statement with Locke's discussion of the state of nature:

> And being furnished with like faculties, sharing all in one community of nature, there cannot be supposed any such subordination among us that may authorize us to destroy another, as if we were made for one another's uses as the inferior ranks of creatures are for ours. (*The Second Treatise on Government*, ch. 2.)

Yet Locke ostensibly also maintained the rationalistic, self-interested approach to individual action. This conflict points to the important role that residual categories play in Locke's argument, an issue about which Parsons is particularly insightful (*The Structure of Social Action*, pp. 95–102). Whether or not Locke's description of social order was actually more realistically correct—if this description is viewed as an empirical proposition—is not our concern here.

111. Halévy, *Philosophic Radicalism*, p. 478.

112. "He remained faithful to . . . his criticism of the theory of natural rights. For it is absurd [Bentham thought] to wish to impose on a nation an everlasting respect for certain abstract rights" (ibid., p. 431).

113. Ibid., pp. 431–432.

The most famous and most important later discussion of Hobbes and the order question is, of course, that found in Parsons' *The Structure of Social Action* (pp. 89–94, and passim). Parsons drew on Halévy's description of the "artificial identity of interest" concept of Hobbes and reformulated it in more self-consciously presuppositional terms as the problem of order. From the present perspective, however, this analysis by Parsons presents several distinctive problems, which parallel the problems I noted above in his discussion of the Lockean approach. Parsons ambiguously views the Hobbesian problem of order both "generically" and presuppositionally, and as a matter of empirical equilibrium.

He also conflates Hobbes' decisions about order with decisions about action. Most importantly for this present discussion, however, is the normative bias which cross-cuts Parsons' treatment of the Hobbesian approach to order, a problem which causes him to radically deemphasize the great accomplishment of Hobbes' notion of the sovereign. Basically, Parsons can praise Hobbes only in a negative way, for exposing the inadequacies of a rationalist and individualist approach. This aspect of Parsons' discussion in *The Structure of Social Action* makes it much less valuable for analyzing the problem of rational action than Halévy's discussion.

114. The significance of the action question helps to explain why the ontological nature of collective elements does not alone decide their conditional status. The issue is not the corporeality of collective elements, but the relation of that reality to the actor. If action is assumed to be purely instrumental, then *all* collective elements must be treated as external and constraining. If action has a nonrational dimension, then ideal elements—though not material ones—may occupy an internal status and, therefore, may sustain voluntarism as I have defined that term. For the asymmetry of the ontological question in rational and nonrational action, see n. 34 above.

115. Ibid., p. 449. By noting Halévy's explicit concern with political rather than presuppositional issues per se, I refer to the fact that Halévy doesn't explicitly identify the conflict between individual and collective rationalism as a problem of order, although that is certainly the basic point of his treatment. Instead, he speaks of "the great problem of morals, to identify the interest of the individual with the interest of the community" (*Philosophic Radicalism*, p. 18). This is another manifestation of Halévy's concern with the specific political implications of the problem of order, which I have described in n. 97 above. For those who are familiar with the detail of Halévy's famous argument, it should perhaps be noted that Halévy himself occasionally refers to the "artificial identity of interest" position as an "individualistic" one (*Philosophic Radicalism*, pp. 499–508). In these instances he is actually referring not to the problem of order as defined here but to the problem of nominalism and realism, which is related but not by any means identical. If collectivist theory is rationalistic it also retains strong elements of nominalism, i.e., the philosophical belief that the only "real" elements in society are individuals, or, more precisely atomized, discrete elements rather than general forms. This problem will be discussed in more detail in the consideration of nonrational collectivism in sec. 3.4, for in its sociological form the nominalism/realist position actually involves the problem of action as well as the problem of order (cf. n. 87 above). The reason, therefore, that Halévy refers to the artificial identity theory as individualistic is that, like Parsons, he often conflates the issues of order and action.

116. Ibid., p. 405.

117. Ibid.

118. Ibid.

119. Although the political irony of the artificial identity position is particularly clear only in the later, democratic phase of Bentham's career, the logical interconnection between this position and the denial of voluntarism relates to the whole of Bentham's work. At least in his political if not his economic theory, Bentham was always a rationalist collectivist; only later in his life was he also democratic. For example, the inspiration for Bentham's early (1784) proposal of the centralized prison-control arrangement called the Panopticon can be understood as rooted in the notion that law is purely a means to an end rather than an end in itself. Law, and the instruments for enforcing it, Bentham believed, need not be regulated by any nonrational normative order in order to efficiently attain their desired effect, which is control. In theoretical terms, the hoary, dictatorial design of the Panopticon emerges because collective order is not related to any norms or seen as emerging from any voluntaristic commitment from the individuals themselves. As Halévy comments on this proposed prison reform:

> This pedagogic idea raises many objections. Would not the spirit of liberty and the energy of a free citizen be changed into the mechanical discipline of a soldier, or the austerity of a monk? Would not this ingenious contrivance have the result of constructing a set of *machines* under the similitude of *men?* . . . Liberty is not, according to Bentham, an *end* of human activity; the doctrine of utility is not, in origin and in essence, a philosophy of liberty. (Halévy, *Philosophic Radicalism*, p. 84, italics added.)

120. Parsons, *The Structure of Social Action*, p. 64. Parsons' equation here of positivism and rationalism should not be allowed to confuse the point he is making. As I mentioned in ch. 1, sec. 2, throughout *The Structure of Social Action* he conflates methodological and presuppositional issues.

121. Ibid., pp. 64–69. For instance, Parsons follows Halévy in describing the role of Malthus' "population growth" as a deterministic construction that undermines voluntarism, yet he does so in terms that are more systematic, abstract, and self-consciously epistemological and presuppositional.

> . . . so far as the principle of population determines social conditions it is, ultimately, the effect of the conditions of action, not of men's ends or any other normative element. But so far as this is so the scope of variation open to human volition is narrowed down and the limit of a radical positivist theory is approached. (Ibid., p. 111.)

122. For Rex's expressed intention to develop a theory that combines norms and conditions, see *Key Problems in Sociological Theory* (n. 16

above), p. 112. For a description of how Rex reduces the notion of "purposive action" to instrumental action, see my discussion in sec. 2.3.1. above.

123. *Key Problems*, p. 113.

124. Ibid., p. 123, italics added.

125. Ibid., pp. 123–129.

126. C. Wright Mills, *The Sociological Imagination* (New York, 1961), p. 37; more generally see pp. 35–42.

127. Ludwig von Mises, *Human Action* (n. 61 above), p. 20. For an analysis of von Mises' equation of purposive action with instrumentally efficient action, see sec. 2.3.1.

128. See Parsons' *The Structure of Social Action*, pp. 65–67, for a good discussion of the logic of this "error strategy."

129. Peter M. Blau, "Structural Effects," *American Sociological Review* 25, no. 2 (1960): 178–193. Blau himself asserts that these feared sanctions can be either ideal or material; but persons do not fear supra-individual sanctions in the instrumental way Blau describes unless these sanctions are material or, at least, are treated by the actor *as if* they were, i.e., as part of action's unmoveable "conditions." For a direct confrontation with such a perspective on social structure, see my "The Concept of Social Structure in Social Science," in Donald E. Stokes, ed., *Paradigm Development in Political and Social Science* (forthcoming).

130. Poggi, *Images of Society: Essays on the Sociological Theories of Tocqueville, Marx, and Durkheim* (Stanford, Calif., 1972) pp. 147–149.

131. Despite the fact that Hobbes in his historical context was not one of these ideological reformists, it should not be forgotten that even his collectivist rationalist theory was linked in his own mind to a positive theory of freedom:

> Liberty, or Freedome signifieth (properly) the absence of Opposition; (by Opposition, I mean externall Impediments of motion;). . . . A freeman, is he, that in those things, which by his strength and wit he is able to do, is not hindered to doe what he has a will to. (*Leviathan*, ch. 21.)

From the perspective here, the crucial phrase in the ultimate elimination of voluntarism from Hobbes' theory of the sovereign is his emphasis here on "externall Impediments" alone.

132. Jürgen Habermas, *Toward a Rational Society* (n. 21 above), p. 92.

133. Idem, *Knowledge and Human Interests* (n. 21 above), p. 157.

134. "The community that is based on the intersubjective validity of . . . symbols makes both possible: reciprocal *identification* and *preservation of the non-identity* of one another. In the dialogue relation a dialectical relation of the general and the individual, without which ego identity cannot be conceived, is realized." (Ibid., p. 157, italics in original.)

Despite the clarity with which Habermas sees the complementarity between internal order and voluntarism, there remains a certain ambiguity in his presentation. He has still, to a significant although not dominant extent, "reified" his conception of the individual—a problem which I will be addressing shortly. He presents the problem of voluntarism as if the individual gains freedom in two ways that are actually in tension with one another: both through his reciprocal identification with another individual and in spite of it. A further problem is that Habermas conflates voluntarism at the presuppositional level and freedom at the ideological level, so that he illegitimately equates presuppositional voluntarism with the achievement of individual autonomy in the sense of Enlightenment ideology. I will discuss this problem in more detail at the end of this subsection.

135. This underlying connection is made very clear in Martin Hollis' *Models of Man* (n. 12 above). "I shall impose a simple dichotomy," Hollis writes. "Social theories will be grouped by whether they treat human nature as *passive* or as *active*. [This] idea is as old as the problem of free will ..." (P. 4, italics in original.) For Hollis, a social philosopher who draws on the British "philosophy of action," voluntarism can be maintained only if the determining locus of action is, en toto, the individual himself. Operating within a similarly particularistic understanding of "action," Alan Dawe takes the same position in "The Two Sociologies," *British Journal of Sociology* 21, no. 2 (1970): 207–218, and in "Theories of Social Action," in Bottomore and Nisbet, eds., *A History of Sociological Analysis* (n. 12 above), pp. 362–417; so does Anthony Giddens in his later work (*New Rules of Sociological Method* and *Central Problems in Social Theory* [both, n. 12 above]). But insufficiently generalized theoretical schemes often include empirical observations that implicitly burst the narrow confines of their formal logic, and these individualistic theorists are no exception. Hollis, e.g., eventually concludes that his autonomous, active individuals may behave in an "expressively rational" way, such that they perform actions from a spontaneous identification with rules which they value in themselves (pp. 136–139). Yet does not the comprehension of this individual expressivity necessarily depend upon the realization that individual voluntary action can be imbedded in a collective, normative order? (Cf. the penetrating criticism of the debilitating individualism of Hollis' argument in the review of *Models of Man* by Ian Jarvie in the *Canadian Journal of Sociology* 4 [1979] pp. 325–328.) Giddens similarly admits to the existence of a collective normative order, but he insists that the "acting" individual can gain voluntarism only by his freedom vis-à-vis this order rather than being sustained by it. The only truly significant collective pressure elaborated in Giddens' later work, therefore, is the material one; if collective normative order is just as coercive, Giddens implies, theory might just as well focus on an order whose coercive quality is perfectly manifest.

136. For an excellent brief discussion of the philosophical arguments involved in this position, see Richard Taylor's *Metaphysics* (Englewood Cliffs, N.J., 1963), particularly in his chapter on "Freedom and Determinism," the discussions of causal versus logical necessity, freedom, soft determinism, and simple indeterminism (pp. 33–53, passim).

In speaking of such purely philosophical argument, it is relevant to note that in certain of its strands English action philosophy is not nearly as individualistic as the sociological theory which claims to follow it, e.g., the theories of Hollis, Dawe, and Giddens referred to in the preceding note. Wittgenstein himself can be interpreted as giving a large role to tradition and normative constraint in the exercise of human agency, and this is clearly manifest in the work of one of his distinguished followers, *Free Action*, by A. I. Meldon (London, 1961). Meldon maintains that action is distinguished from behavior—the latter is for him completely instinctual or physical movement—by virtue of the fact that actors give reasons for their actions, that all action involves "knowing why." The exercise of such reasoning capacity means that there is always the chance for the actor to do something else, hence that there is free will, and it is this possibility that distinguishes causality in the social from that in the natural sciences (p. 207). Yet while insisting on such free will, Meldon does not separate the exercise of human agency from external cultural factors; indeed, he argues that it is precisely the inculcation of human beings into social roles that allows them to reason and to rise above the merely behavioral and physical.

> The activities in which we have been trained to engage in our dealings with one another constitute the substratum upon which our recognition of the actions of others rests. We have then no mere system of abstract concepts of the understanding which we apply to some alien material of experience, but a complex of activities we have been trained to perform, in the context of which the discourse we employ plays its role in communication and by virtue of which we see as we do the [mere] bodily movements of others as the *actions* of persons. It is this training that is of central importance both to our understanding of the concepts of action and agent and to our perception of the actions of those about us. . . . [For example,] the child needs to be trained, by participation in the various forms of activity in which it engages with its mother, to recognize *this* bodily movement of its mother in *this* transaction in which it engages as *this* action, *that* bodily movement in *that* transaction as *that* action. Only in the context of the specific activities which it has been trained to perform, as it grows into its changing roles with respect to its mother and to the other members of the family, is it possible for it to understand the bodily movements [i.e., the mere physical behavior] of these participating in their diverse ways in the life of the family as the actions they are, and to understand what it is to be a mother, a father, a sister, or a brother. . . . [T]he concepts of action and agent are enriched by relating

to the wider scenes of social intercourse in which in diverse ways various social and moral institutions, conventions, statutes, etc., are relevant
to the background activities against which bodily movements are understood as the actions they are and agents the familiar sorts of persons we
understand them to be: employers and employees, sellers and pur-
chasers, motorists, strangers, friends. . . . It is in these transactions in
which, by the training and the instruction we have received, we have
come to participate with others, that the explanation of the concepts of
person and agent come ultimately to rest." (Pp. 187–197, italics altered.)

The crucial distinction between agency and action, on the one hand, and
behavior, on the other, can clearly be seen to rest on the distinction between the social and the biological and physical realms, not on the more
individualistic distinction between action whose motivation involves collective constraints and that which emerges purely through individual
choice and decision.

The classic social-scientific statement of the compatibility of order
and freedom is John Stuart Mill's refutation of the "free-will metaphysi-
cians" in his defense of a social science in *A System of Logic* (1843). One of
the staunchest defenders of individual liberty, Mill argued, nonetheless,
that causality does not have the same status in the natural as the social
sciences. "For the expression of the simple fact of causation," he wrote,
"so extremely inappropriate a term as Necessity" is an incorrect association, because necessity "involves much more than mere uniformity of sequences: it implies irresistibleness."

> The application of the same term to the agencies on which human ac-
> tions depend as is used to express those agencies of nature which are
> really uncontrollable . . . is a mere illusion. There are physical sequences
> which we call necessary. . . . [But it] is apt to be forgotten by people's
> feelings, even if remembered by their understandings, that human ac-
> tions are . . . never . . . ruled by any one motive with such sway that there
> is no room for the influence of any other. The causes, therefore, on
> which action depends are never uncontrollable. (Bk. 5, ch. 2, sec. 3.)

Nonetheless, Mill insists, we may still say there are causation and "laws"
in social life. In this insistence he differs from Meldon, though the substance of his argument is much the same.

137. Nagel, *The Structure of Science* (New York, 1961), pp. 466–476,
547–606. Following Nagel, William R. Catton Jr., has particularly emphasized the compatibility between free will, nonrational collective order,
and scientific determinism. See *From Animistic to Naturalistic Sociology*
(New York, 1966), pp. xi–xv, 30–33, 124–194. A complementary and ad-
mirably succinct account of the relation between sociological methodology and the philosophical problems of causality and determinism can be
found in Rex's *Key Problems in Sociological Theory* (n. 16 above). Rex
demonstrates that the construction of scientific laws, in any branch of

science, is not a matter of absolute determinism but rather the association of observed behavior with a prediction based on generalized, theoretical reasoning:

> [In constructing scientific "laws"], the key to the matter appears to be that we assert that the connection is not merely a repeated temporal one, but that it is, in some sense, necessary. Can we then give any clear meaning to this notion of necessity? The view taken here is that, once we have understood the nature of the relationship between general laws and basic statements reporting empirical events, the meaning of the necessity of a relationship between two events is obvious. When we say that something happened necessarily, rather than accidentally, what we mean is that it was what we would have expected to happen in terms of our deductions from accepted or established laws. (P. 23.)

This statement, however, would have to be qualified by the strictures about physical necessity articulated by Mill (n. 136).

138. Whereas earlier I presented only "negative," indirect evidence against the individualist position, I am here presenting a direct critique. Before this positive critique could be presented, it was necessary to develop the notion of nonrational internal order, because it is this presuppositional option that allows us to perceive what is missing from the individualist position.

139. Atkinson, *Orthodox Consensus and Radical Alternative* (n. 52 above), p. 181.

Obviously, Coleman's identical portrayal of man as "wholly free" and as "not constrained" (sec. 3.2 above) is similarly rooted in the reification of the free-will notion.

Atkinson's section on "Voluntarism and Determinism" provides an interesting example of the double, apparently self-contradictory meaning that the term "voluntarism" can assume when the understanding of free will is reified. Atkinson writes first that "actors act voluntarily with respect to the expectancies of others and the demands of the social system." He then describes this same situation as one in which "the individual is allowed no real choice but to do as he does." As an illustration he offers the fact that "if the actor should step out of line then there are internal and external mechanisms to ensure that he adjusts very quickly." In such a situation, he goes on, the actor is "submitting voluntarily but deterministically to the authority he disregarded." He concludes that "if we are to consider the possibility of free choice as we normally understand it, then all human action as conceived in sociological terms excludes it" (*Orthodox Consensus*, pp. 125–126). We can understand the obvious tensions in this discussion only if we recognize that Atkinson is working with a definition of "voluntarism" as any internally directed activity—much like the definition employed in the present work—while he is using the word "determinism" to denote any action that is subject to collective order, whether its location is internal or external.

140. See Mead's "The 'I' and the 'Me,'" in Anselm Strauss, *George Herbert Mead on Social Psychology* (n. 32 above), pp. 228–233; Herbert Blumer, *Symbolic Interactionism* (Englewood Cliffs, N.J., 1969), passim; Erving Goffman, *Encounters* (Indianapolis, 1961), particularly pp. 107–110.

141. Wilson, "Normative and Interpretive Paradigms in Sociology," in Jack D. Douglas, ed., *Understanding Everyday Life* (Chicago, 1970), pp. 57–79. For Sartre, see, e.g., *Search for a Method* (New York, 1963), passim.

142. "Concepts like culture pattern, subculture, social roles, recipro-cal expectation, social class, status group, communication, human rela-tions and many others make it appear that individuals act as group-influences dictate" (Reinhard Bendix and Bennett Berger, "Images of Society and Problems of Concept Formation in Sociology," in Bendix, *Embattled Reason* [New York, 1970], p. 121).

143. Martindale, *The Nature and Types of Sociological Theory* (n. 35 above), passim. See particularly Martindale's discussion of Weber him-self, pp. 377–393. For a discussion of the nominalism in Martindale's treatment of Weber, see vol. 3, ch. 1.

144. Alain Touraine, "Towards a Sociology of Action" and "Raison d'être of a Sociology of Action," in Anthony Giddens, ed., *Positivism and Sociology* (London, 1974), pp. 75–100, 115–127.

The intellectual origins of Touraine's usage is clearly Marx's concept of "praxis." Among theorists in the neo-Marxist tradition, there is a strong tendency, for ideological reasons, to identify praxis only with cre-ative revolutionary activity, e.g., Avineri's statement that, for Marx, "praxis revolutionizes existing reality through human action" (*The So-cial and Political Thought of Karl Marx* [n. 6 above], p. 139). Although I will take up this general problem at great length in vol. 2, its relation to the individualism issue should be discussed here. The problem, as I de-scribed it earlier, is that Marx's own definition of praxis can be taken only as an epistemological dictate—as describing a multidimensional rela-tionship in which subjective and objective forces are interpenetrated—but it is not yet a sociological one. Interpreting praxis as denoting only a particular type of radical activity is not, then, inconsistent with Marx's praxis concept, but neither is it a necessary correlary of it. The problem with this usage, however, is that it attempts to make general presupposi-tions identical with ideological commitments: if action is praxis, it is also radical. It represents, in other words, a subtle form of ideological confla-tion. More importantly, it is ideological conflation of a particular type, for in attempting to match this ideological conception of revolutionary ac-tivity it develops an approach to voluntarism which can be viewed as "individualistic." I do not mean individualist in the sense of selfishness, for clearly the Marxist use of the term implies the opposite: praxis is conceived as a realization of cooperative "species being." Its use is individualistic in the presuppositional sense I have described above: it implies that voluntarism comes about only as the result of a withdrawal from collective determination, ideal or material.

In avoiding such problematic aspects of the term "praxis," Marxists have contributed to the ambiguity of interpretation that surrounds the concept. For example, the French Marxist sociologist Henri Lefebvre asserts that there are actually three levels of praxis: repetitive, mimetic, and innovative. They are described as constituting a continuum from habitual action, on the one side, to revolutionary action on the other. (*The Sociology of Marx* [New York, 1969], pp. 52–53.) "Praxis" here is *both* presuppositional and ideological, for in a sense, Léfèbvre is actually taking praxis as a generic, fully generalized concept and using three subcategories of it to denote different political situations—a perfectly acceptable relationship between these two levels of the scientific continuum. The same kind of ad hoc theoretical function is performed in neo-Marxist theory by the concept of "reification," which denotes praxis that is alienated from itself and is, in effect, not really praxis. For example, in *Strategy for Labor*, the French theorist André Gorz writes that "whenever individuals meet the overall result of their praxes as an external and hostile process, their praxis is 'alienated' and its result 'estranged' " (Boston, 1967, p. 92). The source of this residual category in Marxist theory goes back to Lukacs and will be discussed at some length in vol. 2, ch. 10.

145. Parsons, *The Structure of Social Action*, pp. 343–359; see also pp. 72–74.

146. Atkinson, *Orthodox Consensus and Radical Alternative*, (n. 52 above), pp. 181, 213.

147. To make my own position as explicit as possible, I should state that, in my view, every empirical act contains elements of free will and contingency as well as a "voluntaristic" (that is, more structured) reference to normative order. Each act also occurs within the context of limiting external conditions. There is no necessity that either type of collective order need be internally integrated or that they be complementary with one another. This position is merely a schematic description of the position set out earlier in this chapter.

148. Hughes, *Consciousness and Society* (n. 24 above), passim, but particularly ch. 2.

149. Bay, *The Structure of Freedom* (Stanford, Calif., 1958), p. 49, italics in original.

150. Ibid., p. 88.

Although Bay uses the term "empiricist" to refer to those political philosophers who have taken a behaviorist orientation to the problem of freedom, in the present context the term can also be seen as referring to a theoretical perspective which takes only a "concrete" perspective on the individual, seeing only the empirical individual in the materialist sense. In fact, Bay does intend to include in the category of empiricists all thinkers who define freedom only in terms of the absence of external, supra-individual restraints (pp. 27–47). However, Bay's term "external" has a double meaning. See n. 154 below.

151. If the presentation of this kind of theoretical distinction were to be historically complete, it would incorporate the attention of Durkheim, Weber, and Parsons to the problem of voluntary individualism and collective, internal control. Within the internal order tradition, these classical theorists stand between the theological and Romantic writers I will describe below (sec. 3.4.3) and the more recent commentators in both individualist and nonindividualist camps. However, since their writings on this question form a major part of the focus in subsequent volumes, I do not deal with their relationship to this theoretical development here. As I mentioned earlier with respect to the position of Marx and Weber in relation to the development of rationalistic collectivist theory, the present chapter should be considered as attempting an analytic statement of theoretical logic, a historical presentation of this logic in theoretical debate, and an overview of its contemporary manifestations.

Since Georg Simmel is a major classical figure in sociology whose work will not be one of the primary concerns of this study, I might mention here that, in my view, it is entirely inappropriate to incorporate his work into the individualistic tradition of social theorizing, as so many contemporary writers in the "exchange" and "conflict" traditions attempt to do. Simmel often worked on the level of microsociology, but as has been emphasized earlier this term describes merely the institutional focus of empirical propositions: it does not describe more generalized commitments as such. In fact, even when he is most insistent on exchange, conflict, and "self-interest," Simmel implicitly conceives the individual in an analytical rather than a concrete way. In his famous injunction that competition can actually increase social integration, for example, he underscores that nonrational and normative considerations are as significant as instrumental ones. Though individuals engage in competition to fulfill their own subjective sense of self-interest, any conception of such individual self-interest is necessarily mediated by the collective context of which the individual is simply a very small part. Thus, Simmel is sharply critical of the classical economic understanding of "the harmony of interests between society and the individual" which empirically results from competition. Actually, he insists, "individual activity is *predesigned and regulated by norms* in order to carry on and develop the legal, moral, political, and cultural conditions of man." This internalization, however, is difficult to observe empirically because these social forces are funneled through the "interests" of *individuals*. Indeed, social force "is possible only because the individual's own eudamonistic, moral, material, and abstract interests appropriate these super-individual values as means." Simmel offers science as an example of this interpenetration of the concrete individual by analytic "social" facts: "Thus, for instance, science is a content of objective culture and, as such, a self-sufficient, ultimate purpose of societal development; but for the individual, all extant science, including the portion he himself adds to it, is only a means for the satisfaction of his cognitive drive." ("Conflict," pp. 11–123 in Simmel, *Conflict and the Web of Group Affiliations* [New York, 1955]; I quote p. 61, n. 1, italics added.)

152. A striking illustration of Blumer's denial of the relevance of variations in collective order can be seen in his interpretation of Parsons' pattern-variable schema. For him its significance lies not in its attempt to measure different kinds of voluntary processes in the manner of Tönnies' *Gemeinschaft/Gesellschaft* distinction; he emphasizes rather the schema's assumption that individuals do act in patterned ways. Thus Blumer's evaluation is that the schema describes the high degree of conformist behavior in human societies. See "Comments by Herbert Blumer," in "Exchange on Turner's 'Parsons as a Symbolic Interactionist,'" *Sociological Inquiry* 45, no. 1 (1975): 59–62. (Cf. my earlier discussions of Schutz and Garfinkel.) In my view, this completely ignores the fundamentally voluntaristic thrust of this element of Parsons' collectivist sociology. For a good discussion of this point, see François Bourricaud, *L'Individualisme Institutionnel* (Paris, 1977); see also my essay on that work, "The French Correction: Revisionism and Followership in the Interpretation of Parsons" (*Contemporary Sociology* 10 [1981]:500–505).

153. There is another error which can prevent theory from perceiving the different consequences for freedom of different *types* of social constraint—although this error manifests itself in the description of almost all collectively controlled action as voluntary rather than as determined. For example, in the classificatory schema that I have referred to above, Wallace places alongside the subjective/objective dimension of his basic "property space" a dimension of theoretical conflict over "free will" and "determinism." A theory, he holds, is deterministic if it views the causes of action as "imposed on the individual" by a nonsocial force, like geography or climate. On the other hand, a theory guarantees free will if it views such causes as related to "conditions that are generated by the social itself" ("Overview of Contemporary Sociological Theory" [n. 14 above], p. 11). The problem with the latter category is that within it Wallace includes every causal factor that is human rather than nonhuman. Thus, technological and most materialistic theories are described by him as guaranteeing free will and as not being determinant. (He can classify Marx and Parsons as antivoluntary only by describing them as

generating "asocial" theories.) From our perspective, to the contrary, both technological and materialistic theories would be deterministic, for the question is not whether but how the social is achieved. To recognize the true scope of theoretical conflict over freedom and determinism, theoretical logic must differentiate the category of "social" action further than Wallace has proposed. This can be done by recognizing the importance of different *kinds* of socially generated determinism, i.e., by cross-cutting conceptions of order with conceptions of action.

In terms of other major schemas of classification, Effrat's is more parallel to the approach to order developed here. Effrat cross-cuts his subjective/objective criterion by the category "levels of analysis," which basically corresponds to the individual/collective division. ("Power to the Paradigms" [n. 30 above], passim.)

154. It is interesting in this regard that all of the theorists whom Christian Bay describes as "empiricist" are, in my terms, also members of the rationalist tradition of social thought. In fact, Bay actually labels this approach the "empiricist-utilitarian" tradition. He is combining, in other words, an approach to social order and an approach to social action. It is for this reason that Bay's use of the word "external" (see n. 150 above) has an unintended double meaning, referring both to supra-individual location and to material composition. He classifies an "external" definition of freedom as being concerned only with freedom's "opportunity" aspects. He criticizes this approach in the following way:

> The empiricists all were concerned with [external] opportunity only; this was for them the whole problem of freedom. External restraints on expression can make up only one of the facets of the freedom problem: these are only one type of phenomena interfering with man's ability to express what he actually or potentially is capable of. . . . (*The Structure of Freedom*, pp. 47–48.)

The other, nonempiricist approach to freedom Bay calls the "idealist" approach and defines as one "in which the problem of freedom has been considered as primarily a problem of the state of affairs *inside* the individual" (p. 48, italics in original). This is basically the division between the rationalist and nonrationalist approaches to voluntarism which have been described here. Bay's book is particularly interesting because he attempts an approach to freedom that not only specifies the presuppositional and ideological criteria for its achievement, but also proposes an elaborate theory of the empirical conditions that would be necessary if freedom were to be realized.

Louis Dumont has written in an illuminating way about the concrete individualism of the instrumental collectivist tradition in *From Mandeville to Marx* (Chicago, 1977).

155. This discussion can be viewed as providing an additional, over-

lapping explanation—in reference specifically to his treatment of Parsons' work—for Gouldner's ideological reductionism as discussed in ch. 2. At that point, I discussed the problem in terms of his conflationary approach to science in general. Here I have described the problem in terms of a particular kind of conflation between the presuppositional and ideological levels of Gouldner's approach.

156. In vol. 2, I criticize Marx's mistaken identification of idealism with any systematic reference to normative order.

157. Karl Marx, "Critique of Hegel's Dialectic and General Philosophy," in *Early Writings*, ed. T. B. Bottomore, pp. 202–203, italics in original.

158. Ibid., pp. 204, 214.

159. See, for example, Karl Marx and Frederick Engels, *The Holy Family* (Moscow, 1956), p. 15.

160. Marx (n. 158 above), p. 198.

161. For an analysis of Augustine's theological writing in terms of the kinds of general presuppositional issues I have described, see Bellah's article, "Religion and Polity in America" (n. 3 above). As Bellah writes, Augustine recognized the two "cities," one the normatively governed City of God, where the principle of *caritas* reigned, the other the instrumentally oriented City of Man, the *civitas terrena* governed mainly by *cupiditas*. It was only an orientation or relationship to the City of God which could provide the voluntarism necessary for salvation—by maintaining in mankind some "impression" of the divine norms. Augustine can be compared to Hobbes in that while he recognizes, as Hobbes did, the reign of *cupiditas* in the *civitas terrena*, his reference to the influence of *caritas* allowed him to take into account the normative sources of social order. It was only the former which could provide the voluntarism that would bring salvation.

162. Nisbet (n. 40 above).

163. Edward Shils, "Center and Periphery," "Charisma, Order, and Status," "The Integration of Society," in *Center and Periphery: Essays in Macro-Sociology* (Chicago, 1975), pp. 3–16, 256–275, and 49–90 respectively.

CHAPTER FOUR

1. Kuhn, *The Structure of Scientific Revolutions* (Chicago, [1962] 1970), p. 94.

2. Ibid.

3. Members of the positivist persuasion cannot, of course, accept the pivotal role of such "translation" in theoretical argument, even as they are themselves engaged in the task. For example, at about the same time

that Kuhn was codifying this standard scientific practice, Homans was sharply criticizing functionalism in the following way:

> What the functionalists actually produced was not a theory but a new language for describing social structure, one among many possible languages; and much of the work they called theoretical consisted in showing how the words of other languages . . . could be translated into theirs. . . . But what makes a theory is deduction, not translation. ("Bringing Men Back in," *American Sociological Review* 29 [1964]:813.)

The irony is that, in arguing against other theories and in constructing his own, Homans has been very much engaged in the translation of key statements of rival theorists. See, for example, his later attempt in this same essay to translate Smelser's functionalist statements about social change in the Industrial Revolution into the utilitarian presuppositions of his own perspective.

4. Karl Popper, "Normal Science and Its Dangers," in Imre Lakatos and Alan Musgrove, eds., *Criticism and the Growth of Knowledge* (London, 1970), p. 56.

5. Habermas, *Toward a Rational Society* (Boston, 1970), p. 7.

6. Ibid.

7. In presenting these criteria, I am drawing on a number of discussions of the problem of such postpositivist objectivity: Polanyi's emphasis on self-discipline and the personal acceptance of extra-individual impersonal standards (see ch. 1, sec. 4.1); Stephen Toulmin's analysis of the "degree of mutual interrelatedness" as the characteristic of objectivity (*Human Understanding* [Princeton, N.J., 1972], pp. 489–503); Bernard Barber's discussion of the role of "generality" and "scope" in defining the basis of theoretical advance in science (*Science and the Social Order* [New York, 1952], pp. 36–40); the notion of internal elegance and simplicity supplied by Abraham Kaplan (*The Conduct of Inquiry* [New York, 1964], pp. 314–319); and the notion of external explanatory complexity proposed by Ian Barbour (*Myths, Models, and Paradigms* [London, 1974], p. 92.

8. Noam Chomsky, *Language and Mind* (New York, 1968).

9. Contrast this, for example, with Mills' historicist discussion of the order problem, in which he argues that the nature of "order" must be considered only in terms of the particular kind of integration or social arrangement at a given historical moment. No theoretical decisions about order, he contends, are made a priori. Rather, the variety of historic social structures suggests "that whatever these societies may have in common must be discovered by empirical examination" (*The Sociological Imagination* [New York, 1961], p. 44). Yet for all the historical variation that Mills described in his work, his conception of social struc-

ture was usually informed by certain rational collectivist understandings of the source of social arrangements.

The alternative description of the status of presuppositional problems I have presented recalls Parsons' attitude toward the "action frame of reference" in *The Structure of Socal Action* (New York, [1937] 1968). Harold Bershady, in fact, has drawn attention to the parallels between Chomsky's use of structure and Parsons' understanding in that work of the role of the elements of action—norms, ends, means, and conditions (*Ideology and Social Knowledge* [New York, 1973], ch. 1). Parsons describes this action frame of reference—which should not be confused with the "problem of action" as I have defined it here—as having a "phenomenological status" in Husserl's sense (*Structure*, p. 733). My intention here also parallels the purpose of Nisbet's distinction between "unit ideas" and "isms" or "overt systems." He defines the former as those ideas that "provide [the] fundamental, constitutive substance of sociology among all the manifest differences among its authors" (*The Sociological Tradition* [New York, 1966], p. 5).

10. Habermas, *Knowledge and Human Interests*, p. 311. Habermas talks about the need for categories of "invariant," " quasi-transcendental status" that "determine the aspect[s] under which reality is objectified and can thus be made accessible to reality to begin with" (*Theory and Practice* [Boston, 1973], pp. 8–9).

11. Kuhn, *Scientific Revolutions*, p. 94.

12. Ibid., p. 109.

13. Through universality and synthesis, in other words, I am trying to approach the realist model of science through a relativist, or conventionalist, framework. The possibility of achieving such qualified realism is the point of the extremely interesting discussion by the philosopher of science Yehuda Elkana: "There is no difficulty—epistemologically speaking—in holding the two following views simultaneously: one is the impossibility of objectively ordering different conceptual frameworks according to their degree of rationality or their degree of approximation to a context-*independent* Truth; the other is that once a framework is given we can define criteria of rationality and truth *relative* to that framework, and order the world inside that framework according to these criteria." This epistemological reconciliation can only be achieved, in Elkana's view, by "two-tiered" philosophical thinking, where realism is pursued within a more specific level than the frameworks which create commitments at a more general level—precisely, in other words, the understanding of science as a two-directional continuum pursued here. If both the realist and relative positions are considered to be so epistemologically reconcilable, Elkana maintains, "then the problem of translation from one framework to another becomes feasible (though

not easier for that): a third framework of greater generality is determined in which the previous two are fully or partially embedded, or into which the two frameworks between which the translation is to take place both fit to the best of our knowledge; by the criteria of this third embracing framework, the components of the first two frameworks can be ordered." Thus "having selected (or being part of) a framework, relative to it we seek objective truth—factual reality," for "inside this framework we will not be able to distinguish our argumentation from that of the realist." To commit oneself to a prior framework, however, is still necessary, despite the element of relativism it implies, for "unless we find a common framework relative to which we can order our universe, we shall not [be] able to find out whose reality is true" ("Two-Tier Thinking: Philosophical Realism and Historical Relativism," *Social Studies of Science* 8 [1978]: 313).

14. Blau, "Structural Effects," *American Sociological Review* 25 (1960): 178–193.

15. Coleman, "Foundations for a Theory of Collective Decisions," *American Journal of Sociology* 71 (1966): 615–627. Actually, as mentioned above (ch. 3, sec. 2.3.1), Coleman's analysis is not really a collectivist one, but his definition of it as such allows one to focus on this reduction in a perfectly satisfactory manner.

16. Homans, "Bringing Men Back in" (n. 3 above), p. 816, italics added, referring to Neil J. Smelser, *Social Change in the Industrial Revolution* (Chicago, 1959).

17. Ekeh, *Social Exchange Theory: The Two Traditions* (Cambridge, Mass., 1974), passim.

18. Nisbet, *The Sociological Tradition* (New York, 1966), ch. 1 and passim.

19. Shils, *Center and Periphery: Essays in Macrosociology* (Chicago, 1975), "Introduction."

20. Habermas, *Knowledge and Human Interests* (Boston, 1971), e.g., p. 157.

21. See the "Conclusion" to Halévy's *Growth of Philosophic Radicalism* (New York, [1901–1904] 1972). Halévy acknowledges an emphasis on collective representations as an alternative to utilitarianism's coercively collectivist theory, but he rejects this on the grounds that it does not explain how an individual actually acts in a voluntary way. Instead, Halévy suggests that the theory of "imitation" may be a fruitful alternative. (Although Halévy is probably referring here to the debate between Durkheim and Tarde, he does not explicitly acknowledge it.)

22. Apter and Andrain, *Contemporary Analytic Theory* (Englewood Cliffs, N.J., 1972), p. 5.

23. This is not to say that Apter and Andrain do not perceive the dif-

ferences between types of order; that they do is indicated by their distinction between structure and norm. But they do not provide for these differences in their formal classification scheme.

24. Stark, *The Fundamental Forms of Social Thought* (New York, 1963). In fact, Stark not only conflates presuppositional questions with one another, but with a number of other levels on the scientific continuum as well, identifying the presuppositional conflict of organicism/mechanism with divisions over ideology, methods, and empirical propositions about equilibrium and conflict. I have discussed this problem in Stark's work in the analysis of conflation in approaches to science (ch. 2, sec. 1). Lewis' and Smith's more recent attempt to utilize the social nominalist/social realist distinction in *American Sociology and Pragmatism: Mead, Chicago Sociology, and Symbolic Interactionism* (Chicago, 1980), despite its great theoretical insight, manifests a similarly conflationary quality.

25. For the similar problem in Lewis and Smith (n. 24 above), see Ch. 3, n. 87, above. Another important example of such simplifying conflation occurs in the so-called action theories of sociology. Alan Dawe, e.g., believes there are "two sociologies," each completely differentiated simply according to differing commitments to an individualistic-versus-collectivist assumption. "Throughout . . . history," he writes, "there has been a manifest conflict between two types of social analysis, variously labeled as being between the organismic and mechanistic approaches, methodological collectivism and individualism, holism and atomism, the conservative and emancipatory perspectives." "At root," he argues, "they are all different versions of the fundamental debate about the abiding conflict between the domination of the system and the exertion of human agency" ("Theories of Social Action," in Tom Bottomore and Robert Nisbet, eds., *A History of Sociological Analysis* [New York, 1978], p. 366). From the commitment to "action" versus "behavior," Dawe believes, emerge commitments to methodology (scientific versus interpretive), empirical propositions (equilibrium versus conflict), models (functional versus institutional), ideology (conservative versus radical); see pp. 367, 369–370, 373. This mode of conflation resembles the one that informs Don Martindale's discussion of action in *The Nature and Types of Sociological Theory* (Cambridge, Mass., 1960); see ch. 2, n. 72, above.

26. The most generalized—and in the terms employed here, therefore, the most objective classificatory analysis of sociological theory and its history—is the one presented by S. N. Eisenstadt and M. Curelaru in *The Form of Sociology: Paradigms and Crises* (New York, 1976). They introduced four distinctive problems, and their work is fundamentally organized around the relationship of social theories to these questions: (1) the nature of the basic unit—individual, society, culture, ecological

organization; (2) degree of systematization; (3) bases of individual acceptance of order—coercion, identification, self-interest, solidarity; (4) description of conflict or equilibrium. The overlap between these categories and the ones presented in chs. 2–3 of this volume should be evident,
and with important qualifications, which have been noted above, their
analysis of contemporary theoretical conflict is often similar as well—
even to the point of emphasizing how contemporary debates so often
"cross-cut" one another. The problem with this classification, in my view,
is that these major categorizations are not still differentiated enough:
they are not related to the different elements of the scientific continuum
and, as a result, they themselves partly overlap one another. The upshot
of this difficulty is that the crucial criteria of what actually produces an
"open" versus a "closed" sociological theory—the major goal of theoretical development, in the authors' view—remains ultimately unclear. The
present work, in effect, gives to the notion of "open theory" an explicit
and detailed content.

27. There are, of course, reasons for this bias in addition to the misunderstandings on the presuppositional level I am describing here.
Often the bias will complement a writer's ideological assumptions. For
example, an ideological antipathy to the social conflict identified with
Marxism, which is for the most part an instrumentalist theory, will lead
to the belief that to solve the presuppositional order problem, theories
must be normative. To take another example, if individualism is equated
with the rationalist emphasis of conservative classical economics, a collectivist emphasis may be proposed by an ideological liberal as the only
way of articulating a welfare state perspective on social problems. This
conflation on the presuppositional level can also be viewed as the only
possible outcome of certain empirical findings. I do not believe, however,
that such commitments at any other nonpresuppositional level of the scientific continuum actually can explain the general conflationary problem here described.

28. In his analysis of this important precursor of Marx—at least that
aspect of Marx which can be formulated as an empirical analysis of political economy—Halévy quotes from Hodgkins' *Natural and Artificial
Right of Property:*

> Most of our domestic and civil rights, the dearest and best, are not guar-
> anteed by any law, and have no other security but the natural respect of
> man for man, or the moral feelings of individuals (Halévy [n. 21 above],
> p. 123.)

Halévy recognizes this is not a reliance on coercion and thus not an emphasis on "artificial identity." But instead of realizing that such an emphasis on "moral feelings" and "mutual respect" can refer to normative

influence, he sees it only as emerging from individualist emphasis within the rationalist tradition, namely, from the "natural identity of interest" notion.

29. There is actually one possible permutation which though *logically* produced by cross-cutting action and order does not exist *empirically*. This is the combination of rational action and internal collective order. The reason is the peculiar properties of instrumentally rational action that I have described above: when couched within a collectivist framework, the order created by rational action must be conceived as external to the actor. The failure to recognize such a combination does not, therefore, indicate the failure to appreciate presuppositional differentiation but rather the nature of substantive theoretical reasoning as such.

30. For an attempt to include some of the empirical illuminations of individualistic theorizing in a more acceptable theoretical framework, see my "The Concept of 'Social Structure' in Social Science," in Donald E. Stokes, ed., *Paradigm Development in Political and Social Science*, forthcoming.

31. Habermas, *Knowledge and Human Interests* (n. 20 above), p. 310. A notable irony of Habermas' work is that he rarely attempts to specify the nature of these practical-cognitive interests. Instead, he usually describes them as a nonempirical commitment to purely technical cognition. Perhaps the reason for this paradox is Habermas' contention that by operating only in a positivist manner, contemporary social science actually has surrendered all cognitive interests other than technical control (e.g., *Theory and Practice*, pp. 114–115, 254–256, 258 or *Toward a Rational Society*, pp. 62–122). Yet this contention is incorrect, particularly in light of Habermas' own hermeneutically inspired critique of the possibilities for positivism. Despite the self-understanding of the positivist persuasion, its scientific practice is as guided by presuppositions, or practical-cognitive interests, as any other.

32. Holton, *Thematic Origins of Science: Kepler to Einstein* (Cambridge, Mass., 1973), p. 24.

33. Karl Mannheim, *Man and Society in an Age of Reconstruction* (New York, 1940), p. 153.

34. Jay, *The Dialectical Imagination* (New York, 1973), p. 54.

35. Clifford Geertz, "Ideology as a Cultural System," in Geertz, *The Interpretation of Cultures* (New York, 1973).

36. Seymour Martin Lipset, *Revolution and Counter-Revolution* (New York, 1968), pp. 210 ff.

37. Abner Cohen, *Two Dimensional Man* (Berkeley and Los Angeles, 1974).

38. Barber, "Social Stratification: Introduction," *Encyclopedia of the Social Sciences* (New York, 1968), 15: 288, 296.

39. I am grateful to Professor Edward G. Swanson for this apt formulation.

Author-Citation Index

This index is intended as a combination bibliography/name index. Every article and book referred to in the text and notes is included here, but authors are included only if their work is specifically cited. If the work of an author mentioned in the text is cited only in the notes, the page of both text and note references is indexed.

Subject Index

Action, the elements of, 214; ends and goals, 66–68, 74, 82, 104; means, 66–67, 82, 100, 110; norms, 66, 68, 74, 76, 82, 99, 102–104, 107, 209
———, instrumentally rational, 72–75, 85, 93, 99–100, 110, 117, 121, 169, 184–187, 199–200, 211; conditional environment of, 65–68, 83, 100, 103–104, 111; its individualist forms, 95–96; its collectivist forms, 98ff; relation to determinism, 99–100; different approaches to, 80ff
———, multidimensional, 66–68, 104, 112, 187
———, nonrational, 75–79; internal subjective reference, 66, 73, 76, 104, 109, 200; normative environment of, 67–68, 74, 76, 82, 90, 104–105; individualist forms of, 97–99; collectivist forms of, 103ff; and idealism, 110–112; different approaches to, 80ff. See also Nonrationality
———, the "problem" of: reductionist approaches to, 71; its

generalized status, 72, 114–116, 122, 125, 184
———, the problem of the rationality of, 41, 65–70, 72, 74, 80, 90, 92, 181
———, and relation to issues of freedom/constraint, 70, 89–90, 100, 103–105, 107, 109; and voluntarism, 67–69, 79, 83, 85, 89, 103–105, 109–110, 200, 206; and determinism, 67, 69, 74, 90, 104–105, 110, 201, 207
——— theory: English, 203–204; Parsonian, 67, 71; Weberian, 183
Ad hoc explanations, 31–32, 96, 102, 146, 156–157, 159, 167, 197, 207
Analytical v. concrete frames of reference. See Concrete v. analytic frames of reference
Antivoluntaristic, 59, 85, 99, 100, 110, 201
A priori aspect of science, 146; positivist criticism of, 135
Artificial identity of interests, 98, 100, 119, 197, 199, 200, 201, 217
Asymmetry: between levels of scientific continuum, 4; between

229